Assessment and Learning

Edited by John Gardner

SAGE Publications
Los Angeles • London • New Delhi • Singapore

UNIVERSITY OF CHICHESTER

SAGE Publications Ltd
1 Oliver's Yard
55 City Road
London EC1Y 1SP

SAGE Publications India Pvt Ltd
B1/I 1 Mohan Cooperative Industrial Area
Mathura Road, New Delhi 110 044
India

SAGE Publications Inc
2455 Teller Road
Thousand Oaks
California 91320

SAGE Publications Asia-Pacific Pte Ltd
33 Pekin Street #02-01
Far East Square
Singapore 048763

British Library Cataloguing in Publication Data

A catalogue record for this book is available from the British
Library

ISBN: 978-1-4129-1050-7 (hbk)
ISBN: 978-1-4129-1051-4 (pbk)

Library of Congress Control Number: 2005929007

Typeset by Dorwyn Ltd, Wells, Somerset
Printed on paper from sustainable resources
Printed in Great Britain by Athenaeum Press, Gateshead,
Tyne & Wear

CONTENTS

CONTRIBUTORS' DETAILS

Paul Black

Paul is Emeritus Professor at King's College, London. He has published extensively on science education, curriculum development and educational assessment. He is co-author, with Professor Dylan Wiliam, of *Inside the Black Box: raising achievement through formative assessment* (King's College, London) and *Assessment and Classroom Learning* (Assessment in Education 5(1)) which was commissioned by the Assessment Reform Group.

Richard Daugherty

Richard is Emeritus Professor in the School of Education and Lifelong Learning at the University of Wales, Aberystwyth. His research interests are in the field of assessment, education policy and geography education. In recent years his work has focused on National Curriculum assessment policies in Wales and England and on education policy in Wales. His publications include *National Curriculum Assessment: a review of policy 1987-1994* (1995), *Education Policy in Wales* (edited, with Robert Phillips and Gareth Rees, 2000) and the *Review of National Curriculum assessment arrangements in Wales at Key Stages 2 and 3* (2004).

Kathryn Ecclestone

Kathryn is a senior lecturer in post–compulsory education and director of the MSc in Educational Research at the University of Exeter. Her teaching and research interests encompass post–16 professional development, post–16 assessment policy in further and adult education, the effects of formative assessment on learners' motivation and autonomy and the impact of action research on post–16 teachers' assessment practice. She is currently carrying out research on quality assurance in post–16 qualifications for the Qualifications and Curriculum Authority (QCA), formative assessment for the Learning and Skills Development Agency (LSDA), improving formative assessment in the 14–19 curriculum (funded by Nuffield) and is convener of an Economic and Social Research Council (ESRC) seminar series.

John Gardner

John is Professor of Education in the School of Education at Queen's University, Belfast. His main research areas include policy and practice in assessment and information technology in education. Since 1990, he has been principal investigator in over 20 large- and small-scale projects involving over £1.6 million including research on the reliability and validity of the 11-plus tests in Northern Ireland. He is currently part of a team conducting an Economic and Social Research Council (ESRC)-funded project on pupils' participation in the assessment of their own learning.

Wynne Harlen

Wynne's main professional interests have been science education and assessment and over the past 20 years she has been Sidney Jones Professor of Science Education at the University of Liverpool, then Director of the Scottish Council for Research in Education and is currently Visiting Professor at the University of Bristol. Her experience in assessment includes working for eight years as deputy director of the UK-wide Assessment of Performance Unit and chair of the Science Expert Group of the OECD Programme for International Student Assessment (PISA) from 1998–2003. She is a founder member of the British Educational Research Association (BERA) and of ARG. She is currently directing, on behalf of ARG, the Nuffield-funded Assessment Systems for the Future (ASF) project and is a member of the Evidence for Policy and Practice Information and Co-ordinating Centre (EPPI-Centre) review group on assessment. Her publications include 25 research reports, over 140 journal articles and 27 books of which she is author or co-author.

Mary James

Mary is Professor in Education at the Institute of Education, University of London and Deputy Director of the Economic and Social Research Council (ESRC) Teaching and Learning Research Programme (TLRP), the largest programme of educational research ever mounted in the UK. She has also recently completed a major research and development project on 'Learning How to Learn – in classrooms, schools and networks', funded within the TLRP. Major recent publications include a series of papers (in press) arising from the Learning How to Learn project and a book for school managers entitled *Using Assessment for School Improvement*, published by Heinemann in 1998.

Dave Pedder

Dave has ten years of classroom teaching experience, gained in schools in Japan and Indonesia, and extensive experience in providing INSET opportunities for serving teachers. He has also written textbooks for teaching secondary school English in Indonesia. In 1995, he made a career change from teaching into research covering his key interests in classroom teaching and learning, the professional development of teachers and school improvement. He has carried out research into the effects of class size on processes and outcomes of teaching and learning at Key Stage 3, and into how teachers consult pupils and respond to their views about teaching and learning. Dave worked full time as senior research associate on the Learning How to Learn project until 2005, when he took up his current post as lecturer in School Leadership, at the University of Cambridge.

Judy Sebba

Judy is Professor of Education at the University of Sussex where she leads the teaching, learning and assessment research, including assessment for learning in the Portsmouth Learning Community Programme. Previously, she had been Senior Adviser (Research) for the Standards and Effectiveness Unit, Department for Education and Skills (DfES), with responsibilities which included work on using assessment for learning research to inform policy and practice. Previous research while in the universities of Cambridge and Manchester included work on school improvement and inspection, self- and peer assessment and special needs and inclusion. She is currently a member of the Evidence for Policy and Practice Information and Co-ordinating Centre (EPPI-Centre) review group on assessment.

Gordon Stobart

Gordon is Reader in Assessment at the University of London, Institute of Education having moved from the Qualifications and Curriculum Authority (QCA) where he worked on both national tests and examinations. His membership of the Assessment Reform Group reflects his commitment to the use of assessment for learning as well as of learning. He co-authored, with Caroline Gipps, *Assessment: a Teacher's Guide to the Issues* (3rd edition, 1997) and is currently editor of the journal *Assessment in Education*.

Dylan Wiliam

Dylan directs the Learning and Teaching Research Center at the Educational Testing Service (ETS) in Princeton, New Jersey. After teaching in secondary schools in London for seven years, he joined King's College, London in 1984 and continued teaching at college level until 2003, when he joined ETS. He served as dean and head of the School of Education at King's before taking up the position of assistant principal there. He is co-author, with Paul Black, of *Inside the Black Box: raising achievement through formative assessment* (King's College, London) and *Assessment and Classroom Learning* (Assessment in Education 5(1)), which was commissioned by the Assessment Reform Group.

Assessment and Learning: An Introduction

John Gardner

On first inspection, the title of this book arguably places learning, one of the most fundamental processes in a person's lifecourse, secondary to one of the most contrived processes, the assessment of that learning. Our intention, however, is quite the opposite. As members of the Assessment Reform Group we have accumulated over seventeen years of collective research into assessment policy and practice, and many more years as individuals. *Assessment and Learning* is a book, therefore, that places learning at the centre of our concerns but unambiguously underscores the importance of assessment in that learning.

The Assessment Reform Group is based in the UK and though it is natural for us to turn to our own contexts to illustrate analyses of assessment practice, the key aspiration throughout the group's existence has been to collate and use research from around the globe to develop a better understanding of how assessment can significantly contribute to learning. The reader will therefore find a liberal sprinkling of research-informed insights from a wide variety of international contexts in addition to chapters that specifically consider the policies in relation to assessment for learning in a variety of countries. Here and there, throughout the book, we refer to various types of learning contexts in these countries but it is fair to say that we draw heavily on the compulsory phases of education (roughly 4–16 years in most countries) to contextualize the practice of assessment for learning. It is also fair to say that it is in this context that the majority of research and experimentation has been recorded. We recognize that it is beyond the capacity of any one book to cover the huge span of educational endeavour in a world in which lifelong learning is the name of the game but we hope that the concepts and processes we illuminate throughout the chapters, such as learner engagement, feedback, motivation and pedagogic style, are key to any learning environment facilitated by teaching or instruction. Translating them to other learning contexts such as work-based learning, adult and community education or post-compulsory education, is not straightforward but the principles and practices will be relevant.

In most developed countries, the pursuit of reliable and valid means of assessing people's learning generates high volumes of published discourse and, not infrequently, dissent; the documentation on the various assessment policies, practices and theories could conceivably fill whole libraries. Some of the discourse and much of the dissent relate to whether the use to which assessment is put is valid or, to put it more mundanely, useful to the learners themselves or to other audiences. Our pursuit is somewhat different. We would argue that learning should take centre stage and we address the role that assessment should play in this. Assessment is our focus but learning is the goal.

Two phrases, 'formative assessment' and 'assessment for learning', are throughout all of the chapters that follow. The older phrase, 'formative assessment', can be traced back to Scriven's (1967) concepts of formative and summative evaluation, distinguished at the time solely on the basis of when the evaluation in question is carried out. While timing is merely one of the distinctions today, formative assessment remains a widely used concept in education. However, it is sometimes used to describe a process in which frequent ad hoc assessments, in the classroom or in formal assessment contexts such as practical skills work, are carried out over time and collated specifically to provide a final (summative) assessment of learning. Such assessments potentially do not contribute to the students' learning. The second phrase, 'assessment for learning', came into use in the late 1980s and early 1990s and may therefore be considered a somewhat 'newer' concept.

In truth, though, assessment for learning comprises the same time-honoured practices as formative assessment, that is, 'what good teachers do' (AAIA, 2005b) and have always done when using assessment to assist students to take the next steps in their learning. In contrast to the term 'formative assessment', however, assessment for learning is arguably less likely to be used to describe the summative use of multiple assessments of learning. The words focus squarely on the essence of our pursuit: the promotion of assessment to support learning and this is neatly contra-distinct from assessment *of* learning. In the final analysis there is little of substance to distinguish the two terms 'formative assessment' and 'assessment for learning', but for the wider educational and policy-making audiences we feel, as Daugherty and Ecclestone report in Chapter 9, that the latter is more accessible than the more technical term, 'formative assessment'. That said, we are content to use both phrases interchangeably, when there is no ambiguity in the type of assessment process being described.

In order to ensure we remain consistent in how we describe the type of process that assessment for learning is, we have defined it to be:

> *the process of seeking and interpreting evidence for use by learners and their teachers, to identify where the learners are in their learning, where they need to go and how best to get there. (ARG, 2002a)*

Unpacking this deceptively simple definition, in terms of classroom practice, reveals a complex weave of activities involving pedagogic style, student-teacher interaction, self-reflection (teacher and student), motivation and a variety of assessment processes. For example, teachers need to plan the learning environment and activities, students need to engage in the assessment of their learning and teachers need to assess the extent of the students' understanding as they are learning. They then need to challenge and support these students to enable them to reach the next stage in their learning progress. An analysis of such a complex learning approach could never be exhaustive but we have tried to make it accessible through a previous publication entitled *Assessment for Learning: 10 Principles*. These principles are mentioned in various places in the chapters that follow and are summarized below:

Assessment for learning

- Is part of effective planning;
- Focuses on how students learn;
- Is central to classroom practice;
- Is a key professional skill;
- Is sensitive and constructive;
- Fosters motivation;
- Promotes understanding of goals and criteria;
- Helps learners know how to improve;
- Develops the capacity for self-assessment;
- Recognizes all educational achievement. (ARG, 2002a)

All of these qualities, which we attribute collectively to assessment for learning, appear in various guises throughout the book – in their practice, in the theories underlying them and in the educational policies that relate to them.

Practice, theory and policy

Under these generic headings the structure of the book proceeds in four parts, which in turn address how assessment for learning manifests itself in the classroom, its theoretical underpinnings, how it relates to summative assessment and how national policies in a selection of nations do (or do not) reflect its role in learning. Chapter 1 by Black and Wiliam draws empirical evidence from the King's-Medway-Oxfordshire Formative Assessment Project (KMOFAP) to portray how the findings from formative assessment research may be translated to classroom practice. In addition to significant changes to pedagogy, the chapter demonstrates that a full espousal of assessment for learning creates inevitable changes in teachers' and learners' understanding and attitudes to learning itself. James and Pedder pick up the story in Chapter 2, which draws on a second project, Learning How to Learn, to tackle how such changes can be promoted and supported through teachers' professional learning. Central to the findings is the observation that very often, in an assessment for learning context, there is little to distinguish between the processes of learning for students and teachers. These initial chapters comprise Part I, *Practice*.

Part II, *Theory*, takes readers to chapters that consider the existing knowledge and understanding that underpin assessment for learning as a concept and its close relationship to pedagogy. In Chapter 3 James considers three major clusters of learning theory: behaviourist, constructivist and socio-cultural. Acknowledging the overlaps, the chapter deals with the implications these theories have for assessment and teaching generally and establishes the basis by

3

which the baton, of explaining the processes fostered by assessment for learning, is passed to Chapters 4 and 5. Harlen's Chapter 4 addresses a key element of formative assessment's armoury. Drawing on research from around the world, Harlen argues that some summative assessment practices may have a negative impact on learners while steps that ameliorate the worst effects, by developing and sustaining learner motivation, are often based on the principles of assessment for learning. Black and Wiliam return in Chapter 5 to propose a tentative four component model, developed using Engeström's Activity System (1987), as a theoretical framework for formative assessment. Central to the model is the triangle of teacher-tools-outcomes; the way that 'tools' (a term that includes procedures such as feedback and peer assessment) alter the teacher-student interaction; the role of the teacher in the regulation of learning and the student's own role in their learning; and how such changes bear upon the outcomes of learning work.

Part III, *Formative and Summative Issues*, continues the theoretical theme but with a focus on more technical aspects of the distinctions and overlaps between assessment for learning and summative assessment. In Chapter 6 Harlen explores whether it is feasible for evidence gathered for one purpose to be used for another. Proposing a spectrum of possibilities that allows an overlap of purposes in its middle region, the chapter highlights the pitfalls of blithely advocating dual usage of the same information and suggests the conditions under which its integrity may be preserved. However, the question of whether teachers' assessments are reliable looms in the background. Black and Wiliam's Chapter 7 specifically deals with this issue of a perceived lack of reliability in any assessment carried out by teachers, whether formative or summative. The chapter debunks the corresponding folk-myth that external assessments (statutory tests and so on) are highly reliable and argues that dependability in context is the key attribute for any assessment. Stobart's Chapter 8 picks up the validity issue and concludes that there is a simple test for the validity of any assessment for learning process: did learning take place as a consequence? A negative response suggests that the formative assessment is invalid because it did not achieve its purpose of promoting learning.

The book thus far seeks to build a platform of discourse, informed by practice and research, on which to articulate the processes and proclaim the benefits of assessment for learning. Part IV, *Policy*, turns to the thorny issue of how governments and national educational organizations reflect developments in assessment for learning in their policies. In Chapter 9 Daugherty and Ecclestone analyse the recent assessment policy activities in England, Scotland, Wales and Northern Ireland in terms of the key policy texts and the discourse surrounding policy development. Wiliam's Chapter 10 charts the emphasis in the USA on high stakes tests and the psychometric dimensions of reliability and validity as primary concerns. Although there is an emerging interest in monitoring student progress current moves involving portfolio assessment, for example, are limited and formative assessment is generally better understood as 'early warning' summative measures in relation to predicting performance in annual state tests. Concluding Part IV, Sebba's Chapter 11 acknowledges the problems inherent in any attempt to compare practices across cultures but points to the commonalities of understanding and practice across several nations.

Finally Gardner's Chapter 12 serves as a concluding discussion on the main messages the book offers.

The Assessment Reform Group

Ever since its establishment in 1988, as the then Assessment Policy Task Group of the British Educational Research Association (BERA), the group has occasionally changed in personnel but has doggedly pursued the agenda of improving assessment in all of its forms. The founding members were Patricia Broadfoot, Bryan Dockrell, Caroline Gipps, Wynne Harlen and Desmond Nuttall and its first task was to consider the implications of the 1988 Education Reform Act. Following Bryan Dockrell's retirement, Mary James and Richard Daugherty joined the group in 1992 and, in 1994, after the untimely death of Desmond Nuttall the previous year, Gordon Stobart and John Gardner also joined. The membership then remained more or less unchanged until Caroline Gipps and Patricia Broadfoot moved on, in 2000 and 2002 respectively.

Very able replacements were on hand and the current group now includes Paul Black, Kathryn Ecclestone and Judy Sebba. Dylan Wiliam was also a member for a short time before leaving to take up a post in the USA. In this book we are very pleased to welcome him back as a guest contributor, along with Dave Pedder as a co-author of a chapter with Mary James. Since 1997, when BERA ceased to sponsor policy task groups, we have continued to work as an independent group. Our primary source of funding has been the Nuffield Foundation, which has generously supported a variety of our activities including group meetings, regional seminars and the dissemination of our work. This funding has been vital and we would be very remiss if we did not take the opportunity here to acknowledge our grateful appreciation of both BERA's and, in more recent times, the Foundation's support.

This introduction to the book would be seriously deficient if acknowledgement of our sources and influences was not formally recorded. Over the period of its existence, the group has worked with many people including teachers, academics and curriculum and assessment agency personnel from around the world, local authority advisers and district superintendents, government officials, politicians and, most importantly, students in a variety of national and local contexts. There are too many to name and it would be inappropriate to single out specific people. However, the content of this book has been influenced by them all and we humbly record our thanks to everyone with whom we have had the privilege to work.

Part I Practice

Chapter 1

Assessment for Learning in the Classroom

Paul Black and Dylan Wiliam

Assessment in education must, first and foremost, serve the purpose of supporting learning. So it is fitting to start a study of assessment with an exploration of the meaning and practices of assessment which serve this purpose most directly. This chapter is the story of a development which started with a review of what research had to say about formative assessment. The background to this review, and the main features of its findings, are first described. Its results led to development work with teachers to explore how ideas taken from the research could be turned into practice. A description of this work is followed by reflections on its outcomes and implications. There is then a final discussion of the dissemination of the project's findings and the wider impact.

The research review

The background

Studies over many years have shown that formative assessment is an important aspect of teachers' classroom work and that attention to improving its practice can enhance the learners' achievements. Harry Black, a researcher in Scotland who was unique at the time in working with teachers to develop formative assessment, introduced his account of the subject by pointing out that formative assessment has always been part of the practice of teachers, quoting in evidence a letter written by the principal of Greenwich Hospital School (quoted in Chadwick, 1864) and calling attention to its neglect in the following trenchant terms:

> *Consider the amount of time, energy and money spent by both individual teachers, and schools in general, on setting and marking continuous assessment tests, end of session examinations and mock 'O' levels. Reflect on the money spent by examination boards and the number of assessment specialists employed by them. Read, if you can find a sabbatical term, the literature on the technology of assessment for reporting and certification. Compare these in turn with the complete lack of support normally given to teachers in devising and applying procedures to pinpoint their students' learning problems, with the virtual absence of outside agencies to develop formative assessment instruments and procedures, and the limited literature on the topic. (Black, 1986: 7)*

Linn, writing three years later, made a different and prophetic point about what might be involved:

> *the design of tests useful for the instructional decisions made in the classroom requires an integration of testing and instruction. It also requires a clear conception of the curriculum, the goals, and the process of instruction. And it requires a theory of instruction and learning and a much better understanding of the cognitive processes of learners. (Linn, 1989)*

These extracts should not be misunderstood: it is clear from Harry Black's work that his terms 'procedures' and 'instruments' were not references to conventional summative tests, and it should also be clear that Linn's 'tests useful for instructional decisions' was not a reference to such tests either. However, despite such insights in the writing of several authors, formative assessment was not regarded as a more than marginal component by many of those involved in public debates on education. The report of the government's Task Group on Assessment and Testing (DES/WO, 1988a) made teachers' formative assessment a central plank for its proposals for the new national assessment in the UK. While this was accepted in principle, however, in practice it was brushed aside by ministers and their advisers (Daugherty, 1995) as either already in place, or as a dangerous fall back to discredited ideas on child centred learning, or as a mere nod towards teachers' classroom work before focusing on the serious business of raising standards through national tests.

Yet there was accumulating in the research literature on formative assessment practices a formidable body of evidence that could support claims for its importance. Early reviews by Natriello (1987), Crooks (1988) and Marshall and Hodgen (2005) drew attention to this evidence, but these were neither sufficiently comprehensive in scope, nor targeted directly at making the argument that formative assessment was a powerful way to raise standards. In particular, the TGAT group was not even able to call on the body of research already published by 1987 with sufficient strength to support its argument for giving priority to teachers' formative assessment, to offset the general belief in the promise that external testing with public accountability would be the sure way to raise standards (Black, 1997).

The Assessment Reform Group, however, whose main concern was consideration of research evidence as a basis for formation of assessment policy, judged that further exploration of formative assessment was essential and in 1996 obtained funding from the Nuffield Foundation to support a review of the research. The group then invited us to carry out this review, and because of our long-standing interest in formative assessment, we were happy to agree to undertake the task.

The review

Our survey of the research literature involved checking through many books plus the issues of over 160 journals for a period of nine years and studying earlier reviews of research (Crooks, 1988; Natriello, 1987). This process yielded about 580 articles or chapters to study. Out of this we prepared a lengthy review, which used material from 250 of these sources. The review was published (Black and Wiliam, 1998a) together with comments on our work by experts from five different countries. In studying these articles our initial focus was on those describing empirical work, whether with quantitative or qualitative evidence, which were exploring some aspect of on-going assessment and feedback between teachers and students. As the work progressed, our view of the issues relevant to the field also changed as our searches led us to look at work on issues related and relevant to the practices and understanding of formative assessment.

A first section of the review surveyed the evidence. We looked for studies which showed quantitative evidence of learning gains by comparing data for an experimental group with similar data from a control group. We reported on about 30 such studies, all of which showed that innovations, which included strengthening the practice of formative assessment, produced significant and often substantial learning gains. They ranged over various age groups (from 5-year-olds to university undergraduates), across several school subjects and involved several countries.

The fact that such gains had been achieved by a variety of methods which had, as a common feature, enhanced formative assessment indicated that it is this feature that accounted, at least in part, for the successes. However, it did not follow that it would be an easy matter to achieve such gains on a wide scale in normal classrooms, in part because the research reports lacked enough detail about the practical use of the methods, detail that would be needed if replication was envisaged. More significantly, successful implementation of methods of this kind is heavily dependent on the social and educational cultures of the context of their development, so that they cannot be merely 'replicated' in a different context.

A second section covered research into current teacher practices. The picture that emerged was that formative assessment was weak. In relation to *effective learning* it seemed that teachers' questions and tests encouraged rote and superficial learning, even where teachers said that they wanted to develop understanding. There was also evidence of the *negative impact* of a focus on comparing students with one another, so emphasizing competition rather than personal improvement. Furthermore, teachers' feedback to students often seemed to serve social and managerial functions, often at the expense of the learning functions.

A third section focused on research into the involvement of students in formative assessment. Students' beliefs about the goals of learning, about the risks involved in responding in various ways, and about what learning work should be like, were all shown to affect their motivation. Other research explored the different ways in which positive action could be taken, covering such topics as study methods, study skills and peer and self-assessment.

A fourth section looked at ideas that could be gleaned from the research about strategies that might be productive for teachers. One feature that emerged was the potential of the learning task, as designed by a teacher, for exploring students' learning. Another was the importance of the classroom discourse, as steered by teachers' questions and by their handling of students' responses.

A fifth section shifted attention to research into comprehensive systems of teaching and learning in which formative assessment played a part. One example was mastery learning programmes. In these it was notable that students were given feedback on their current achievement against some expected level of achievement (the 'mastery' level), that such feedback was given rapidly and that students were given the opportunity to discuss with their peers how to remedy any weaknesses.

A sixth section explored in more detail the literature on feedback. The review of empirical evidence by Kluger and DeNisi (1996) showed that this can have positive effects only if the feedback is used as a guide to improvement, whilst the conceptual analysis of the concept of feedback by Ramaprasad (1983) and the development of this by Sadler (1989) emphasized that learners must understand both the 'reference level' – that is, the goal of their learning – and the actual level of their understanding. An equally important message here came from the research on attribution theory (for example by Vispoel and Austin, 1995) showing that teachers must aim to inculcate in their students the idea that success is due to internal unstable specific factors such as effort, rather than on stable general factors such as ability (internal) or whether one is positively regarded by the teacher (external).

Overall, the features which seem to characterize many of the studies were :

- Formative work involves new ways to enhance feedback between those taught and the teacher, ways which require new modes of pedagogy and significant changes in classroom practice;
- Underlying the various approaches are assumptions about what makes for effective learning – in particular that students have to be actively involved;
- For assessment to function formatively, the results have to be used to adjust teaching and learning – so a significant aspect of any programme will be the ways in which teachers do this;
- The ways in which assessment can affect the motivation and self-esteem of students, and the benefits of engaging students in self-assessment, both deserve careful attention.

The structure of the six sections outlined above did not emerge automatically; it was our chosen way to summarize the relevant literature. Our definition of 'relevance' expanded as we went along, so we had to find ways of organizing a widening field of research and of making new conceptual links in order to be able to combine the various findings into as coherent a picture as possible. We believe that our review generated a momentum for work in this field by providing a new framework that would be difficult to create in any other way.

Moving into action

Setting up a project

The second stage of our story followed the first almost inevitably. Given that our review had shown that innovations in formative assessment could raise standards of student achievement, it was natural to think about ways to help schools secure these benefits. However, even if a recipe for practice could have been derived from the variety of research studies, our own experience of teachers' professional development had taught us that the implementation of practices in classrooms, which would be new to most of the teachers involved, could not be a straightforward matter of proclaiming a recipe for them to follow. We believed that new ideas about teaching and learning could only be made to work in particular contexts, in our case that of teachers in (initially) secondary schools in the UK, if teachers are able to transform these and so create a new practical knowledge relevant to their task.

So we obtained funding initially from the UK's Nuffield Foundation and later from the USA, for a two year development project. To find schools and teachers to work with, we talked with assessment specialists from two local (district) education authorities (LEAs) whom we knew would understand and support our aims and whose districts, Oxfordshire and Medway, were within easy reach of London. Six schools who taught students in the age range 11 to 18 years were then chosen by the LEA specialists, the criterion agreed with us being that they were to avoid schools that were either in serious difficulties or unusually successful. They agreed to collaborate with us and each selected two science and two mathematics teachers. In the second year of the project we added two teachers of English, from each of the same schools, and one additional mathematics and science teacher, so that in all 48 teachers were involved. The LEA specialists supported and were involved with the work throughout. The project was called the King's-Medway-Oxfordshire Formative Assessment Project (KMOFAP) to highlight our close collaboration with these partners (Black and Wiliam, 2003).

The teachers within the schools were chosen by the schools themselves, with advice from the LEA staff. As a result, they ranged across the spectrum to include heads of subject departments, a teacher close to retirement, one that was reputed to have been chosen on the grounds of 'needing some INSET' and a newly qualified teacher. However, the majority were experienced and well qualified. Before the start of the project's work, each school was visited by us, with the LEA adviser, so that we could explain the aims and the requirements to the head teacher. We chose to work with secondary mathematics and science because we were specialists in those two subjects at this level and believed that the nature of the subject matter was important. English teachers were brought in when a colleague specializing in education in English was able to join the King's team.

We advised the teachers to focus on a few focal classes, and to eventually choose only one, to try out their specific innovations with a caveat that they might do well to avoid those age groups (14- and 16-year-olds) where statutory national tests could inhibit freedom to experiment. In the event some ignored this advice, so that the classes involved ranged over ages 11 to 16. Whilst support from each school's senior management was promised in principle, it varied in practice. Moreover, within the school subject faculty or department some had stronger support from subject colleagues than others, and in fact the collegial support that would be essential in an endeavour of this kind was largely provided by the meetings – once every five weeks – when the project teachers all spent a day together with the staff at King's. There was evidence of interest and support from other school colleagues and several productive ideas were injected into the group from this type of source. It was soon clear that the ideas in the project were also influencing teachers more widely, to the extent that in some cases it was difficult to find suitable 'control' classes for comparison of their test performance with those of students in the focal classes of the project.

The practices that developed

These practices will be described here under four headings: oral feedback in *classroom questioning* (more recently relabelled as *dialogue*), *feedback through marking, peer and self-assessment*, and the *formative use of summative tests*. The account given will be brief – more detailed accounts have been published else-where (Black et al., 2003). These were defined and developed in the course of the project, the process being one where we drew from the research findings a variety of ideas for which there was evidence of potential value and then the teachers selected from these and developed them in their own ways. Whilst the focus of the first of these and of some aspects of the other three was on class-room practice, it was not a criterion for selecting our inputs. The four themes discussed below were an outcome of the project. Although they were related to our inputs, we could not have predicted at the outset that this model of four groups of activities would emerge in the way that it did.

For *classroom dialogue* the aim was to improve the interactive feedback that is central to formative assessment. One account of wait time research (Rowe, 1974) motivated teachers to allow longer time after asking a question so that students would have time to think out responses. They could thus be expected to become actively involved in question and answer discussions and would make longer replies. Increased participation by students also required that all answers, right or wrong, be taken seriously, the aim being to develop thoughtful improvement rather than to evoke expected answers. A consequence of such changes was that teachers learnt more about the pre-knowledge of their students and about any gaps and misconceptions in that knowledge, so that their next move could be to address a learner's real needs.

As they tried to develop this approach, teachers realized that more effort had to be spent in framing questions that would evoke, and so help to explore, crit-ical indicators of students' understanding. They also had to listen carefully to students and then formulate meaningful responses and challenges that would help them to extend that understanding.

The task of developing an interactive style of classroom dialogue required a radical change in teaching style from many teachers, one that they found chal-lenging not least because it felt at first as if they were losing control. Some were well over a year into the project before such change was achieved. Subsequent work with other schools has shown that it is this aspect of formative work that teachers are least likely to implement successfully.

To address *feedback through marking*, teachers were first given an account of research studies which had established that whilst students' learning can be advanced by feedback through comments, the giving of marks or grades has a negative effect because students ignore comments when marks are also given (Butler, 1988). These results surprised and worried the teachers because of concern about the effect of returning students' work with comments but no marks. However, potential conflicts with school policy were resolved as experience showed that the provision of comments gave both students and their parents advice on how to improve. It also set up a new focus on the learning issues involved rather than on trying to interpret a mark or grade. To make the most of the learning opportunity created by feedback on written work, procedures that required students to follow up comments had to be planned as part of the overall learning process.

One consequence of this change was that teachers had to think more carefully in framing comments on written work in order to give each student guidance on how to improve. As the skills of formulating and using such feedback were developed, it became more clear that the quality of the tasks set for written homework or classwork was critical. As for oral questions, tasks had to be designed to encourage students to develop and express key features of their understanding.

For *peer and self-assessment*, the starting point was Sadler's (1989) argument that self-assessment is essential to learning because students can only achieve a learning goal if they understand that goal and can assess what they need to do to reach it. Thus the criteria for evaluating any learning achievements must be made transparent to students to enable them to have a clear overview both of the aims of their work and of what it means to complete it successfully. Insofar as they do so they begin to develop an overview of that work so that they can manage and control it; in other words, they develop their capacity for meta-cognitive thinking. A notable example of the success of such work is the research of White and Frederiksen (1998).

In practice, peer assessment turned out to be an important stimulus to self-assessment. It is uniquely valuable because the interchange is in language that students themselves would naturally use, because they learn by taking the roles of teachers and examiners of others (Sadler, 1998), and because students appear to find it easier to make sense of criteria for their work if they examine other students' work alongside their own. A typical exercise would be on the marking of homework. Students were asked to label their work with 'traffic lights' as an indicator of their confidence in their learning, that is, using red or amber if they were totally or partially unsure of their success and green where they were confident. Those who had used amber or green would then work in mixed groups to appraise and help with one another's work, while the teacher would pay special attention to those who had chosen red.

Teachers developed three ways of making *formative use of summative tests*. One way was to ask students, in preparation for a test, to 'traffic light' a list of key words or the topics on which the test would be set, an exercise which would stimulate them to reflect on areas where they felt their learning was secure and where they needed to concentrate their efforts. One reason for doing this was that teachers had realized that many students had no strategy in preparing for a test by formulating a strategic appraisal of their learning.

A second way was to mark one another's test papers in peer groups, in the way outlined above for the marking of homework. This could be particularly challenging when they were expected to invent their own marking rubric, for to do this they had to think about the purpose of a question and about which criteria of quality to apply to responses. After peer marking, teachers could reserve a time for discussion of those questions that give particular difficulty.

A further idea was introduced from research studies (Foos et al., 1994; King, 1992) that have shown that students trained to prepare for examinations by generating and then answering their own questions out-performed comparable groups who prepared in conventional ways. Preparation of test questions calls for, and so develops, an overview of the topic.

The teachers' work on summative assessments challenged our expectations that, for the context in which they worked, formative and summative assessments are so different in their purpose that they have to be kept apart. The finding that emerged was quite different – that summative tests should be, and should be seen to be, a positive part of the learning process. If they could be actively involved in the test process, students might see that they can be beneficiaries rather than victims of testing, because tests can help them improve their learning. However, this synergy could not be achieved in the case of high-stakes tests set and marked externally; for these, as currently designed and administered, formative use would not be possible.

Reflections on the outcome

It was clear that the new ideas that had emerged between the teachers and ourselves involved far more than the mere addition of a few tactical tricks. Some reflection was needed to tease out the more fundamental issues that seemed to have been raised.

A focus on learning

One of the most surprising things that happened during the early project meetings was that the participating teachers asked us to run a session on learning theories. In retrospect, perhaps, we should not have been so surprised. Whilst teachers could work out, after the event, whether or not any feedback had had the desired effect, what they needed was to be able to give their students feedback that they knew in advance was going to be useful. To do that they needed to build up models of how students learn.

Thus the teachers came to take greater care in selecting tasks, questions and other prompts, to ensure that the responses made by students actually 'put on the table' the ideas that they were bringing to a learning task. The key to effective learning is to then find ways to help students restructure their knowledge to build in new and more powerful ideas. In the KMOFAP classrooms, as the teachers came to listen more attentively to the students' responses, they began to appreciate more fully that learning was not a process of passive reception of knowledge, but one in which the learners must be active in creating their own understandings. These ideas reflect some of the main principles of the constructivist view of learning – to start where the student is and involve them actively in the process.

Students also changed, coming to understand what counted as good work by focusing on the criteria and their exemplification. Sometimes this was done through concentrated whole-class discussion around a particular example; at other times it was achieved through students using criteria to assess the work of their peers. The activities, by encouraging students to review their work in the light of the goals and criteria, were helping them to develop meta-cognitive approaches to learning.

Finally, the involvement of students both in whole-class dialogue and in peer group discussions, all within a change in the classroom culture to which all four activities contributed, was creating a richer community of learners where the social learning of students was becoming more salient and effective.

A learning environment and changes of role

Reflection on the experiences described above led to more profound thinking by participants about their role as teachers and about the need to 'engineer' learning environments in order to involve students more actively in learning tasks. The emphasis had to be on the students doing the thinking and making that thinking public. As one teacher said:

> There was a definite transition at some point, from focusing on what I was putting into the process, to what the students were contributing. It became obvious that one way to make a significant sustainable change was to get the students doing more of the thinking. I then began to search for ways to make the learning process more transparent to the students. Indeed, I now spend my time looking for ways to get students to take responsibility for their learning and at the same time making the learning more collaborative.

This teacher had changed his role, from a presenter of content to a leader of an exploration and development of ideas in which all students were involved. One of the striking features of the project was the way in which, in the early stages, many described the new approach as 'scary', because they felt that they were losing control of their classes. Towards the end of the project, they described this same process not as a loss of control, but one of sharing responsibility for the class's learning with the class – exactly the same process, but viewed from two very different perspectives.

The learning environment envisaged requires a classroom culture that may well be unfamiliar and disconcerting for both teachers and students. The effect of the innovations implemented by our teachers was to change the rules, usually implicit, that govern the behaviours that are expected and seen as legitimate by teachers and by students. As Perrenoud (1991) put it:

> *Every teacher who wants to practise formative assessment must reconstruct the teaching contract so as to counteract the habits acquired by his pupils.*

From the students' viewpoint, they have to change from behaving as passive recipients of the knowledge offered to becoming active learners who can take responsibility for their own learning. These students become more aware of when they are learning and when they are not. One class, who were subsequently taught by a teacher not emphasizing assessment for learning, surprised that teacher by complaining: 'Look, we've told you we don't understand this. Why are you going on to the next topic?'

What had been happening here was that everybody's role expectations, that is, what teachers and students think that being a teacher or being a student requires you to do, had been altered. Whilst it can seem daunting to undertake such changes, they do not have to happen suddenly. Changes with the KMOFAP teachers came slowly – over two years rather than one – and steadily, as experience developed and confidence grew in the use of the various strategies for enriching feedback and interaction.

A collection of individual and group discussion data near the end of the project did expose one unresolved problem; the tension between the formative approach and summative demands. Some, but not all, teachers were confident that the new work would yield better test results than 'teaching to the test'. However, for their in-school summative tests many felt impelled to use questions from the Key Stage 3 and GCSE tests despite doubts about the validity of these in relation to the improved student learning achieved in the project. The general picture was that, despite developing the formative use of their summative tests, teachers felt that they could not reconcile the external test and accountability pressures with their investment in improved formative assessment.

Research and practice

Explaining success – the focus of the project

We were surprised that the project was so successful in promoting quite radical changes in the practices of almost all of the teachers involved and wondered whether lessons could be learned from it about the notoriously difficult problem of turning research into practice. One relevant factor is that the ideas which the project set before the teachers had an intrinsic acceptability to them. We were talking about improving learning in the classroom, which was central to their professional identities, as opposed to bureaucratic measures such as predicting test levels. One feature of our review was that most of it was concerned with such issues as students' perceptions, peer and self-assessment, and the role of feedback in a pedagogy focused on learning. Thus it helped to take the emphasis in formative assessment studies away from systems, with a focus on the formative-summative interface, and to relocate it on classroom processes. Acceptability was also enhanced by our policy of emphasizing that it was up to each teacher to make his or her own choice between the different formative practices; so teachers developed their own personal portfolios, supplementing or dropping components as their own experience and that of their colleagues led them to change.

Linked to the previous factor is that through our choice to concentrate on the classroom processes, we had decided to live with the external constraints operating at the formative-summative interface: the legislated attempts to change the system, in the 1980s and 1990s in England, were set aside. Whilst it might have been merely prudent to not try to tilt at windmills a more fundamental strength was that it was at the level chosen, that of the core of learning, that formative work stakes its claim for attention. Furthermore, given that any change has to work itself out in teachers' practical action, this is where reform should always have started. The evidence of learning gains, from the literature review and from our project, restates and reinforces the claim for priority of formative work that earlier policy recommendations (DES, 1988a) tried in vain to establish.

Another factor that appears to have been important is the credibility that we brought as researchers to the process. In their project diaries, several of the teachers commented that it was our espousal of these ideas, as much as the ideas themselves, that persuaded them to engage with the project. Part of that credibility is that we chose to work with teachers in the three subjects – English, mathematics and science – when in each of these one or two members of the team had both expertise and a reputation in the subject community. Thus, when specific issues such as 'Is this an appropriate question for exploring students' ideas about the concept of photosynthesis?' arose, we could discuss them seriously.

Explaining success: the process strategy

The way in which teachers were involved was important. They all met with the researchers for a whole day every five weeks and over two years in all. In addition, two researchers were able to visit the schools, observe the teachers in their classrooms, give them feedback, collect interview data on their perceptions and elicit ideas about issues for discussion in the whole day meetings. The detailed reports of our findings (Black et al., 2002, 2003) are based on records of these meetings, on the observations and records of visits to classrooms by the King's team, on interviews with and writing by the teachers themselves, on feedback from the LEA advisers who held their own discussions with their teachers and on a few discussions with student groups. As the project developed, the King's team played a smaller part as the teachers took over the agenda and used the opportunity for their own peer learning.

In our development model, we attended to both the content and the process of teacher development (Reeves et al., 2001). We attended to the process of professional development through an acknowledgement that teachers need time, freedom and support from colleagues, in order to reflect critically upon and to develop their practice whilst also offering practical strategies and techniques about how to begin the process. By themselves, however, these are not enough. Teachers also need concrete ideas about the directions in which they can productively take their practice and thus there is a need for work on the professional development of teachers to pay specific attention to subject-specific dimensions of teacher learning (Wilson and Berne, 1999).

One of the key assumptions of the project was that if the promise of formative assessment was to be realized, a research design in which teachers are asked to test out and perhaps modify a scheme worked out for them by researchers would not be appropriate. We presented them with a collection of ideas culled from research findings rather than with a structured scheme. We argued that a process of supported development was an essential next step. In such a process, the teachers in their classrooms had to work out the answers to many of the practical questions which the research evidence we had presented could not answer. The issues had to be reformulated in collaboration with them, where possible in relation to fundamental insights and certainly in terms that could make sense to their peers in ordinary classrooms.

The key feature of the INSET sessions was the development of action plans. Since we were aware from other studies that effective implementation of formative assessment requires teachers to renegotiate the 'learning contract' that they had evolved with their students (Brousseau, 1984; Perrenoud, 1991), we decided that implementing formative assessment would best be done at the beginning of a new school year. For the first six months of the project (January 1999 to July 1999), therefore, we encouraged the teachers to experiment with some of the strategies and techniques suggested by the research, such as rich questioning, comment-only marking, sharing criteria with learners and student peer and self-assessment. Each teacher was then asked to draw up an action plan of the practices they wished to develop and to identify a single focal class with whom these strategies would be introduced at the start of the new school year in September 1999. (Details of these plans can be found in Black et al., 2003.) As the teachers explored the relevance of formative assessment for their own practice, they transformed ideas from the research and from other teachers into new ideas, strategies and techniques and these were in turn communicated to teachers thus creating a 'snowball' effect. As we have introduced these ideas to more and more teachers outside the project, we have become better at communicating the key ideas.

Through our work with teachers, we have come to understand more clearly how the task of applying research into practice is much more than a simple process of 'translating' the findings of researchers into the classroom. The teachers in our project were engaged in a process of knowledge creation, albeit of a distinct kind, and possibly relevant only in the settings in which they work (Hargreaves, 1999). We stressed this feature of our approach with the teachers right from the outset of the project. We discovered later that some of them did not, at that stage, believe us: they thought that we knew exactly what we wanted them to do but were leaving them to work it out for themselves. As they came to know us better they realized that, at the level of everyday classroom practice, we really did not know what to do.

20

The arguments in this section are addressed only to the specific question with which it started – why did this project work? – with the intent of thereby illuminating the vexed issues of the relationship between research and practice. They cannot claim to address the question of whether an innovation with similar aims would succeed in different circumstances. Any attempt to answer such a question would have to relate the context and particular features of our work to the context and features of any new situation, bearing in mind that any such innovation will start from where our work finished and not from where it started.

Dissemination and impact

Publicity

Publicity designed to make a case for formative assessment started, alongside the publication of the research review, in 1998. Although we tried to adhere closely to the traditional standards of scholarship in the social sciences when conducting and writing our review, we did not do so when exploring the policy implications in a booklet entitled *Inside the Black Box* (Black and Wiliam, 1998b) that we published, and publicized widely, alongside the academic review. This raised a great deal of interest and created some momentum for our project and for subsequent dissemination. While the standards of evidence we adopted in conducting the review might be characterized as those of 'academic rationality', the standard for *Inside the Black Box* was much closer to that of 'reasonableness' advocated by Toulmin for social enquiry (Toulmin, 2001). In some respects *Inside the Black Box* represented our opinions and prejudices as much as anything else, although we would like to think that these are supported by evidence and are consistent with the fifty years of experience in this field that we had between us. It is also important to note that its success – it has to date sold about 50,000 copies – has been as much due to its rhetorical force as to its basis in evidence. This would make many academics uneasy for it appears to blur the line between fact and value, but as Flyvbjerg (2001) argues, social enquiry has failed precisely because it has focused on analytic rationality rather than value-rationality (see also Wiliam, 2003).

The quantitative evidence that formative assessment does raise standards of achievement was a powerful motivator for the teachers at the start of the project. One aspect of the KMOFAP project was that the King's team worked with each teacher to collect data on the gains in test performance of the students involved in the innovation and comparable data for similar classes who were not involved (Wiliam et al., 2004). The project did not introduce any tests of its own; the achievement data used were from the tests that the schools used for all students whether or not they were involved in the project. The analysis of these data showed an overall and significant gain in achievement outcomes. Thus the evidence from the research review can now be supplemented by evidence of enhanced performance in the UK national and in schools' own examinations. This evidence was incorporated, with an account of the practical lessons learnt in the KMOFAP project, in a second small booklet entitled *Working Inside the Black Box* (Black et al., 2002) which has also been widely successful with about 40,000 copies sold to date, whilst a detailed account of the project's work (Black et al., 2003) has also been very well received. Other publicity for formative assessment, further research results and practical advice notably from the Assessment Reform Group (ARG, 1999, 2002a,b) have added to the impact.

Dissemination

Following this project, members of the King's team have responded to numerous invitations to talk to other groups: in the space of three years they have made over 200 such contributions. These have ranged across all subjects and across both primary and secondary phases. In addition, there has been sustained work with four groups of primary schools. The King's team has also been involved as advisers to large-scale development ventures in several local government districts in the UK, with education ministries in Scotland and in Jersey, and in a recent exploration of classroom outcomes for a government programme which aims to improve teaching and learning practices in schools.

One reason for many of these requests is that assessment for learning was adopted as one of several key areas in the UK government's Key Stage 3 initiative, a programme focusing on improvements in methods of teaching and learning for students in the age range 11- to 14-years-old. The work of the ARG and of the King's group has been quoted and used in the documents for schools and in the training for local advisers that form the basic tools for this initiative. It has turned out to be the area that schools in general have been most ready to adopt.

The Education Department of the Scottish Executive, which has full legislative powers for education in Scotland, has also taken up the work as one of several projects in its Assessment is for Learning Development Programme. This project, entitled 'Support for Professional Practice in Formative Assessment', involved four groups of 8 or 9 schools, including both secondary and primary. They were supported by one development officer and staff from two university faculties and also by contributions from the King's project staff. The work started in May 2002 and an evaluation project, conducted by the London Institute of Education, completed its work in summer 2004. The evaluation (Hallam et al., 2004) reported the following findings regarding impact on students:

- A substantial increase in perceptions of pupils' engagement with learning, with particular notable impact on lower attainers, shy and disengaged pupils in a special school for pupils with complex learning needs;
- Better motivation, more positive attitudes to learning and, for many, enhanced confidence;
- Some improvements in behaviour and more co-operation in class in teamwork and in learning;
- Dramatic improvements in pupils' learning skills, in learning about their strengths and weaknesses and about what they needed to do to make progress, so encouraging them to take more responsibility for their learning.

As for the teachers, they reported greater awareness of the needs of individual students and improvement in their motivation, confidence and enjoyment of their work. They believed that their capacity for self-evaluation, reflection and continuous improvement had been enhanced. A positive impact on their schools as a whole was also reported and similar benefit for parents was reported by the primary schools.

Just as these features reflected the experience of the KMOFAP project (which was not independently evaluated), so did most of the points that were judged to contribute to the success. These included the provision of time out of class for teachers to plan, prepare, reflect and evaluate the action research elements of the project and the commitment of each school's head teacher and senior management team.

The evaluation also revealed several challenges. One was that some staff found that the initiative called for a fundamental change in their pedagogy which they found stressful and for more priority in developing differentiation in implementation of the strategies. A need to meet the demands of external accountability was also a cause for concern, with teachers reporting tension between the requirements of summative assessment and the implementation of new formative practices. Again, in all of these features there was close correspondence with the KMOFAP experience.

Future issues

Many questions arise from this work which await further research enquiry. Some will be taken further in subsequent chapters of this book. The need to co-ordinate all of the above issues in a comprehensive theoretical framework linking assessment in classrooms to issues of pedagogy and curriculum will be tackled in Chapter 5. The tensions and possible synergies between teachers' own assessments and the assessment results and methods required by society will be explored further in Chapter 6.

A further issue exists in the assumptions about learning underlying the curriculum and pedagogy. The beliefs of teachers about learning, about their roles as assessors and about the 'abilities' and prospects of their students, will affect their interpretations of their students' learning work and will thereby determine the quality of their formative assessment. This will be taken further in Chapters 3 and 4. A parallel enquiry is also needed into the perceptions and beliefs held by students about themselves as learners and into their experience of the changes that follow from innovations in formative assessment. Exploration of this issue is a current aim of the ESRC Learning How to Learn (L2L) project.

Light will also be cast by that project on the problem of the generalizability of the findings, from both KMOFAP and the Scottish initiative. The experience so far of schools basing their own innovations on the existing findings of results from research and from recently developed practice is that a sustained commitment over at least two years is needed, that evaluation and feedback have to be built in to any plan and that any teachers involved need strong support, both from colleagues and from their school leadership. The more recent L2L project – a collaboration between Cambridge, King's College and the Open University – has implemented interventions based in part on the findings of our project. This project has given less intensive support to schools, but at the same time has been researching the beliefs and practices of both students and teachers and issues of professional development within and across a large number of schools. This work is reported in Chapter 3.

Other issues that might repay further exploration are :

- The surprising feature – that the research in this field has paid virtually no attention to issues relating to race, class and gender;
- The effect on practice of the content knowledge, and the pedagogical content knowledge, that teachers deploy in particular school subjects. Issues for enquiry would include the way in which these resources underlie each teacher's composition and presentation of the learning work, and the interpretative frameworks that they use in responding to the evidence provided by feedback from students;
- The need to pursue in more detail the many issues about pedagogy that are entailed in formative assessment work, notably the deployment in this context of the results of the numerous studies of classroom dialogue (see for example Alexander, 2004);
- The nature of the social setting in the classroom, as influenced both by the divisions of responsibility between learners and teachers in formative assessment, and by the constraints of the wider school system;
- The need to extend work of this nature to other groups, notably pupils in infant and junior school and students in post-16, tertiary and non-statutory assessment settings (Ecclestone et al., 2004).

More generally, this work raises questions about the 'application' of research to practice and the links between this and the professional development of teachers (Black and Wiliam, 2003). Researching how teachers take on research, adapt it and make it their own is much more difficult than researching the effects of, for example, different curricula, class sizes or the contribution of classroom assistants. Furthermore, the criteria applied in judging the practical value of research aligned to development can easily be made too stringent – if, as we believe is reasonable, an approach in which 'the balance of probabilities' rather than 'beyond reasonable doubt' was adopted as the burden of proof, then this type of educational research would be accepted as having much to say. Thus we take issue with the stance of some policy makers who appear to want large-scale research conducted to the highest standards of analytic rationality, but must also display findings which are relevant to policy. It may often be the case that these two goals are, in fact, incompatible. To put it another way, when policy without evidence meets development with some evidence, development should prevail.

This chapter is based on a story. We claim that it is an important story, in that the success of the project that it describes helped to give impetus to the wider adoption of formative assessment practices and to recognition of their potential. The significance for this book is that those practices, developed with the teachers, helped to put classroom flesh on the conceptual bones of the idea of assessment for learning. Given that serving learning is the first and most important purpose of assessment, this provides an appropriate starting point for the comprehensive picture of assessment that is developed through subsequent chapters.

Chapter 2

Professional Learning as a Condition for Assessment for Learning

Mary James and David Pedder

Chapter 1 described what research has to say about assessment for learning and how the King's-Medway-Oxfordshire Formative Assessment Project (KMOFAP) sought to turn ideas from research into practice. Implications for changes in classroom roles were made explicit. Such changes are not trivial; they involve changes in understanding, values and attitudes as well as behaviour. Moreover, both teachers and students need to change. It was significant that teachers in the KMOFAP were keen to tell their personal stories of change (Black et al., 2003: 80–90). However, this raises questions about the conditions within and across schools that enable such change to take place and, specifically, what kind of professional learning by teachers is most conducive to the development of assessment for learning practice. Such questions were one focus of the Learning How to Learn – in the Classrooms, Schools and Networks Project (funded by the UK Economic and Social Research Council (ESRC)[1]) which sought to build on the work of the KMOFAP and extend it.

This chapter examines further the issue of learning by teachers in support of assessment for learning and reports analysis of a questionnaire to staff in 32 secondary and primary schools in England.[2] The questionnaire explored associations between teachers' reported classroom assessment practices and values, and their own professional learning practices and values. The importance of focusing professional learning on classrooms emerges strongly. The chapter concludes by arguing for an interpretation that draws parallels between processes of assessment for learning for students and inquiry-based learning by teachers.

Assessment for learning: implications for classroom roles

As Chapter 1 made clear, assessment for learning carries much potential for transforming teaching and learning processes in ways that enhance learning outcomes. These outcomes include attainments as conventionally assessed through performance tests and examinations (Black and Wiliam, 1998a) and other valued outcomes such as the development of motivation for learning as an enduring disposition (see Chapter 4). The transformation of classroom processes entails change in what teachers and students do. The focus is particularly on change in pedagogical practice, though the concept of 'practice' as understood in socio-cultural theory (see Chapter 3) involves much more than change in surface behaviours. It implies behaviour imbued with deeper understanding, and values informed by norms associated with particular constructions of appropriate roles for teachers and for learners. What makes assessment for learning both exciting and challenging is that, to be truly effective, it requires teachers and students to change the way they think about their classroom roles and their norms of behaviour.

This was a main message of Chapter 1. In its fullest expression it gives explicit roles to learners, not just to teachers, for instigating teaching and learning. Thus students are not merely the objects of their teacher's behaviour, they are animators of their own effective teaching and learning processes. This has its clearest embodiment in processes of peer and self-assessment when students: (i) individually or collaboratively, develop the motivation to reflect on their previous learning and identify objectives for new learning; (ii) when they analyse and evaluate problems they or their peers are experiencing and structure a way forward; and (iii) when, through self-regulation, they act to bring about improvement. In other words, they become autonomous, independent and active learners. When this happens, teaching is no longer the sole preserve of the adult teacher; learners are brought into the heart of teaching and learning processes and decision making as they adopt pedagogical practices to further their own learning and that of their peers. It gives the old expression of being 'self-taught' a new meaning.

These expanded roles for learners are reflected in the Assessment Reform Group's ten principles for assessment for learning which, although the focus is mainly on what teachers can do, state that the role of teachers should be to help students take on new roles as learners, specifically to:

- Understand the learning goals they are pursuing and to identify the criteria they, and their peers and/or their teacher, will use for assessing progress;
- Understand how they are learning as well as what they are learning;
- Reflect on their learning strengths and weaknesses and to develop approaches to learning that build on these;
- Make progress through constructive formative feedback from peers and their teacher on how to improve upon their work;
- Think about their learning and progress in relation to their own previous performance rather than in comparison with others;
- Develop the skills of peer and self-assessment as an important way of engaging in self-reflection, identifying the next steps in their learning and encouraging their peers to do the same.

In brief, effective assessment for learning involves radical transformation in classroom teaching and learning through the development of two key aspects. First, new understandings and perspectives need to be developed among teachers and students about each other and, therefore, about the nature of teaching and of learning. Second, new attitudes to and practices of learning and teaching, shaped by explicit and critically reflective modes of participation, need to be acquired and implemented. This crucially involves developing a language and disposition for talking about teaching and learning. Just as such transformation requires new dimensions of student learning, so it is essential for teachers to learn if they are to promote and support change in classroom assessment roles and practices. One of the Assessment Reform Group's (ARG, 2002a) ten principles makes this explicit:

> *Assessment for learning should be regarded as a key professional skill for teachers. Teachers require the professional knowledge and skills to: plan for assessment; observe learning; analyse and interpret evidence of learning; give feedback to learners and support learners in self-assessment. Teachers should be supported in developing these skills through initial and continuing professional development.*

However, such learning is not a straightforward matter, any more than it is for students. It is not achieved simply by telling teachers what they have to do, issuing them with ring-binders containing information and advice, showing examples of 'best practice', and reinforcing the messages through inspection. Learning that involves radical transformation in roles always requires change in normative orientations. This, in turn, involves development of frameworks of values and principles to guide action when faced with decisions about how best to act in novel or unpredictable situations. Rational-empirical or power-coercive strategies will not do. But alternative normative-re-educative approaches (Bennis et al., 1961) require opportunities to try out and evaluate new ways of thinking and practising. Thus the metaphor of 'learning as participation' may be important, to set alongside the more familiar metaphor of 'learning as acquisition' of knowledge, skills and understanding (see Sfard, 1998), because teachers need to practise new roles.

This continuous learning in the context of practice is described by a senior teacher from one of the secondary schools in the Learning How to Learn Project. In the following quotation from an interview she explains why teacher learning is essential for the promotion of assessment for learning:

> *Well it won't just happen. I think teacher learning is essential to it ... I think something needs to be invested in order for there to be an outcome. And it needs to keep going because in a way some of these questions imply that it's a sort of finished business. 'We know about that now. You just do rich questioning, do the self and peer assessment, do whatever it might be, feedback without marks and that's all sorted.' Well it isn't, and that's actually at the heart of it. It's a development of permanent reflection and refinement and there's no end if you like. You can't reach the stage where you can say 'OK, done that, got there, sorted, I've done my learning and now I'm teaching OK.' The profession should never be like that anyway and no profession should, actually. For one thing the external circumstances are changing, but also, what we understand about learning is changing all the time. It's*

what we understand professionally, we as a collective profession of teachers, or what we as individuals understand, or what we with that particular group of students understand. It keeps changing; it's quite a dynamic process. And I know that approaches which work with one class may need to be subtly changed in order to work with another class. So if you like, what you're learning is judgment and you're learning more about how to judge within a set of principles.

Questions for research

The thread of the argument so far can be summarized as follows: (i) the effective promotion of assessment for learning in classrooms requires a radical transformation of both teaching and learning roles; (ii) this requires considerable innovation in teachers' practices; (iii) teachers need to learn these new practices; (iv) this, in turn, needs to be encouraged by a supportive culture for continuous professional learning that gives teachers permission and opportunity to develop critically reflective modes of participation, for themselves and for their students.

An investigation of these links between changes in classroom assessment practice, teachers' learning and cultures for continuous professional development is at the heart of the Learning How to Learn Project. For the purposes of the argument we want to develop in this chapter, we will draw on evidence from one particular dataset to explore a main empirical research question arising from the discussion above: What kinds of relationships are there between teacher learning and classroom assessment practice? More specifically:

- How are different aspects of teachers' classroom assessment practices influenced by teacher learning practices?
- Which teacher learning practices are most strongly related to teachers' classroom assessment practices?
- How do teachers and school managers construe the relationship between teacher learning and the promotion of assessment for learning?

Evidence from responses to the Learning How to Learn staff questionnaire

The Learning How to Learn Project sought to develop understandings of the organizational conditions of schools in which teachers are successful in developing students' knowledge and practices in learning, and in learning how to learn through assessment for learning. This reflected our aspiration to bring insights from classroom-level and school-level research into closer alignment with one another. James et al. (2003: 3) argue that such alignment offers our best chance of furthering understanding of effective learning, its nature, the teaching practices that promote it and the kinds of professional learning and institutional conditions that help teachers to adopt new practices. These avenues of investigation constitute an enormous range of inquiry and much more than we can report here (see www.learntolearn.ac.uk for other publications from the project as they emerge). However, one salient aspect of this inquiry was our attempt to conceptualize teacher learning practices and values. We wanted to find out how teachers value and practise professional learning (see Pedder et al., 2005, for details about the literature and findings) and how teacher learning practices and classroom assessment practices are related. This second question is the particular focus of this chapter.

Here we draw on the first (baseline) administration of the 'staff question-naire' – a survey intended for all staff (managers, teachers and teaching assistants) in project schools. The use of this questionnaire enabled us to make some generalizations across our sample and insofar as we had over 1,000 responses from teachers across 32 primary and secondary schools, they may be representative of the views of teachers in other schools in England. Unlike observation data, which the project also collected but from a smaller sample of teachers, the questionnaire relied on self-report of practices and values. We acknowledge the possibility of a discrepancy between what teachers say they do, and what they actually do, although other evidence from this survey suggests they were open and honest about values-practice gaps (Pedder et al., 2005).

The staff questionnaire was designed to generate systematic data on teachers' views about classroom assessment, professional learning and school management, and to enable analysis of the patterns of associations in these three areas. It therefore consists of three sections: Section A with 30 statements about classroom assessment; Section B with 28 statements about teachers' professional learning; and Section C with 26 statements about school management practices and systems. The focus in this chapter is on data generated from sections A and B of the questionnaire – and the relationships between them. Some 1,397 teachers and managers at 32 schools were included in the first administration of this questionnaire and 1,018 completed questionnaires were returned, representing a return rate of 73 per cent.

Section A: classroom assessment

Staff were asked to make two kinds of responses[3] to each of the 30 questionnaire items in Section A. The first response focused on assessment practices. We asked respondents to tell us, with reference to their own practices in the case of teachers with no managerial responsibility (n = 558) or with reference to perceived practice across the school in the case of senior and middle managers (n = 460), whether particular practices were never true, rarely true, often true or mostly true. They were then asked to make a second response, this time about their values, and to indicate how important they felt any given practice was in creating opportunities for students to learn. The response categories were: not at all important, of limited importance, important or crucial. A fifth option was provided enabling respondents to record particularly strong negative value if they considered the statement to constitute bad practice. Figure 2.1 below provides an illustration of the dual-format scales which enabled us to compare practices (scale X) with values (scale Y) and identify practice-value gaps.

Figure 2.1: *Dual scale format for Section A of the teacher questionnaire*

Scale X This school now (About you)				Section A Teachers' assessment practices	Scale Y How important are your assessment practices for creating opportunities for students to learn? (About your values)				
Never true	Rarely true	Often true	Mostly true		Not at all important	Of limited importance	Important	Crucial	Bad practice
				I provide guidance to help my students assess their own work.					

In formulating Section A items, we operationalized conceptual and empirical insights from the assessment literature. We drew on distinctions between assessment *of* learning (summative assessment) and assessment *for* learning (formative assessment) and associations with performance versus learning (mastery) goal orientations (Ames, 1984; Dweck, 1986; Watkins, 2000) as well as notions of convergent and divergent approaches to assessment (Torrance and Pryor, 1998) and constructive alignment of pedagogy and assessment (Biggs, 1999). Particular attention was given to assessment *for* learning practices such as planning, questioning, feedback, sharing objectives and criteria, peer and self-evaluation (Black and Wiliam, 1998a; ARG, 2002a), underpinned by constructivist and social constructivist models of assessment and learning (see Chapter 3).

Section B: teachers' professional learning

As in Section A, teachers were asked to make two kinds of response to each of the 28 items in Section B. All teachers and managers were asked to make judgements about current practice, not by reference to their own practices, but according to their perceptions of these practices as: true of no staff, few staff, some staff or most staff. Respondents could choose to tick a fifth box labelled 'don't know'. Teachers were also asked to make a second response about their own values using the same Likert scale as in Section A, scale Y.

Again, theoretical and empirical insights influenced the construction of questionnaire items. On the basis of a review of over thirty years of research into teachers' professional learning, four hypotheses were developed: (i) teachers' learning is an embedded feature of teachers' classroom practice and reflection; (ii) teachers' learning is extended through consulting different sources of knowledge; (iii) teachers' learning is expanded through collaborative activity; (iv) teachers' learning is deepened through talking about and valuing learning. By construing teacher learning in terms of these four characteristics we were able to develop questionnaire items to operationalize them (see Pedder et al., 2005, for details). This enabled Section B to reflect a balanced interest in individual and social, interpersonal and intrapersonal, public and private processes of teacher learning.

Dimensions of classroom assessment and teacher learning

The data generated by the total of 58 items in two sections of our questionnaire provided opportunities for different kinds of analysis. However, in order to relate responses in Section A to those in Section B we found it helpful to reduce the data through factor analysis. Factor analysis was carried out separately for each section and was based on respondents' practice scores (derived from scale X). Analysis of Section A data yielded three factors with four from the Section B data. Cronbach's alpha values demonstrated that the internal consistency of the main factors was good (values greater than 0.7) with, as might be expected, the last factor in each group being a little less stable. The items underpinning dimensions to classroom assessment practices (Section A factors) are set out in Tables 2.1 to 2.3. It should be noted that our questionnaire attempted to capture a wide range of classroom assessment practices, although it was perceptions of formative assessment that were of particular interest. The three factors were interpreted as: making learning explicit; promoting learning autonomy and performance orientation. The interpretations and the constituent items of the factors are set out in three tables as follows:

Table 2.1 *'Making Learning Explicit' (Factor A1) items*

Factor A1: Making Learning Explicit: eliciting, clarifying and responding to evidence of learning; working with students to develop a positive learning orientation (alpha = 0.7302)

Item No	Item Text
1	Assessment provides me with useful evidence of students' understandings which they use to plan subsequent lessons.
10	Students are told how well they have done in relation to their own previous performance.
11	Students' learning objectives are discussed with students in ways they understand.
14	I identify students' strengths and advise them on how to develop them further.
15	Students are helped to find ways of addressing problems they have in their learning.
16	Students are encouraged to view mistakes as valuable learning opportunities.
18	I use questions mainly to elicit reasons and explanations from students.
20	Students' errors are valued for the insights they reveal about how students are thinking.
21	Students are helped to understand the learning purposes of each lesson or series of lessons.
27	Pupil effort is seen as important when assessing their learning.

Table 2.2 *'Promoting Learning Autonomy' (Factor A2) items*

Factor A2: Promoting Learning Autonomy: widening of scope for students to take on greater independence over their learning objectives and the assessment of their own and each other's work (alpha = 0.7636)

Item No	Item Text
6	Students are given opportunities to decide their own learning objectives.
13	I provide guidance to help students assess their own work.
19	I provide guidance to help students to assess one another's work.
24	I provide guidance to help students assess their own learning.
29	Students are given opportunities to assess one another's work.

Table 2.3 *'Performance Orientation' (Factor A3) items*

Factor A3: Performance Orientation: concern to help students comply with performance goals prescribed by the curriculum, through closed questioning, and measured by marks and grades (alpha = 0.5385)

Item No	Item Text
2	The next lesson is determined more by the prescribed curriculum than by how well students did in the last lesson.
3	The main emphasis in my assessments is on whether students know, understand or can do prescribed elements of the curriculum.
7	I use questions mainly to elicit factual knowledge from my students.
8	I consider the most worthwhile assessment to be assessment that is undertaken by the teacher.
12	Assessment of students' work consists primarily of marks and grades.

For Section B, four factors were developed from the teachers' responses to items about their professional learning practices. The four factors were interpreted as: inquiry, building social capital, critical and responsive learning and value learning. The interpretations and the constituent items of the factors are set out in the next four tables (Tables 2.4 to 2.7).

Relationships between assessment practices and teacher learning practices

Three separate multiple regression analyses were carried out in order to explore relationships between three teacher learning practice 'independent' variables; B1: inquiry; B2: building social capital and B3: critical and responsive learning (the fourth variable, valuing learning, was excluded from this analysis because the scores were not normally distributed) and each of the three classroom assessment practice 'dependent' variables; A1: making learning explicit; A2: promoting learning autonomy and A3: performance orientation. We wanted to find out how much variance in each of the three classroom assessment practice

Table 2.4 *'Inquiry' (Factor B1) items*

Factor B1: Inquiry: using and responding to different sources of evidence; carrying out joint research and evaluation with colleagues (alpha = 0.7675)

Item No	Item Text
2	Staff draw on good practice from other schools as a means to further their own professional development.
3	Staff read research reports as one source of useful ideas for improving their practice.
4	Staff use the web as one source of useful ideas for improving their practice.
5	Students are consulted about how they learn most effectively.
6	Staff relate what works in their own practice to research findings.
12	Staff modify their practice in the light of published research evidence.
15	Staff carry out joint research/evaluation with one or more colleagues as a way of improving practice.

Table 2.5 *'Building Social Capital' (Factor B2) items*

Factor B2: Building social capital: learning, working, supporting and talking with each other (alpha = 0.7476)

Item No	Item Text
16	Staff regularly collaborate to plan their teaching.
19	If staff have a problem with their teaching they usually turn to colleagues for help.
20	Teachers suggest ideas or approaches for colleagues to try out in class.
21	Teachers make collective agreements to test out new ideas.
22	Teachers discuss openly with colleagues what and how they are learning.
23	Staff frequently use informal opportunities to discuss how students learn.
24	Staff offer one another reassurance and support.

variables was accounted for by our selected teacher learning variables. Separate models were tested for teachers without managerial responsibility and for middle and senior managers.

Results for teachers without managerial responsibility

As Table 2.8 shows, the teacher learning practices, taken together, accounted for a rather low proportion of the variance in all three variables of classroom assessment practices.

Table 2.6 *'Critical and Responsive Learning' (Factor B3) items*

Factor B3: Critical and responsive learning: through reflection, self-evaluation, experimentation and by responding to feedback (alpha = 0.7573)

Item No	Item Text
7	Staff are able to see how practices that work in one context might be adapted to other contexts.
9	Staff reflect on their practice as a way of identifying professional learning needs
10	Staff experiment with their practice as a conscious strategy for improving classroom teaching and learning.
11	Staff modify their practice in the light of feedback from their students.
13	Staff modify their practice in the light of evidence from self-evaluations of their classroom practice.
14	Staff modify their practice in the light of evidence from evaluations of their classroom practice by managers or other colleagues.

Table 2.7 *'Valuing Learning' (Factor B4) items*

Factor B3: Valuing learning: believing that all students are capable of learning; the provision by teachers of an affective environment in which students can take risks with their learning, and teachers contributing to the learning orientation of their schools by identifying themselves as well as their students as learners (alpha = 0.6252)

Item No	Item Text
1	Staff as well as students learn in this school.
25	Staff believe that all students are capable of learning.
26	Students in this school enjoy learning.
27	Pupil success is regularly celebrated.

Table 2.8 *The proportion of variance in each of the three dimensions of classroom assessment accounted for by teacher learning practices (teachers' responses)*

Dependent Variables	Variance (%)
Making learning explicit	13.0
Promoting learning autonomy	4.0
Performance orientation	0.1

Independent variables: inquiry, building social capital, critical and responsive learning

However, when we compared the strength of association between each of the teacher learning variables and each of the classroom assessment variables we found that 'inquiry' (teachers' uses of and responses to evidence, and their collaboration with colleagues in joint research and evaluation activity) was most strongly associated with 'making learning explicit' and the 'promotion of learning autonomy'. 'Building social capital' and 'critical and responsive learning' had only weak and non-significant associations with all three classroom assessment variables. None of the teacher learning variables was significantly related to the 'performance orientation' variable.

Results for middle and senior managers

As Table 2.9 shows, when we analysed the school managers' responses, the three teacher learning variables accounted for much more of the variance in each of the three classroom assessment practices than was the case with data from teachers without managerial responsibility.

Table 2.9 *The proportion of variance in each of the three dimensions of classroom assessment accounted for by teacher learning practices (managers' responses)*

Dependent Variables	Variance (%)
Making learning explicit	36
Promoting learning autonomy	29
Performance orientation	7

Independent variables: inquiry, building social capital, critical and responsive learning

All teacher learning variables were significantly associated with 'making learning explicit'. 'Critical and responsive learning' and 'Inquiry' had the strongest associations. 'Inquiry' was the only teacher learning variable that was significantly related to the 'promotion of learning autonomy' and here the relationship was strong. 'Building social capital' and 'critical and responsive learning' had only weak and non-significant relationships with 'performance orientation'.

Discussion

A number of themes of considerable interest arise from this analysis. First, there are the differences between the responses of teachers and managers. There is a stronger relationship between managers' perceptions of teacher learning practices and classroom assessment practices in their schools than there is between 'ordinary' teachers' perceptions of learning by teachers in their school and their own classroom practices. On the surface this might be expected because managers with some responsibility for the work of others are likely to perceive these aspects more clearly, or may even want to 'talk them up'. However, we have been cautious about coming to any such conclusion because teachers and managers were asked different questions about classroom assessment (related to teachers' own practices but managers' perceptions of others practices) which render direct comparisons problematic. Also we know that a few managers,

37

including one head teacher, either through choice or misunderstanding, actually completed the teachers' version of the questionnaire.

More interesting are the areas where results for both teachers and managers are similar, although the strength of association differs. Four points are worthy of note. First, the three teacher learning variables account only poorly for the variance in 'performance orientation' in classroom assessment. This suggests a weak association and might reasonably lead to a conclusion that any performance orientation in classroom assessment derives very little from teachers' learning practices, and probably owes more to structural constraints in the environment such as curriculum prescriptions and performance management.

Second, and in contrast, teacher learning variables do seem to account for variance in the two classroom assessment variables most closely allied with assessment for learning: 'making learning explicit' and 'promoting learning autonomy'. The fact that the strongest associations are with 'making learning explicit' is not surprising. Although this 'baseline' questionnaire was administered in 2002, before project development work was properly begun in Learning How to Learn schools, there was already considerable activity in England under the banner of assessment for learning: some stimulated by national initiatives such as the DfES Key Stage 3 and Primary Strategies, and some promoted by researchers, such as the King's College, London assessment group (see Chapter 1), or by consultants (Sutton, 1995; Clarke, 1998, 2001). The national strategies put particular emphasis on making learning objectives and success criteria explicit, as does Clarke in her advice to primary schools.

Third, the relationship of 'inquiry' to 'promoting learning autonomy' is particularly interesting. The strength of the relationship is not as strong for teachers as it is for managers but the clear association suggests that teachers' uses of, and responses to, different sources of evidence (from more formal research and their own inquiries) together with their collaboration with colleagues in joint research and evaluation activity, are important for the development of assessment practices that lead to autonomous, independent and active learning among their students. This insight may be a key finding because other analyses of Section A data (to be reported in detail in other publications) suggest that 'promoting learning autonomy' (for example, giving students opportunities to decide their own learning objectives and to peer and self-assess) was the dimension of classroom assessment practice that teachers were having the greatest difficulty implementing, despite believing it to be important or crucial.

Finally, and perhaps surprisingly, 'building social capital' does not appear to be strongly related to change in classroom assessment practice, at least not in a straightforward, linear kind of way. This implies that teacher learning practices focused on building social capital through, for example, team building, networking, building trust and mutual support, may be of limited value without a clear focus on specific changes to be brought about in classrooms. In other words, processes need content (a point made in Chapter 1). So, we may need to be cautious about allocating time, energy and resources to building social capital if it lacks an explicit classroom focus. Indeed, teachers might develop and use social capital as a 'polite' way of protecting their classroom privacy. By agreeing to collaborate with colleagues in 'safe' aspects of their work, such as giving and receiving moral support, exchanging resources and the like, they can effectively keep colleagues at 'arm's length' from the classroom issues that really need attention. In particular, classroom-based modes of collaboration can be avoided.

Conclusion: the centrality of learning by teachers for the development of assessment for learning

These interpretations of results from the Learning How to Learn Project carry three strong messages for teachers' professional learning if it is intended to support the development of assessment for learning. First, classroom assessment for learning practices are underpinned most strongly by teachers' learning in the contexts of their classrooms with a clear focus on change in teacher and learner roles and practices and on interactions between assessment, curriculum and pedagogy. Insights from work in other projects, as described in Chapters 1 and 5, are thus corroborated by evidence from the Learning How to Learn Project's survey of 1,000 teachers. This implies that programmes of professional development, whether school-based or course-based, should be focused on classrooms and classroom practice.

The growth of interest in 'research lessons' (Stigler and Hiebert, 1999) offers one possible approach. The idea derives from Japan where teams of teachers identify an aspect of their teaching which is likely to have an impact on an area of need in students' learning. They spend between one and three years working in groups, planning interventions which may prove effective, closely observing these 'research lessons' and deconstructing and writing up what they learn – from failures as well as successes. At the end of a cycle of studies they may teach a 'public research lesson' before an audience of peers from local schools and colleges in order to share the practice and widen the critique. These studies are widely read by Japanese teachers who contribute more than 50 per cent of the educational research literature produced in the country (Fernandez, 2002). Lesson study has been developed in a number of locations in the USA over the past seven years. It is also used in the National College for School Leadership's Networked Learning Communities Projects in England and is the particular focus of a research training fellowship linked to the Learning How to Learn Project (Dudley, 2004). There are other possible approaches, of course, and the Learning How to Learn Project will report some of these in other publications.

Second, as the above account of research lessons demonstrates, both individual and social processes of teacher learning are to be valued. Our survey findings indicate that both are important conditions for the promotion of assessment for learning in classrooms. This justifies the approach taken in the KMOFAP and the Learning How to Learn Project in providing, or encouraging, opportunities for teachers to learn together in in-school teams, departmental teams and across-school groups.

Third, if 'promoting learning autonomy' is the ultimate goal but the greatest challenge, as our evidence suggests it is, and if 'inquiry' approaches to teacher learning are productive in this respect, then more emphasis needs to be placed on providing opportunities and encouragement to teachers to engage with and use research relevant to their classroom interests, and recognizing the value of, and supporting, teachers' collaborative inquiries into their own practices. The first was a strength of the way that the findings of the 1998 Black and Wiliam review of classroom assessment research was disseminated to teachers and used as a basis for in-service work (see Chapter 1). The second reflects Stenhouse's (1975) belief that 'it is teachers who, in the end, will change the world of the school by understanding it' and that a 'research tradition which is accessible to teachers and which feeds teaching must be created if education is to be significantly improved' (p. 208). He argued for teacher research on the grounds that, 'It is not enough that teachers' work should be studied, they need to study it themselves' (p. 208). In the thirty years since he wrote these words, many forms of teacher research and inquiry have flourished, some more focused on student learning than others. Our research suggests that classroom-based teacher research and inquiry is not only an important strand of teachers' continuing learning, as Stenhouse argued, but also an important factor in helping students develop independence and autonomy in their learning. The explanation for this might be quite simple, yet profound. If teachers are prepared and committed to engage in the risky business of problematizing their own practice, seeking evidence to evaluate in order to judge where change is needed, and then to act on their decisions, they are thus engaging in assessment for learning with respect to their own professional learning. Helping students to do the same with respect to their learning becomes less challenging because teachers are familiar with the principles and processes through inquiry into their own practices. In other words, they are well on the way to conceptualizing, developing and valuing expanded roles for themselves and their students in teaching and learning.

Assessment for learning and inquiry-based learning by teachers as parallel processes

In a presentation on the theme of 'Conditions for Lifelong Learning', to an audience of policy makers from the UK Department for Education and Skills and related agencies in July 2003, we argued that teachers and schools needed to develop the processes and practices of learning how to learn if they are to create the conditions for students to learn and to learn how to learn. We saw assessment for learning at the heart of this. For teachers this implied that they need to: value learning and engage with innovation; draw on a wide range of evidence, for example peer observation, student consultation, research results and web resources; reflect critically on and modify their practice; and engage in both individual and collective learning, in an atmosphere of confidence that they can help students improve. We made reference to the Assessment Reform Group's (ARG, 2002a) definition of assessment for learning and argued that: 'Whether learners are students, teachers or schools, learning how to learn is achieved when they make sense of where they are in their learning, decide where they need to go, and how best to get there'. We hypothesized that the processes are parallel for both students' learning and teachers' learning. The evidence of analysis of responses to the Learning How to Learn Project's teacher questionnaire, suggests that this hypothesis was well founded.

Implications

In the context of this book, the implications of this study are substantial because there is still evidence that classroom assessment practices need to be improved. The Annual Report of Her Majesty's Chief Inspector of Schools for 2003/04 states that teaching and learning could be improved by the better use of assessment in primary schools. In secondary schools the situation is even worse: 'The use of assessment in meeting individual students' needs remains a weakness generally and is unsatisfactory in well over a tenth of schools' (see OFSTED, 2005). If this situation is to be remedied, our evidence suggests that proper attention needs to be given to teachers' professional development in this area. However, current approaches to 'rolling out' the lessons from effective small-scale research and development may not meet the need. As the Learning How to Learn Project has discovered, whilst some changes in practice, such as sharing learning objectives with students, have been achieved by many teachers there is a danger that these can remain at the level of surface changes in procedures. Deeper changes, and those that are perhaps even more fundamental, such as promoting independent and autonomous learning, remain more difficult. These changes do not happen through the agency of consultants and the distribution of ring-binders full of material, although these can have a role. In the end, change can only be embedded if teachers actively engage with the ideas and principles underpinning the advocated practices and if the environments in which they work are supporting such engagement.

Our evidence suggests that the encouragement and support required to make classrooms the focus and site of individual and collective professional development are vital. In this way teachers can, in the context of reflective practice, develop the principles for action that provide frames of reference when confronted with unexpected circumstances. For this reason, an inquiry-based approach is also vital, although it has profound implications for school leadership and policy more widely. Not only do teachers need access to relevant knowledge and skills for drawing on research and developing their own inquiries, they also need permission to experiment, and occasionally to fail, and then to learn from these failures. In the current climate of accountability this is difficult – but not impossible. As one infants' teacher involved in the Learning How to Learn Project claimed:

The focus on learning how to learn enabled professional dialogue to flourish, promoted collaborative learning opportunities for children and adults and developed a deeper understanding of some of the elements that contribute to successful learning. It has been one of the most powerful professional development opportu-nities in my career and has enhanced my teaching and learning.

Likewise, a secondary school head teacher:

Assessment for learning has been a joy. It is intellectually profound, yet eminently practical and accessible. [It] has enhanced the learning of us all. I have no doubt that our children are now better taught than ever before. It has been the best edu-cational development of my career.

What is particularly interesting about these two statements is that neither clearly distinguishes between the learning of students and the learning of teach-ers. The two are closely associated. Moreover, the classroom and school become the environment for effective learning by both groups, and assessment for learning is at the heart of this.

Notes

1 The Learning How to Learn – in Classrooms, Schools and Networks Project was a four year development and research project funded from January 2001 to June 2005 by the UK Economic and Social Research Council as part of Phase II of the Teaching and Learning Research Programme (see http://www.tlrp.org). The Project (ref: L139 25 1020) was directed by Mary James (Institute of Education, University of London) and co-directed by Robert McCormick (Open University). Other members of the research team were Patrick Carmichael, Mary-Jane Drummond, John MacBeath, David Pedder, Richard Procter and Sue Swaffield (University of Cambridge), Paul Black, Bethan Marshall (King's College, London), Leslie Honour (University of Reading) and Alison Fox (Open University). Past members of the team were Geoff Southworth, University of Reading (until March 2002), Colin Conner and David Frost, University of Cambridge (until April 2003 and April 2004 respectively) and Dylan Wiliam and Joanna Swann, King's College, London (until August 2003 and January 2005 respectively). Further details are available at http://www.learntolearn.ac.uk.

2 Forty-three schools were initially recruited to the project from five local edu-cation authorities (Essex, Hertfordshire, Medway, Oxfordshire, Redbridge) and one virtual education action zone (Kent and Somerset VEAZ). During the lifetime of the project five schools withdrew. The criteria used for selection of schools were:

- A willingness by schools to be involved in the project for the duration, and actively to contribute to project ideas;
- Six schools to be chosen from each main LEA (fewer for Redbridge and the VEAZ) with the proportion of one secondary school to two primary schools, preferably in cluster groups;
- A range of contexts to be represented in the overall sample: urban/rural; small/large; mono-ethnic/multi-ethnic;

- Schools' performance at one or two key stages to have been allocated a 'C' benchmark grade, in the Office for Standards in Education Performance and Assessment (PANDA) Report, at the beginning of the project, that is, based on their results in 2000. This is a crude measure of 'averagely' performing schools. Not all schools in Redbridge, which were added to the sample in response to a special request from the LEA, conformed to this criterion;
- Schools to be located within a reasonable distance from the university bases of researchers.

3 The dual scale format adopted for all three sections of this questionnaire was shaped by assumptions similar to those that informed the design of the 'teacher questionnaire' used in the Improving School Effectiveness Project (ISEP) (MacBeath and Mortimore, 2001).

Part II Theory

Chapter 3

Assessment, Teaching and Theories of Learning

Mary James

The discussion of formative assessment practice and implications for teachers' professional learning, in Chapters 1 and 2, draws attention to the close relationship between assessment and pedagogy. Indeed, the argument in both chapters is that effective assessment for learning is central and integral to teaching and learning. This raises some theoretical questions about the ways in which assessment and learning are conceptualized and how they articulate. This chapter considers the relationship between assessment practice and the ways in which the processes and outcomes of learning are understood, which also has implications for the curriculum and teaching.

Starting from an assumption that there should be a degree of alignment between assessment and our understanding of learning, a number of different approaches to the practice of classroom assessment are described and analysed for the perspectives on learning that underpin them. Three clusters of theories of learning are identified and their implications for assessment practice are discussed. The point is made that learning theorists themselves rarely make statements about how learning outcomes within their models should be assessed. This may account for the lack of an adequate theoretical base for some assessment practices and, conversely, for a lack of development of assessments aligned with some of the most interesting new learning theory. The chapter concludes with a discussion of whether eclectic or synthetic models of assessments matched to learning are feasible. The intention here is to treat the concepts broadly and to provide a basis for more specific consideration of particular issues in the two chapters following this one, and indeed in the rest of the book. Thus Chapter 4 examines the role of assessment in motivation for learning and Chapter 5 focuses on the theory of formative assessment.

Alignment between assessment and learning?

The alignment (Biggs, 1996; Biggs and Tang, 1997) of assessment with learning, teaching and content knowledge is a basis for claims for the validity of assessments (see Chapter 8), but the relationship is not straightforward and cannot be taken for granted. Indeed there are plenty of examples of assessment practices that have only tenuous or partial relationships with current understanding of learning within particular domains. Take, for instance, short answer tests in science that require a recall of facts but do not begin to tap into the understanding of concepts or the investigative processes, which are central to the 'ways of thinking and doing' (Entwistle, 2005) that characterize science as a subject discipline. Nor do assessment practices always take sufficient account of current understanding of the ways in which students learn subject matter, the difficulties they encounter and how these are overcome.

Historically, much assessment practice was founded on the content and methods of psychology, the kind of psychology especially that deals with mental traits and their measurement. Thus classical test theory has primarily been concerned with differentiating between individuals who possess certain attributes, or in determining the degree to which they do so. This 'differential-ist' perspective is still very evident in popular discourse (see for example, Phillips, 1996). The focus tends to be on whether some behaviour or quality can be detected rather than the process by which it was acquired. However, during the twentieth century our understanding of how learning occurs has developed apace. It is no longer seen as a private activity dependent largely, if not wholly, on an individual's possession of innate and usually stable characteristics such as general intelligence. Interactions between people, and mediating tools such as language, are now seen to have crucial roles in learning. Thus the assessment of learning outcomes needs to take more account of the social as well as the individual processes through which learning occurs. This requires expansion of perspectives on learning and assessment that take more account of insights from the disciplines of social-psychology, sociology and anthropology.

Similarly, insofar as assessments are intended to assess 'something', that is, some content, account needs to be taken also of the way the subject domain of relevance is structured, the key concepts or 'big ideas' associated with it, and the methods and processes that characterize practice in the field. This is an important basis for construct validity without which assessments are valueless (see Chapter 8). This requirement implies some engagement with ideas from the branch of philosophy that deals with the nature of knowledge, that is, epistemology. Thus psychological, social-psychological, sociological and epistemological dimensions all need to be taken into consideration at some level in the framing of assessment practice. This is no easy task for assessment experts and may seem far too great an expectation of classroom teachers; yet one might expect their training to provide them minimally with pedagogical content knowledge (Shulman, 1987), a basic understanding of how people learn (learning theory), and some assessment literacy (Earl et al., 2000) in order to put these things together. The difficulty, in the climate that has developed around initial teacher training over the last fifteen years, has been the reduction of teaching to a fairly atomistic collection of technical competences. This is antithetical to the synoptic and synthetic approach that teachers may need to acquire in order to align their teaching and assessment practice with their understanding of learners, learning and subject knowledge.

Teachers are not helped by the fact that formal external assessments – often with high stakes attached to them – are often not well aligned either. Whilst exciting new developments in our understanding of learning unfold, developments in assessment systems and technology sometimes lag behind. Even some of the most innovative and novel developments, say, in e-assessment, are underpinned by models of learning that are limited or, in some cases, out-of-date. This is understandable too because the development of dependable assessments – always an important consideration in large-scale testing – is associated with an elaborate technology which takes much time and the skills of measurement experts, many of whom having often acquired their expertise in the very specialist field of psychometrics. This is especially true in the USA which has a powerful influence on other anglophone countries (see Chapter 10).

In this book we are primarily interested in classroom assessment by teachers, but research tells us that teachers' assessment practice is inevitably influenced by external assessment (Harlen, 2004) and teachers often use these assessments as models of their own, even if they do not use them directly. By using models of assessment borrowed from elsewhere, teachers may find themselves subscribing, uncritically or unwittingly, to the theories of learning on which they are based. Some teachers do have clear and internally consistent theories of learning to underpin their assessment practice, and they are able to articulate them, as teachers involved in the KMOFAP (Black et al., 2003; see Chapter 1) and others investigated by Harlen (2000) illustrate. But some disjunction between 'espoused theory' and 'theory-in-practice' (Schön, 1983) is common, as is a lack of theoretical coherence. This raises a question about whether it really matters which conceptions of learning underpin classroom assessment practices if they are deemed to 'work' well enough, and whether the need for consistency between teaching, learning and assessment might be overrated.

My view is that it does matter because some assessment practices are very much less effective than others in promoting the kinds of learning outcomes that are needed by young people today and in the future (see James and Brown, 2005, for a discussion of questions for assessment arising from different conceptions of learning outcomes). As Chapter 4 makes clear, the most valuable learning outcomes in enabling human flourishing – as citizens, as workers, as family and community members and as fulfilled individuals – are those that allow continued learning, when and where it is required, in a rapidly changing information- and technology-rich environment. There is a need, therefore, for teachers to have a view about the kinds of learning that are most valuable for their students and to choose and develop approaches to teaching and assessment accordingly.

Helping teachers to become more effective may therefore mean both changes in their assessment practice and changes in their beliefs about learning. It will entail development of a critical awareness that change in one will, and should, inevitably lead to the need for change in the other. So, for instance, implementing assessment for learning/formative assessment may require a teacher to rethink what effective learning is, and his or her role in bringing it about. Similarly, a change in their view of learning is likely to require assessment practice to be modified. While the focus of this book is mainly on formative assessment, a good deal is relevant to classroom-based summative assessment by which teachers summarize what has been achieved at certain times.

Examples of different classroom assessment practices

So, what might classroom assessments practices, aligned with different theories of learning, look like? Consider the following examples. They are written as caricatures of particular approaches in order to provide a basis for subsequent discussion. In reality, the differences are unlikely to be so stark and teachers often blend approaches. The focus of the examples is a secondary school teacher who has just received a new student into her English class. He has recently arrived in the country and English is an additional language for him although he speaks it reasonably well. The teacher wants to assess his writing. If she chooses one of the following approaches what would it say about her model of knowledge, learning and assessment?

Example 1

She sits him in a quiet room by himself and sets him a timed test that consists of short answer questions asking him, without recourse to reference material or access to other students, to: identify parts of given sentences (nouns, verbs, articles, connectives); make a list of adjectives to describe nouns; punctuate sentences; spell a list of ten words in a hierarchy of difficulty; write three sentences describing a favourite animal or place; write the opening paragraph of a story. She then marks these using a marking scheme (scoring rubric) which enables her to identify incorrect answers or weaknesses and compare his performance with others in the class. As a result she places him in a group with others at a similar level and then provides this group with additional exercises to practise performance in areas of weakness. When he shows improvement she is liberal with her praise and then moves on to the next set of skills to be learnt. Learning by rote and practice is a dominant feature of this approach.

Example 2

As part of her class teaching, she has been covering work on 'genre' in the programme of study. Her current focus is narrative and especially the aspect of temporal sequencing. The class has been reading Tolkien's *The Hobbit* and she used this as a stimulus for their own writing of stories of journeys in search of treasure. The students discuss the qualities of *The Hobbit* that make it a good story, including structure, plot, characterization, use of language and dramatic tension (all key concepts to be understood). These they note as things to consider in their own writing. Using a writing frame they first plan their stories and then try out opening paragraphs. They write their stories over a series of lessons. At draft stages they review their work, individually with the teacher and through peer discussion using the criteria they have developed. Then they redraft to improve their work using the feedback they have received.

The teacher monitors this activity throughout and observes that her new student has a rich experience of travel to draw on, although some of those experiences have been negative and need to be handled sensitively. With English as an additional language he knows more than he can say and needs to be helped to acquire a wider vocabulary. He also has problems with sequencing which she thinks could indicate a specific learning difficulty or a different cultural conception of time. She makes a mental note to observe this in future activities. In the meantime she decides to provide lots of opportunities for him to engage in classroom talk to help with the first difficulty. To help with the sequencing difficulty, she suggests that he writes topic sentences on card and cuts them out so that he can physically move them round his table until he gets them in a satisfactory order. When his story is complete, the student is asked to record his own self-evaluation and the teacher makes comments on this and his work which they discuss together to decide next steps. She does not make much use of praise or numerical scores or grades because, by making learning explicit, he understands the nature and substance of the progress he has made.

Example 3

The teacher regards one of her main aims as helping to develop her students as writers. To this end she constructs her classroom as a writing workshop. The new student is invited to join this workshop and all participants including the teacher and any learning support assistants are involved, on this occasion, in writing stories for children of a different age to themselves. Although their own writing or that of others including established authors is used to stimulate thinking and writing, all members in the group, from the most expert to the most novice, are encouraged to set their own goals and to choose an individual or group task that will be challenging but achievable with the help of the knowledge and skill of others in the group. There is no concept of a single specific goal to be achieved or a performance 'gap' to be closed but rather a 'horizon of possibilities' to be reached. The broad learning goal is for all members of the group to develop their identities as writers.

By participating together in the activity of writing, each member of the group has the opportunity to learn from the way others tackle the tasks (rather than being told how to do things). Different members of the group take on the role of student and teacher according to the particular challenges of a given activity. For example, if the teacher wants to write a story for young people she might need to learn about street language from her students. Thus they become her teachers. At intervals the members of the group read their work to the rest and the group appraise it, drawing on the criteria they use to judge what counts as good work. These criteria may be those shared by writers more generally (as in Examples 1 and 2 above) but the dynamic of the group might allow new criteria to emerge and be accepted as norms for this group. For example, the introduction of a new student member with a different cultural background could encourage more experimental work in the group as a whole.

The model is in some respects similar to apprenticeship models, although these tend to be associated with the preservation and maintenance of guild knowledge. In other respects it goes beyond this and, like the University of East Anglia's well-known creative writing course, it seeks to foster creativity. Our new student begins by being a peripheral participant in this writing workshop, observing and learning from what others do, but gradually he is brought into the group and becomes a full participating member. Assessment in this context is ongoing, continuous and shared by all participants (not just the preserve of the teacher) but linked very specifically to the particular activity. There is often less concern to make general statements about competence and more concern to appraise the quality of the particular performance or artefact, and the process of producing it. It is considered especially important to evaluate how well the student has used the resources (tools) available to him, in terms of materials, technology, people, language and ideas, to solve the particular problems he faced.

The learning is focused on an authentic project so one of the most important indicators of success will be whether the audience for the stories produced (other children) responds to them positively. Their response will also provide key formative feedback to be used by the individual student and the group in future projects. The role of the English teacher is therefore not as final arbiter of quality but as 'more expert other' and 'guide on the side'. Learning outcomes are best recorded and demonstrated to others through portfolios of work, rather like those produced by art students, or through the vehicle of the 'masterpiece' (the 'piece for the master craftsman' designed to be a demonstration of the best of which an apprentice is capable – also a model for the doctoral thesis).

Each of these examples looks very different as a model of teaching, learning and assessment, yet each is internally consistent and demonstrates alignment between: a conception of valued knowledge in the sub-domain (writing in English); a view of learning as a process and its implications for teaching; and an appropriate method for assessing the process and product of such learning. Of course, each of these elements may be contested, as are the theories on which they are founded. These theories are elaborated in the next section.

The theoretical foundations of learning and assessment practice

In this section I will consider three views of learning, identifying their manifestation in classroom practice and the role of assessment in each. The three examples given in the previous section were attempts to portray what each of these might look like in the real world of schools: to put flesh on theoretical bones. In reality however, teachers combine these approaches by, for instance, incorporating elements of Example 1 into Example 2, or combining elements of Example 2 with Example 3. Thus boundaries are blurred. Similarly, the perspectives on learning considered in this section are broad clusters or families of theories. Within each cluster there is a spectrum of views that sometimes overlaps with another cluster, therefore it is difficult to claim exclusivity for each category. For example, constructivist rhetoric can be found in behaviourist approaches and the boundary between cognitivist constructivism and social constructivism is indistinct. This may be helpful because, in practice, teachers often 'cherry-pick'. Whilst theorists can object that this does violence to the coherence of their theories and their intellectual roots I will argue, in the next section of this chapter, that teachers may have grounds for combining approaches.

In the US literature (Greeno et al., 1996; Bredo, 1997; Pellegrino et al., 2001) the three perspectives are often labelled 'behavorist', 'cognitive', and 'situated', but within the UK, drawing more on European literature, the labels 'behaviourist', 'constructivist', and 'socio-cultural' or 'activist' are sometimes preferred. These two sets of labels are combined in the descriptions below because they are roughly equivalent. Each of these perspectives is based on a view of what learning is and how it takes place; it is in respect to these key questions that they differ. However, and this is an important point – they do not necessarily claim to have a view about the implications for the construction of learning environments, for teaching or assessment. This has sometimes created problems for learning theorists because practitioners and policy makers usually expect them to have a view on these matters, and if this is not the case then there are those who will try to fill the gap; some successfully and others less so.

The Learning Working Group set up in 2004 by David Miliband, the then Minister for School Standards in England, noted this with respect to Gardner's theory of multiple intelligences:

> *In the case of multiple intelligences there have undoubtedly been consequences in education that Gardner did not intend, and soon he began to distance himself from some of the applications in his name that he witnessed in schools:*
>
> *' ... I learned that an entire state in Australia had adopted an educational program based in part on MI theory. The more I learned about this program, the less comfortable I was. While parts of the program were reasonable and based on research, much of it was a mishmash of practices, with neither scientific foundation nor clinical warrant. Left-brain and right-brain contrasts, sensory-based learning styles, "neuro-linguistic programming", and MI approaches commingled with dazzling promiscuity.' (Hargreaves, 2005: 15)*

The theory of multiple intelligences is not a theory of learning, strictly speaking, but a theory of mental traits. The point is an important one because the scholarship of learning theorists is, by definition, focused on learning per se and not necessarily the implications and application of their ideas for pedagogic practice. To take this second step requires applications to be equally rigorously investigated if they are to be warranted (see James et al., 2005). In Gardner's case this was the reason for his key role in Harvard's Project Zero which applied his ideas to practice (Project Zero, 2005).

Bearing these cautions in mind the following account summarizes, in a schematic and necessarily brief way, the key ideas associated with each of the three families of learning theories. First, how learning takes place (the process and environment for learning) and second, how achievement (the product of learning) is construed. This is as far as some theories go. However, and very tentatively, I will also extract some implications for teaching and assessment that would seem to be consistent with the theory, as illustrated in the examples in the section above.

Behaviourist theories of learning

Behaviourist theories emerged strongly in the 1930s and are most popularly associated with the work of Pavlov, Watson, Skinner and Thorndike. Behaviourism remained a dominant theoretical perspective into the 1960s and 1970s, when some of today's teachers were trained, and can still be seen in behaviour modification programmes as well as everyday practice. Bredo (1997), who is particularly interesting on the subject of the philosophical and political movements that provide the background to these developments, notes the association with the political conservatism that followed the end of World War I and the growth of positivism, empiricism, technicism and managerialism.

According to these theories the environment for learning is the determining factor. Learning is viewed as the conditioned response to external stimuli. Rewards and punishments, or at least the withholding of rewards, are powerful ways of forming or extinguishing habits. Praise may be part of such a reward system. These theories also take the view that complex wholes are assembled out of parts, so learning can best be accomplished when complex performances are deconstructed and when each element is practised, reinforced and subsequently built upon. These theories have no concept of mind, intelligence, ego; there is 'no ghost in the machine'. This is not necessarily to say that such theorists deny the existence of human consciousness but that they do not feel that this is necessary to explain learning; they are only interested in observable behaviour and claim that this is sufficient. From this perspective, achievement in learning is often equated with the accumulation of skills and the memorization of information (facts) in a given domain, demonstrated in the formation of habits that allow speedy performance.

Implications for teaching construe the teacher's role as being to train people to respond to instruction correctly and rapidly. In curriculum planning, basic skills are introduced before complex skills. Positive feedback, often in the form of non-specific praise, and correction of mistakes are used to make the connections between stimulus and response. As for the environment for learning, these theories imply that students are best taught in homogeneous groups according to skill level or individually according to their rate of progress through a differentiated programme based on a fixed hierarchy of skill acquisition. Computer-based typing 'tutors' are paradigm examples of this although the approach is also evident in vocational qualifications post-16 (for example, the UK General National Vocational Qualification or GNVQ) where learning outcomes are broken down into tightly specified components. In the early days of the national curriculum the disaggregation of attainment levels into atomized statements of attainment reflected this approach. The current widespread and frequent use of Key Stage 2 practice tests to enhance scores on national tests in England also rests on behaviourist assumptions about learning.

Implications for assessment are that progress is measured through unseen timed tests with items taken from progressive levels in a skill hierarchy. Performance is usually interpreted as either correct or incorrect and poor performance is remedied by more practice in the incorrect items, sometimes by deconstructing them further and going back to even more basic skills. This would be the only feasible interpretation of formative assessment according to these theories. Example 1 in the previous section comes close to this characterization.

Cognitive, constructivist theories of learning

As with behaviourist and socio-cultural theories, these derive from a mix of intellectual traditions including positivism, rationalism and humanism. Noted theorists include linguists such as Chomsky, computer scientists such as Simon, and cognitive scientists such as Bruner (who in his later writing moved towards socio-cultural approaches; see Bruner, 1996). Recently, neuroscientists have joined these ranks and are offering new perspectives on theories that began their real growth in the 1960s alongside and often in reaction to behaviourism.

Learning, according to these theories, requires the active engagement of learners and is determined by what goes on in people's heads. As the reference to 'cognition' makes clear, these theories are interested in 'mind' as a function of 'brain'. A particular focus is on how people construct meaning and make sense of the world through organizing structures, concepts and principles in schema (mental models). Prior knowledge is regarded as a powerful determinant of a student's capacity to learn new material. There is an emphasis on 'understanding' (and eliminating misunderstanding) and problem solving is seen as the context for knowledge construction. Processing strategies, such as deductive reasoning from principles and inductive reasoning from evidence, are important. Differences between experts and novices are marked by the way experts organize knowledge in structures that make it more retrievable and useful. From this perspective, achievement is framed in terms of understanding in relation to conceptual structures and competence in processing strategies. The two components of metacognition – self-monitoring and self-regulation – are also important dimensions of learning.

This perspective on learning has received extensive recent attention for its implications in relation to teaching and assessment. The two companion volumes produced by the US National Research Council (Bransford et al., 2000; Pellegrino et al., 2001) are perhaps the best examples of the genre currently available. With the growth of neuroscience and brain research, there are no signs that interest will diminish. The greatest danger seems to be that the desire to find applications will rush ahead of the science to support them (see the quote from Gardner above). Cognitivist theories are complex and differentiated and it is difficult to summarize their overall implications. However, in essence, the role of the teacher is to help 'novices' to acquire 'expert' understanding of conceptual structures and processing strategies to solve problems by symbolic manipulation with 'less search'. In view of the importance of prior learning as an influence on new learning, formative assessment emerges as an important integral element of pedagogic practice because it is necessary to elicit students' mental models (through, for example, classroom dialogue, open-ended assignments, thinking-aloud protocols and concept-mapping) in order to scaffold their understanding of knowledge structures and to provide them with opportunities to apply concepts and strategies in novel situations. In this context teaching and assessment are blended towards the goals of learning, particularly the goal of closing the gap between current understanding and the new understandings sought. Example 2 in the previous section illustrates some aspects of this approach. It is not surprising therefore that many formulations of formative assessment are associated with this particular theoretical framework (see Chapter 5). Some experimental approaches to summative assessment are also founded on these theories of learning , for example, the use of computer software applications for problem-solving and concept-mapping as a measure of students' learning of knowledge structures (see Pellegrino et al., 2001; and Bevan, 2004, for a teacher's use of these applications). However, these assessment technologies are still in their infancy and much formal testing still relies heavily on behavioural approaches, or on psychometric or 'differentialist' models. As noted earlier, these are often not underpinned by a theory of learning as such because they regard individual ability to learn as being related to innate mental characteristics such as the amount of general intelligence possessed.

Socio-cultural, situated and activity theories of learning

The socio-cultural perspective on learning is often regarded as a new development but Bredo (1997) traces its intellectual origins back to the conjunction of functional psychology and philosophical pragmatism in the work of James, Dewey and Mead at the beginning of the twentieth century. Associated also with social democratic and progressivist values, these theoretical approaches actually stimulated the conservative backlash of behaviourism. Watson, the principal evangelist of behaviourism, was a student of Dewey at Chicago but admitted that he never understood him (cited in Bredo, 1997: 17). The interactionist views of the Chicago school, which viewed human development as a transaction between the individual and the environment (actor and structure), derived from German (Hegel) and British (Darwin) thought but also had something in common with the development of cultural psychology in Russia, associated with Vygotsky (1978) and derived from the dialectical materialism of Marx (see Edwards, 2005, for an accessible account). Vygotsky was in fact writing at the same time as Dewey and there is some evidence that they actually met (Glassman, 2001).

Vygotsky's thinking has subsequently influenced theorists such as Bruner (1996) in the USA and Engeström (1999) in Finland. Bruner has been interested in the education of children but Engeström is known principally for reconfiguring Russian activity theory as an explanation of how learning happens in the workplace. Other key theorists who regard individual learning as 'situated' in the social environment include Rogoff (1990) and Lave and Wenger (Lave and Wenger, 1991; Wenger, 1998) who draw on anthropological work to characterize learning as 'cognitive apprenticeship' in 'communities of practice'. Given the intellectual roots – deriving as much from social theory, sociology and anthropology as from psychology – the language and concepts employed in socio-cultural approaches are often quite different. For example, 'agency', 'community', 'rules', 'roles', 'division of labour', 'artefacts' and 'contradictions' feature prominently in the discourse.

According to this perspective, learning occurs in an interaction between the individual and the social environment. (It is significant that Vygotsky's seminal work is entitled *Mind in Society*.) Thinking is conducted through actions that alter the situation and the situation changes the thinking; the two constantly interact. Especially important is the notion that learning is a mediated activity in which cultural artefacts have a crucial role. These can be physical artefacts such as books and equipment but they can also be symbolic tools such as language. Since language, which is central to our capacity to think, is developed in relationships between people, social relationships are necessary for, and precede, learning (Vygotsky, 1978). Thus learning is by definition a social and collaborative activity in which people develop their thinking together. Group work is not an optional extra. Learning involves participation and what is learned is not necessarily the property of an individual but shared within the social group, hence the concept of 'distributed cognition' (Salomon, 1993) in which collective knowledge of the group, community or organization is regarded as greater than the sum of the knowledge of individuals. The outcomes of learning that are most valued are engaged participation in ways that others find appropriate, for example, seeing the world in a particular way and acting accordingly. The development of identities is particularly important; this involves the learner shaping and being shaped by a community of practice. Knowledge is not abstracted from context but seen in relation to it, thus it is difficult to judge an individual as having acquired knowledge in general terms, that is, extracted from practice.

These theories provide very interesting descriptions and explanations of learning in communities of practice but the newer ones are not yet well worked out in terms of their implications for teaching and assessment, particularly in the case of the latter and especially in school contexts. Example 3 in the section above is my attempt to extrapolate from the theory. According to my reading, socio-cultural approaches imply that the teacher needs to create an environment in which people can be stimulated to think and act in authentic tasks (like apprentices) beyond their current level of competence (but in what Vygotsky calls their 'zone of proximal development'). Access to, and use of, an appropriate range of tools are important aspects of such an expansive learning environment. It is important to find activities that learners can complete with assistance but not alone so that the 'more expert other', in some cases the teacher but often a peer, can 'scaffold' their learning (a concept shared with cognitivist approaches) and remove the scaffold when they can cope on their own. Tasks need to be collaborative and students must be involved both in the generation of problems and of solutions. Teachers and students jointly solve problems and all develop their skill and understanding.

Assessment within this perspective is weakly conceptualized at present. Since the model draws extensively on anthropological concepts one might expect forms of ethnographic observation and inference to have a role. However, Pellegrino et al. (2001: 101) devote only one paragraph to this possibility and make a single reference to 'in vivo' studies of complex situated problem solving as a model. In the UK, Filer and Pollard (2000) provide an ethnographic account of the way children build learning identities and the role assessment plays in this. As they show, learning can be inferred from active participation in authentic (real-world) activities or projects. The focus here is on how well people exercise 'agency' in their use of the resources or tools (intellectual, human, material) available to them to formulate problems, work productively, and evaluate their efforts. Learning outcomes can be captured and reported through various forms of recording, including audio and visual media. The portfolio has an important role in this although attempts to 'grade' portfolios according to 'scoring rubrics' seems to be out of alignment with the socio-cultural perspective. Serafini (2000) makes this point about the state-mandated Arizona Student Assessment Program, a portfolio-based system, which reduced the possibilities for 'assessment as inquiry' largely to 'assessment as procedure' or even 'assessment as measurement'. Biggs and Tang (1997) argue that judgement needs to be holistic to be consistent with a socio-cultural or situated approach. Moreover, if a key goal of learning is to build learning identities then students' own self-assessments must be central. However, this raises questions about how to ensure the trustworthiness of such assessments when large numbers of students are involved and when those who are interested in the outcomes of such learning cannot participate in the activities that generate them. Clearly, more work needs to be done to develop approaches to assessment coherent with a socio-cultural perspective on learning.

Possibilities for eclecticism or synthesis

The previous two sections have attempted to show the potential to develop consistency between assessment practice and beliefs about learning and to provide a basis for arguing that change in one almost always requires a change in the other. I have noted, however, that assessment practice is sometimes out of step with developments in learning theory and can undermine effective teaching and learning because its washback effect is so powerful, especially in high stakes settings. It would seem, therefore, that alignment between assessment practice and learning theory is something to strive for. But is this realistic and how can it be accomplished? Teachers are very interested in 'what works' for them in classrooms and will sometimes argue that a blend or mix of practical approaches works best. They will wonder if this is acceptable or whether they have to be purist about the perspective they adopt. They might ask: Do I have to choose one approach to the exclusion of others? Can I mix them? Or is there a model that combines elements of all? These questions are essentially about purism, eclecticism or synthesis. An analogy derived from chemistry might help to make these distinctions clear.

The paradigm purist might argue that, like oil and water, these theories do not mix. A theory, if it is a good theory, attempts to provide as complete an account as possible of the phenomena in question. Therefore one good theory should be sufficient. However, if the bounds around a set of phenomena are drawn slightly differently, as they can be with respect to teaching and learning because it is a wide and complex field of study, then a number of theories may overlap. Thus behaviourist approaches seem to work perfectly well when the focus is on the development of some basic skills or habitual behaviours. In these contexts, too much thought might actually get in the way of execution. On the other hand, cognitivist approaches seem to be best when deep understanding of conceptual structures within subject domains is the desired outcome. Thus, 'fitness for purpose' is an important consideration in making such judgements and a blending of approaches, like a mixture of salt and bicarbonate of soda as a substitute for toothpaste, might work well. Such a combination would constitute an eclectic approach. Nonetheless, there are practices that contradict each other and to employ them both could simply confuse students. The use of non-specific praise is a case in point. Whilst the use of such praise to reinforce the desired behaviour may be effective in one context, in another context it can be counter-productive to the development of understanding (see Chapter 4 for more discussion).

The nature of the subject domain might also encourage consideration of whether priority should be given to one approach in preference to another. For example, subject disciplines such as science and mathematics, with hierarchically-ordered and generally-accepted conceptual structures, may lend themselves to constructivist approaches better than broader 'fields' of study with contested or multiple criteria of what counts as quality learning (Sadler, 1987), such as in the expressive arts. It is perhaps no surprise that teaching and assessment applications from a constructivist perspective draw on an overwhelming majority of examples from science and mathematics (see Bransford et al., 2000, and Pellegrino et al., 2001). Many elaborations of formative assessment also do so (Black et al., 2003) although accounts of applications in other subjects are being developed (Marshall and Hodgen, 2005) with a resulting need to critique and adapt earlier models (see Chapter 5).

Most importantly, the constructivist approach in both theory and practice has taken on board the importance of the social dimension of learning: hence the increasing use of the term 'social constructivism'. Similarly, there is now evidence that socio-cultural and activity theory frameworks are involved in a 'discursive shift' to recognize the cognitive potential to explain how we learn new practices (Edwards, 2005). This seems to suggest possibilities for synthesis whereby a more complete theory can emerge from blending and bonding key elements of previous theories. The analogy with chemistry would be the creation of a new compound (for example, a polymer) through the combining of elements in a chemical reaction. Thus synthesis goes further than eclecticism towards creating a new alignment. Could it be that one day we will have a more complete meta-theory which synthesizes the insights from what now appear to be rather disparate perspectives? Could such a theory permit a range of assessment practices to fit different contexts and purposes whilst still maintaining an internal consistency and coherence? Chapter 5 goes some way to meeting this challenge with respect to formative assessment/assessment for learning. Certainly, the possibility for a more complete and inclusive theory of learning to guide the practice of teaching and assessment seems a goal worth pursuing.

In the end, however, decisions about which assessment practices are most appropriate should flow from educational judgements as to preferred learning outcomes. This forces us to engage with questions of value – what we consider to be worthwhile, which in a sense is beyond both theory and method.

Chapter 4

The Role of Assessment in Developing Motivation for Learning

Wynne Harlen

This chapter is about motivation for learning and how assessment for different purposes, used in various ways, can affect it, both beneficially and detrimentally. It begins with a brief discussion of some key components of motivation for learning and some of the theories relevant to it. This is followed by reference to research evidence relating to the impact of summative assessment on motivation for learning. Despite the great range and variety in the research studies, their findings converge in providing evidence that some summative assessment practices, particularly high stakes tests, have a negative impact. At the same time, the evidence points towards ways of avoiding such impact. Not surprisingly, these actions suggest classroom practices that reflect many of the features of 'formative assessment', or 'assessment for learning', these two terms being used interchangeably here to describe assessment when it has the purpose and effect of enabling students to make progress in their learning. The chapter ends by drawing together implications for assessment policy at the school, local and national levels.

The importance of motivation for learning

Motivation has been described as 'the conditions and processes that account for the arousal, direction, magnitude, and maintenance of effort' (Katzell and Thompson, 1990: 144), and motivation for learning as the 'engine' that drives teaching and learning (Stiggins, 2001: 36). It is a construct of what impels learners to spend the time and effort needed for learning and solving problems (Bransford et al., 2000). It is clearly central to learning, but is not only needed as an input into education. It is also an essential outcome of education if students are to be able to adapt to changing conditions and problems in their lives beyond formal schooling. The more rapid the change in these conditions, the more important is strong motivation to learn new skills and to enjoy the challenge.

Consequently, developing motivation for learning is seen as an important outcome of education in the twenty-first century and it is essential to be aware of what aspects of teaching and learning practice act to promote or inhibit it. Assessment is one of the key factors that affect motivation. Stiggins claims that teachers can enhance or destroy students' desires to learn more quickly and more permanently through their use of assessment than through any other tools at their disposal (2001: 36). In this chapter we look at this association and take it further to suggest ways of using assessment to enhance motivation for learning. However, it is first necessary to consider the nature of motivation in some detail, for it is not a single or simple entity. By recognizing some of its complexity we can see how assessment interacts with it.

The concept of motivation for learning

In some sense all actions are motivated, as we always have some reason for doing something, even if it is just to fill an idle hour, or to experience the sense of achievement in meeting a challenge, or to avoid the consequences of taking no action.

People read, or even write books, climb mountains or take heroic risks for these reasons. We may undertake unpleasant and apparently unrewarding tasks because we know that by doing so we avoid the even more unpleasant consequences of inaction or, in other circumstances, achieve the satisfaction of helping others. In tasks that we enjoy, the motivation may be in the enjoyment of the process or in the product; a person might take a walk because he or she enjoys the experience or because the destination can only be reached on foot, or because of the knowledge that the exercise will be good for the health. In such cases the goals are clear and the achievement, or non-achievement, of them is made evident in a relatively short time. In relation to learning, however, the value of making an effort is not always apparent to the student. This underlines the importance of understanding how learning contexts and conditions, and particularly the crucial role of assessment, impact on motivation.

Extrinsic and intrinsic motivation

There is a well-established distinction between intrinsic and extrinsic motivation. When applied to motivation for learning it refers to the difference between the learning process being a source of satisfaction itself or the potential gains from learning being the driving force. In the latter case, extrinsic motivation, the benefit derived may be a result of achieving a certain level of attainment but is not related to what is learned; learning is a means to an end, not an end in itself. On the other hand intrinsic motivation describes the situation in which learners find satisfaction in the skills and knowledge that result and find enjoyment in learning them. Intrinsic motivation is seen as the ideal, since it is more likely to lead to a desire to continue learning than learning motivated extrinsically by rewards such as stars, certificates, prizes or gifts in the absence of such external incentives. Most teachers have come across students who constantly ask 'Is it for the examination?' when asked to undertake a new task. This follows years of being told how important it is to pass the examination rather than to become aware of the usefulness and interest in what is being learned.

The distinction between intrinsic and extrinsic motivation for learning is a useful one when one considers the extremes. There are times when effort is made in undertaking a task because of enjoyment in the process and satisfaction in the knowledge or skills that result. There are also times when the effort is made because either there are penalties for not accomplishing a task according to expectations or there are rewards that have little connection with the learning task (such as a new bicycle for passing an examination). However, there is a large area between the extremes where is it difficult to characterize a reward as providing extrinsic or intrinsic motivation. For example, the desire to gain a certificate which enables a learner to pass on to the next stage of learning could be regarded as extrinsic motivation, but on the other hand the certificate can be seen as symbolic of the learning achieved. Similarly praise can be a confirmation that one has achieved something worthwhile or a reason for expending effort.

Furthermore, to regard all extrinsic sources of motivation as 'bad' and all intrinsic motivation as 'good' ignores the reality of the variety of learning, of learning contexts and goals as learning. Hidi (2000) suggests that what may apply to short-term or simple tasks may not apply to long-term and complex activities. She contends that 'a combination of intrinsic rewards inherent in interesting activities and external rewards, particularly those that provide performance feedback, may be required to maintain individuals' engagement across complex and often difficult – perhaps painful – periods of learning' (Hidi and Harackiewicz, 2000: 159). Nevertheless, there is strong evidence, reviewed by Deci et al. (1999), that external rewards undermine intrinsic motivation across a range of activities, populations and types of reward. Kohn has written extensively about the destructive impact of external rewards, such as money, on student learning. From experimental studies comparing rewarded and non-rewarded students he concludes that those students offered external rewards:

> *choose easier tasks, are less efficient in using the information available to solve novel problems, and tend to be answer-orientated and more illogical in their problem-solving strategies. They seem to work harder and produce more activity, but the activity is of a lower quality, contains more errors, and is more stereotyped and less creative than the work of comparable subjects working on the same problems. (1993: 471–2)*

Although the quality of this particular research by Kohn has been criticized (Kellaghan et al., 1996), the findings are supported by similar studies and Kellaghan et al. (1996) themselves report evidence that intrinsic motivation is associated with levels of engagement in learning that lead to conceptual understanding and higher level thinking skills. The review by Crooks (1988) also drew attention to research that indicates the problems associated with extrinsic motivation in tending to lead to 'shallow' rather than 'deep' learning.

'Intrinsic' and 'extrinsic' are descriptions of overall forms of motivation but to understand how to promote intrinsic motivation in individual learners it is necessary to consider some underlying factors. Rewards and punishments are only one way of influencing motivation and people vary in their response to them; the reward has to be valued if it is to promote the effort needed to achieve it. The effort required for learning is influenced by interest, goal-orientation, locus of control, self-esteem, self-efficacy and self-regulation. These are inter-connected components of motivation for learning and there is a good deal of evidence that assessment has a key role in promoting or inhibiting them and hence affects the nature of the learning achieved in particular circumstances.

Components of motivation for learning

Interest

Interest is the result of an interaction between an individual and certain aspects of the environment. It has a powerful impact on learning. Hidi and Harackiewicz suggest that 'it can be viewed as both a state and a disposition of a person, and it has a cognitive, as well as an affective, component' (2000: 152). As it depends on the individual as well as on the environment, studies have identified two aspects: individual or personal interest, and 'situational' interest, residing in contextual factors of the environment. Individual interest is considered to be a relatively stable response to certain experiences, objects or topics that develop over time as knowledge increases and enhances pleasure in the activity. Situational interest resides in certain aspects of the environment that attract attention and may or may not last. Not surprisingly those with personal interest in particular activities persist in them for longer, learn from them and enjoy the activities more than those with less personal interest. Where personal interest is absent, situational interest is particularly important for involvement in learning. Features of learning activities such as novelty, surprise and links to existing experience provide a meaningful context and can therefore help to engage students' interest. Some potentially boring activities can be made interesting through, for example, making them into games. It has also been found that changing the social environment can encourage interest; for instance, some students show more when working with others than by themselves (Isaac et al., 1999).

The aim of creating situational interest is to get students to participate in learning tasks that they do not initially find interesting, in the hope that personal interest may develop, at the same time as some learning taking place. This is more likely to happen if students are encouraged to see the purpose of their involvement as learning. Thus the development of interest that leads to learning is connected with goal orientation and with the type of feedback they receive, both of which are closely connected with assessment as discussed later.

Goal orientation

How learners see the goals of engaging in a learning task determines the direction in which effort will be made and how they will organize and prioritize (or not) time spent for learning. The nature of the goal that is adopted is clearly critical. Goals will only be selected if they are understood, appear achievable, and are seen as worthwhile. As Henderson and Dweck (1990) point out, if students do not value the goals of academic achievement they are unlikely to be motivated to achieve them.

The relationship between the goals embraced by a learner and how they respond to learning tasks is expressed in terms of two main types of goal. These are described as 'learning (or mastery) goals' and 'performance (or ego) goals' (Ames, 1992). Those motivated by goals identified in terms of learning apply effort in acquiring new skills, seek to understand what is involved rather than just committing information to memory, persist in the face of difficulties, and generally try to increase their competence. Those oriented towards goals identified as a level of performance seek the easiest way to meet requirements and achieve the goals, compare themselves with others, and consider ability to be more important than effort.

A good deal of research evidence supports the superiority of goals as learning over goals as performance. For example, Ames and Archer (1988) found those who hold with goals as learning seek challenging tasks and Benmansour (1999) found a particularly strong association between goal orientation and the use of active learning strategies. The use of more passive learning strategies and avoidance of challenge by those who see goals as performance is particularly serious for lower achieving students. Indeed Butler (1992) found that the effects of different goal orientations are less evident among high achieving students or those perceiving themselves as performing well than among those performing less well. But the extent to which goal orientation is a dichotomy has been challenged by evidence that goals as learning and goals as performance are uncorrelated (McInerney et al., 1997) and that there may be students who endorse one or other, both or neither. The fact that researchers have set up experimental situations that induce different goal orientations in order to investigate their effect (as in the study by Schunk, 1996, outlined later) indicates that they are subject to change and manipulation and so can be influenced by classroom culture.

The evident value for school work of goals as learning leads to the question of how students can be oriented or re-oriented towards these rather than goals as performance. This question of how individuals come to embrace goals is discussed by Kellaghan et al. (1996). They cite evidence of the need to ensure that goals are understood, that they are challenging but achievable, seen to be beneficial to the learner and are valued by them, and that the social and cultural context facilitates opportunities for learning. In relation to the last of these conditions they comment:

Social and cultural considerations are important aspects of context because they can influence students' perception of self, their beliefs about achievement, and the selection of goals. Thus a student may, or may not, adopt achievement goals to gain or keep the approval of others. ... If academic achievement is not valued in a student's neighbourhood, peer group, or family, the student will be affected by this in considering whether or not to adopt academic goals. Even if academic achievement and the rewards associated with it are perceived to have value, a student may decide that home and school support are inadequate to help him or her succeed. (1996: 13–14)

This further underlines the interconnectedness of the components of motivation chosen for discussion here. It also draws attention to the extent to which learners feel themselves to be in control of their learning, the 'locus of control', the point to which we now turn.

Locus of control

As just suggested, 'locus of control' refers to whether learners perceive the cause of their success or failure to be under their control (internal locus) or to be controlled by others (external locus). Locus of control is a central concept in attribution theory (Weiner, 1979). A sense of internal control is evident in those who recognize that their success or failure is due to factors within themselves, either their effort or their ability. They see themselves as capable of success and are prepared to invest the necessary effort to meet challenges. Those with a sense of external control attribute their success or failure to external factors, such as their teacher or luck. They have less motivation to make an effort to overcome problems and prefer to keep to tasks where they can succeed.

In addition, the beliefs of learners about whether their ability is something that can or cannot be changed by effort affects their response to challenging tasks (Dweck, 1999). Those with a view that their effort can improve their ability will not be deterred by failure, but will persist and apply more effort. Those with a view of their ability as fixed find, in success, support for their view. But failure casts doubt on the ability they regard as fixed. So risk of failure is to be avoided; when not confident of success, they are likely to avoid challenge. As in the case of goal orientation, the consequences are most serious for those who perceive their ability to be low, for the chance of failure is higher and they learn to expect it. The implication for their feeling of self-worth as a learner, and self-esteem more generally, is clear.

Self-esteem

Self-esteem refers to how people value themselves both as people and as learners. It shows in the confidence that the person feels in being able to learn. Those who are confident in their ability to learn will approach a learning task with an expectation of success and a determination to overcome problems. By contrast, those who have gained a view of themselves as less able to succeed are likely to be tentative in attempting new tasks and deterred by problems encountered. As a result they appear to make less effort to learn and find less and less enjoyment in the learning situation. As noted, this is related to their view of whether they have control over their performance and whether effort can improve it.

Self-efficacy

Self-efficacy is closely related to self-esteem and to locus of control, but is more directed at specific tasks for subjects. It refers to how capable the learner feels of succeeding in a particular task or type of task. It is characterized as 'I can' versus 'I can't' by Anderson and Bourke (2000: 35) who state that it is a learned response, the learning taking place over time through the student's various experiences of success and failure. Clearly, the more a student experiences failure in relation to a type of task the more likely it is that they will become convinced of not being able to succeed. The student develops a condition described as 'learned helplessness', characterized by a lack of persistence with a task or even an unwillingness to put enough effort into it to have a chance of success. Assessment must have a key role in this development, so it is important for learning that the assessment is conducted so as to build self-efficacy.

Self-regulation

Self-regulation in learning refers to the will to act in ways that bring about learning. It refers to learners' consciously controlling their attention and actions so that they are able to solve problems or carry out tasks successfully. Self-regulated learners select and use strategies for learning and evaluate their success. They take responsibility for their own learning and make choices about how to improve. Those not able to regulate their own learning depend on others to tell them what to do and to judge how well they have done it. Young children are able to regulate their learning by adopting simple strategies relevant to learning, such as focusing their attention on key features to detect changes or 'clustering' to aid their memory. Bransford et al. (2000) quote the example of third year school students outperforming college students in memorizing a list of 30 items. The younger students grouped the items into clusters with meaning for them which aided recall. It would appear from examples such as this that learning depends on a control of strategies and not just on an increase in experience and information.

Consciously selecting relevant strategies is a step towards students reflecting on learning and becoming aware of their own thinking, leading to meta-cognition. For this they need a language to use when talking about learning and about themselves as learners. Developing and using this language, in a context where each person is valued, were found by Deakin Crick et al. (2002) to be central in developing students' strategic awareness of their learning. Promoting self-regulation and meta-cognition enables effort to be directed to improve performance.

Assessment and motivation for learning

How learning is assessed is intimately related to views of learning. Behaviourist views of learning, which continue to permeate classrooms and indeed to influence education policy decisions, are based on reinforcing required behaviour with rewards and deterring unwanted behaviour with punishments. Student assessment is generally the vehicle for applying these rewards and punishments. Constructivist views of learning focus attention on the processes of learning and the learner's role. Teachers engage students in self-assessment and use their own assessment to try to identify the learner's current understanding and level of skills. These are matters discussed in detail in Chapter 3. Our focus here is on how assessment affects each of the components of motivation discussed in the last section. As we will see there are both negative and positive effects and by considering both we can draw out, in the next section, the ways in which assessment can promote motivation for learning.

The research studies of how assessment impacts on motivation for learning are variable in design, population studied, and in quality. A systematic review of research on this impact, conducted by Harlen and Deakin Crick (2002, 2003) identified 183 potentially relevant studies, of which 19 remained after successive rounds of applying inclusion and exclusion criteria, and making judgments on the weight of evidence each study provided for the questions addressed. The research discussed here draws heavily on this review, mainly on the 12 studies that provided evidence of high weight for the review questions. The focus was on the impact of summative assessment, some conducted by teachers and some by external agencies. These are the most common forms of assessment encountered by students for, as Black and Wiliam (1998a) point out, current practice of assessment lacks many of the features that are required for assessment to be formative. The findings indicate how assessment can be practised so that, even though its purpose is summative, it can support rather than detract from motivation for learning.

Motivation, as we have seen, is too complex a concept for it to be studied as a single dependent variable. Rather, research studies have concerned one or more of the components indicated in the last section, underlining their interrelatedness. The studies do not fit neatly into categories identified by the components of motivation as dependent variables. Thus the approach taken here is to outline the findings from some key studies grouped according to the independent variable, the assessment being studied, and then to draw together the motivation-related themes emerging from them.

Studies of the impact of the national testing and assessment in England and Wales

Several studies were able to take advantage of the introduction into England and Wales of formal tests and teachers' assessments from the beginning of the 1990s in order to explore the changes associated with the innovation. In primary schools the national curriculum tests represented a considerable change from previous practice and a unique opportunity to compare students' experiences before and after this innovation. Part of one such study was reported by Pollard et al. (2000). The research was one element of a larger longitudinal study, which mapped the educational experiences in a cohort of students as they passed through primary school, beginning just one year before the introduction of the national tests and assessment in England and Wales. Over the eight years of the study, personal interviews with head teachers, teachers and students were some of the most important sources of data. Other procedures included questionnaires for teachers, observation in classrooms using systematic quantitative procedures and qualitative approaches, open-ended or partially structured field notes, and children's cartoon bubble completions. Sociometric data on children's friendship patterns and tape recordings of teachers' interactions with children were also collected.

The study found that in the initial stages of national testing the teachers tried to 'protect' students from the effects of the new assessment requirements, which they saw as potentially damaging. But as time went on, teachers became more accepting of a formal structured approach to student assessment. As the students became older they were aware of assessment only as a summative activity. They used criteria of neatness, correctness, quantity, and effort when commenting on their own and others' work. There was no evidence from students that teachers were communicating any formative or diagnostic assessment to them. Feelings of tension, uncertainty and test anxiety were reported. The researchers concluded that pressure of external assessment had had an impact on students' attitudes and perceptions. Students became less confident in their self-assessments and more likely to attribute success and failure to innate characteristics. They were less positive about assessment interactions that revealed their weaknesses. The assessment process was intimately associated with their developing sense of themselves as learners and as people. They incorporated their teachers' evaluation of them into the construction of their identity as learners.

Another study of the impact of the national curriculum tests in England and Wales focused specifically on students' self-esteem. Davies and Brember (1998, 1999) conducted a study beginning two years before the introduction of national tests and extending for several years afterwards, using successive cohorts of Year 2 (7-year-old) and Year 6 (11-year-old) students. They administered measures of self-esteem and some standardized tests in reading and mathematics. For Year 2 children, self-esteem dropped with each year, with the greatest drop coinciding with the introduction of the national curriculum tests. Although there was a small upturn for the fifth cohort, the level still remained lower than the third and very much below the second cohort. Mean levels of self-esteem for the pre-national test cohorts were significantly higher than for the post-national test cohorts. The difference in self-esteem across cohorts was highly significant for Year 2 children but not for Year 6 children. Before the introduction of the national tests there was no overall relationship between self-esteem and achievement in reading and maths on the standardized tests. However, there was a positive correlation between self-esteem and performance after the introduction of national curriculum tests. The authors suggested that the lack of correlation between achievement and self-esteem before the national curriculum tests meant that the children's view of themselves was apparently less affected by their attainments than in the case of the post-national test group.

A small-scale study by Reay and Wiliam (1999) concerned the experiences of Year 6 (11-year-old) students in one primary school in the term before taking the national tests. The researchers observed in the class for over 60 hours and interviewed students in groups. They described the class as being at 'fever pitch' because of the impending tests. The results of these tests had in fact little consequence for the students, but because the school was held responsible for the levels that they reached and was charged to make improvements in scores from one year to another, the tests had high stakes for the teachers involved. In the observed class, the teacher's anxieties were evident in the way he berated the children for poor performance in the practice tests. Even though the students recognized that the tests were about how well they had been taught, they still worried about their performance and about possible consequences for their own future. They were beginning to view themselves and others differently in terms of test results, equating cleverness with doing well in the tests, and increasingly referring to the levels they expected themselves and others to achieve.

Studies of selection tests in Northern Ireland

While the tests for 11-year-old students in England and Wales were not used for selection until 2003, tests of 11-year-olds in Northern Ireland were used for the highly competitive selection for admission to grammar school. Two studies of contrasting design reported different kinds of evidence abut the impact of the tests on aspects of students' motivation for learning. Johnston and McClune (2000) investigated the impact on teachers, students and students' learning processes in science lessons through interviews, questionnaires and classroom observations. Leonard and Davey (2001) reported the students' perspectives of the process of preparing for taking and coming to terms with the results of these tests, generally known as 11-plus tests.

Johnston and McClune (2000) used several instruments to measure students' learning dispositions, self-esteem, locus of control and attitude to science and related these to the transfer grades obtained by the students in the 11-plus examination. They found four main learning dispositions, using the Learning Combination Inventory (Johnston, 1996). These were described as:

- 'Precise processing' (preference for gathering, processing and utilizing lots of data, which gives rise to asking and answering many questions and a preference for demonstrating learning through writing answers and factual reports);
- 'Sequential processing' (preference for clear and explicit directions in approaching learning tasks);
- 'Technical processing' (preference for hands-on experience and problem-solving tasks; willingness to take risks and to be creative);
- 'Confluent processing' (typical of creative and imaginative thinkers, who think in terms of connections and links between ideas and phenomena and like to see the 'bigger picture').

Classroom observation showed that teachers were teaching in ways that gave priority to sequential processing and which linked success and ability in science to precise/sequential processing. The statistical analysis showed a positive correlation between precise/sequential learning dispositions and self-esteem. The more positive a student's disposition towards precise/sequential or technical processing, the higher is their self-esteem and the more internal their locus of control. Conversely, the more confluent the student's learning orientation, the more external their locus of control and the lower is their self-esteem. Interviews with teachers indicated that they felt the need to teach through highly structured activities and transmission of information on account of the nature of the selection tests. However, the learning dispositions of students showed a preference for technical processing, that is, through first-hand exploration and problem solving. Thus teachers appeared to be valuing precise/sequential processing approaches to learning more than other approaches and in doing so were discriminating against and demoralizing students whose preference was to learn in other ways.

A study by Leonard and Davey, (2001) funded by Save the Children, was specifically designed to reveal students' views on the 11-plus tests. Students were interviewed in focus groups on three occasions, and they wrote stories and drew pictures about their experiences and feelings. The interviews took place just after taking the test, then in the week before the results were announced, and finally a week after the results were known. Thus the various phases of the testing process and its aftermath could be studied at times when these were uppermost in the students' minds. As well as being the cause of extreme test anxiety, the impact on the self-esteem of those who did not meet their own or others' expectations was often devastating. Despite efforts by teachers to avoid value judgements being made on the basis of grades achieved, it was clear that among the students those who achieved grade A were perceived as smart and grade D students were perceived as stupid. The self-esteem of those receiving a grade D plummeted. What makes this impact all the more regrettable is that the measures are so unreliable that many thousands of students are misgraded (see Chapter 7).

Studies of regular classroom assessment in North America

Brookhart and DeVoge (1999) studied US third grade students' perceptions of assessment 'events' taking place in the course of regular classroom work. They collected data by questionnaire from students about their perceptions of a task (as 'easy' or 'difficult', and so on) before attempting it. After the event they asked students about how much effort they felt they had applied. Selected students were then interviewed about their perceptions of the assessment. The results were used to test a model of the role of classroom assessment in student motivation and achievement. The findings indicated that students' self-efficacy judgements about their ability to do particular classroom assessments were based on previous experiences with similar kinds of classroom assessments. Results of previous spelling tests, for example, were offered as evidence of how students expected to do on the current spelling test. Judgemental feedback from previous work was used by students as an indication of how much effort they needed to invest. Students who were sure that they would succeed in the work might not put effort into it. However this would depend on their goal orientation. Those seeing goals as performance might apply effort, if this was how they would be judged, in order to gain approval.

The authors also found that teachers' explicit instructions and how they presented and treated classroom assessment events affected the way students approached the tasks. When a teacher exhorted a student to work towards a good grade that teacher was, on the one hand, motivating students and on the other was setting up a performance orientation that may have decreased motivation.

Duckworth et al. (1986) also studied the impact of normal classroom grading procedures but in this case with high school students in the USA across different subjects. Their aim was to understand the relationship between effort, efficacy and futility in relation to types of teacher feedback at the individual student level, at the class level, and at the school level. Questionnaires were administered to a cross-section of students in 69 schools to provide indices of effort, efficacy and futility. At the individual level they found efficacy positively correlated with effort across all ability levels and subjects. These same relationships were stronger at class level. However, there was only scattered support for the hypothesis that the fit between the tests and what had been studied would be positively associated with efficacy and negatively associated with futility. At the school level, collegiality (amount of constructive talk about testing) among teachers was related to students' perceptions of desirable testing practices and students' feelings of efficacy and effort. School leadership was needed to develop and foster such collegial interaction.

Some of the detailed findings anticipated those of Brookhart and DeVoge (1999). In particular, Duckworth et al. (1986) found students' perceptions of communication, feedback, and helpfulness of their teachers to be strongly related to feelings of efficacy of study and effort to study. They also found that the students' perceptions, in relation to the communication, feedback and helpfulness of their teachers to be strongly related to their feelings of the efficacy versus futility of study and of their own efforts to study. The authors suggested that the difference found between results for specific events and the more general reactions was possibly due to the informal culture of expectations, built up over the year by teachers' remarks and reactions that had operated independently of the specific practices studied. This may be part of a 'halo' effect from desirable class testing practices. They therefore argued that increasing student perceptions of desirable class testing practices may increase feelings of efficacy and levels of effort.

Students' understanding of the grades they were given by their teachers was the subject of a study by Evans and Engelberg (1988). Data were collected by questionnaire from students in grades 4 to 11 in the USA, about understanding of grades, attitude to grades, and attribution. In terms of understanding of grades the authors found, as hypothesized, that older students understood simple grades more than younger ones, but even the older students did not understand complex systems of grades in which judgments about effort and behaviour were combined with academic achievement. The experience of being given a grade, or label, without knowing what it meant seemed likely to lead to a feeling of helplessness. In terms of attitudes to grades, not surprisingly, higher-achieving students were more likely to regard grades as fair and to like being graded more than lower-achieving students. Clearly, receiving low grades was an unpleasant experience which gave repeated confirmation of personal value rather than help in making progress. It was found that younger students perceived grades as fair more than older ones, but they also attached less importance to them. Evans and Engelberg also looked at attribution and found that lower achieving and younger students made more external attributions than higher achieving and older students who used more ability attributions. This suggested that low-achieving students attempted to protect their self-esteem by attributing their relative failure to external factors.

In her study of self-regulated learning conducted in Canada, Perry (1998) divided teachers of grade 2 and 3 students into two groups based on a survey of their classroom activities in teaching writing. One group was of teachers whose natural teaching style encouraged self-regulated learning. In these high self-regulated classrooms teachers provided complex activities, they offered students choices, enabling them to control the amount of challenge, to collaborate with peers, and to evaluate their work. The other group was of teachers who were more controlling, who offered few choices, and students' assessments of their own work were limited to mechanical features (spelling, punctuation and so on). These were described as 'low self-regulated classrooms'. Questionnaires were administered to students in these two groups of classes and a sample of students in each group was observed in five sessions of writing.

Although there were some limitations to this study, the findings were of interest. There was a difference between the responses of children in high and low self-regulated classrooms to being asked what they would want the researcher to notice about their writing whilst looking through their work. Although a large proportion of students in both contexts indicated that the mechanical aspects of writing were a focus for them, many more students in high self-regulated classrooms alluded to the meaningful aspects and intrinsic value of their work. Students in the low self-regulated classrooms also were more likely to respond 'I don't know' or suggest that they did not care. Similarly, in interviews, the students observed in the high self-regulated classrooms indicated an approach to learning that reflected intrinsic motivation. They showed a task focus when choosing topics or collaborators for their writing and focused on what they had learned about a topic and how their writing had improved when they evaluated their writing products. In contrast, the students in the low self-regulated classrooms were more focused on their teacher's evaluations of their writing and how much they got right on a particular assignment. Both the high and low achievers in the low self-regulated classes were concerned with getting 'a good mark'.

Studies of experimental manipulation of feedback and goal orientation

A study by Butler (1988) of the effect of different forms of feedback, involving fifth and sixth grade students in Israel, is well quoted for its results relating to changes in levels of achievement. However, the study also reported on the interest shown in the tasks used in the study following different forms of feedback. The students, first and sixth graders, were randomly allocated to groups and were given both convergent and divergent tasks. After working on these tasks they received feedback on their performance and answered an interest questionnaire. Three feedback conditions were applied to different groups:

- Comments only: feedback consisted of one sentence, which related specifically to the performance of the individual student (task involving);
- Grades only: these were based on the scores after conversion to follow a normal distribution with scores ranging from 40 to 99 (ego-involving);
- Grades plus comments.

High achieving students expressed similar interest in all feedback conditions, whilst low achieving students expressed most interest after comments only. The combined interest of high achieving students receiving grades and grades plus comments was higher than that of the lower achieving students in these conditions. However, the interest of high and low achieving students in the comments only grades did not differ significantly. The author concluded that the results indicated that the ego-involving feedback whether or not combined with task-involving feedback induced ego-involving orientation, that is, a motivation to achieve high scores rather than promoting interest in the task. On the other hand, promoting task involvement by giving task related non-ego-involving feedback may promote the interest and performance of all students, with particular value for the lower achieving students.

In the experimental study of goal orientation and self-assessment by Schunk (1996) in the USA, fourth grade students were randomly assigned to one of four experimental conditions: goals as learning with self-assessment; goals as learning without self-assessment; goals as performance with and without self-assessment. The students studied seven packages of material, covering six major types of skill in dealing with fractions and a revision package, for 45 minutes a day over seven days. The difference between the goal instructions lay in a small change in wording in presenting each package. Self-assessment was undertaken by the relevant groups at the end of each session. Measures of goal orientation, self-efficacy, and skills in the tasks (addition of fractions) were administered as pre- and post-tests. The result of this study was that the effect of goal orientation on achievement was only apparent when self-assessment was absent. Self evaluation appeared to swamp any effect of goal-orientation. Therefore, in a second study all students engaged in self-assessment but only at the end of the programme rather than in each session, to equalize and reduce its effect. With self-assessment held constant, the results showed significant effects of goal orientation for self-efficacy and for skill in the addition of fractions. The scores of the group working towards learning-goals were significantly higher than those of the performance-goals group on both measures.

Of relevance here are several studies, not included in the systematic review, reported by Dweck (1999). When Elliott and Dweck (1988) introduced some tasks to different groups of fifth grade students in the USA, they did this in a way whereby some regarded the goal as performance and others as learning. The two groups performed equally well when they experienced success, but there was some difference in the groups' response to difficult problems. Many of those given goals as performance began to show patterns of behaviour reflecting helplessness and their problem-solving strategies deteriorated, whilst most of those who saw goals as learning remained engaged and continued to use effective strategies.

Dweck and Leggett (1988) found a relationship between students' theories about their general ability (intelligence) and goal orientation. This was one of a series of investigations into the effects of believing, on the one hand, that intelligence is innate and fixed, and on the other, that intelligence can be improved by effort. The view of intelligence by some eighth grade students was identified by asking for their agreement or disagreement with statements such as 'you can learn new things but you can't really change your basic intelligence' (Dweck, 1999: 21). The students were then offered a series of tasks, some of which were described in terms of 'goals as performance' and some in terms of 'goals as learning'. They found a significant relationship between beliefs about their ability and the students' choice of task, with those holding a fixed view of their ability choosing a performance goal task.

These findings suggest that students who are encouraged to see learning as their goal feel more capable, apply effort, and raise their performance. This is less likely to happen where students are oriented to performance which other research shows inevitably follows in the context of high stakes summative assessment. For instance, Pollard et al. (2000) found that after the introduction of national tests, teachers increasingly focused on performance outcomes rather than the learning process. Schunk's (1996) findings, however, suggest that student self-assessment has a more important role in learning than goal orientation, but when it is combined with goals as learning it leads to improved performance and self-efficacy.

Using assessment to promote motivation for learning

In the foregoing sections we have discussed various forms and components of motivation and considered some evidence of how it is affected by assessment. As a start in bringing these together, it is useful to restate the reasons for being concerned with motivation for learning. In plain terms, these are because we want, and indeed society needs, students who:

- Want to learn and value learning;
- Know how to learn;
- Feel capable of learning;
- Understand what they have to learn and why;
- Enjoy learning.

How does assessment affect these outcomes? We will first bring together the features of assessment practice that need to be avoided. Then we will look at the more positive side of the relationship.

Impacts of assessment to be avoided

Assessment, particularly when high stakes are attached to the results, creates a strong reason for learning. But this reason is, for the vast majority of students, to pass the test/examination at the necessary level to achieve the reward. Students who are extrinsically motivated in this way see their goals as performance rather than as learning, and the evidence shows that this is associated with seeking the easiest route to the necessary performance. Students with such goal orientation use passive rather than active learning strategies and avoid challenges; their learning is described as 'shallow' rather than 'deep' (Ames and Archer, 1988; Benmansour, 1999; Crooks, 1988; Harlen and James, 1997). Students are encouraged, sometimes unwittingly, by their teachers in this approach to their work. The way in which teachers introduce tasks to students can orientate students to goals as performance rather than goals as learning (Brookhart and DeVoge, 2000; Schunk, 1996). Repeated tests, in which are they encouraged to perform well to get high scores, teaches students that performance is what matters. This permeates throughout classroom transactions, affecting students' approach to their work (Pollard et al., 2000; Reay and Wiliam, 1999).

Pollard et al. (2000) suggest that making teachers accountable for test scores but not for effective teaching, encourages the administration of practice tests. Many teachers also go further and actively coach students in passing tests rather than spending time in helping them to understand what is being tested (Gordon and Reese, 1997; Leonard and Davey, 2001). Thus the scope and depth of learning are seriously undermined. As discussed in Chapter 8, this may also affect the validity of the tests if coaching in test-taking enables students to perform well even when they do not have the required knowledge, skills and understanding.

Even when not directly teaching to the tests, teachers change their approach. Johnston and McClune (2000) reported that teachers adjusted their teaching style in ways they perceived as necessary because of the tests. They spent the most time in direct instruction and less in providing opportunities for students to learn through enquiry and problem solving. This impairs learning, and the feeling of being capable of learning, for those students who prefer to do this in a more active way.

The research confirms that feedback to students has a key role in determining their feeling of being capable of learning, of tackling their classroom activities and assessment tasks successfully. Feedback can come from several sources: from the reactions of the teachers to their work, from others, including their peers, and from their own previous performance on similar tasks. In relation to teachers' feedback, there is strong evidence that, in an atmosphere dominated by high stakes tests, teachers' feedback is largely judgemental and rarely formative (Pollard et al., 2000). Butler's (1988) experimental study of different kinds of feedback indicated that such feedback encourages interest in performance rather than in learning and is detrimental to interest in the work, and achievement, of lower achieving students.

The feedback that students obtain from their own previous performance in similar work is a significant element in their feeling of being able to learn in a particular situation (Brookhart and DeVoge, 1999). Consequently, if this is generally judgemental in nature it has a cumulative impact on their self-efficacy. The opportunity for past experience to help further learning is lost.

Feedback from these different directions adds to the general impression that students have of their teachers' helpfulness and interest in them as learners. Indeed, Roderick and Engel (2001) reported on how a school providing a high level of support was able to raise the effort and test performance of very low achieving and disaffected students to a far greater degree than a comparable school providing low level support for similar students. High support meant creating an environment of social and educational support, working hard to increase students' sense of self-efficacy, focusing on learning related goals, making goals explicit, using assessment to help students succeed and creating cognitive maps which made progress evident. They also displayed a strong sense of responsibility for their students. Low teacher support meant teachers not seeing the target grades as attainable, not translating the need to work harder into meaningful activities, not displaying recognition of change and motivation on the part of students, and not making personal connections with students in relation to goals as learning. There are implications here and in Duckworth et al's (1986) study for school management. Pollard et al. (2000) and Hall and Harding (2002) also found that the assessment discourse and quality of professional relationships teachers have with their colleagues outside the classroom influence the quality of teaching and learning inside the classroom.

In summary, assessment can have a negative impact on student motivation for learning by:

- Creating an classroom culture which favours transmission teaching and undervalues variety in ways of learning;
- Focusing the content of teaching narrowly on what is tested;
- Orienting students to adopt goals as performance rather than goals as learning;
- Providing predominantly judgmental feedback in terms of scores or grades;
- Favouring conditions in which summative judgements permeate all teachers' assessment transactions.

Assessment practices that preserve student motivation

Each item in the above list indicates consequences to be avoided and so suggests what not to do. However, the research evidence also provides more positive implications for practice. One of the more difficult changes to make is to convince teachers that levels of achievement can be raised by means other than by teaching to the tests. Certainly students will have to be prepared for the tests they are required to take, but this best takes the form of explaining the purpose and nature of the test and spending time, not on practising past test items, but on developing understanding and skills by using assessment to help learning. The work of Black et al. (2003) in development of practical approaches to using assessment for learning has added to the evidence of the positive effect of formative assessment on achievement (see Chapter 1). Since the measures of change in achievement used in this work are the same statutory tests as are used in all schools, the results show that improvement can be brought about by attention to learning without teaching to the test.

The particularly serious impact of summative assessment and tests on lower achieving students results from their repeated experience of failure in comparison with more successful students. There are implications here for two kinds of action that can minimize the negative impact for all students. The first is to ensure that the demands of a test are consistent with the capability of the students, that is, that students are not faced with tests that are beyond their reach (Duckworth et al., 1986). The notion of 'testing when ready' is relevant here. It is practised in the Scottish national assessment programme, where students are given a test at a certain level when the teachers are confident that based on their professional judgement they will be able to succeed. Thus all students can experience success, which preserves their self-esteem and feeling of self-efficacy. The result also helps students to recognize the progress they are making in their learning, noted as important in the research (Roderick and Engel, 2001; Duckworth et al., 1986). The second action is for teachers actively to promote this awareness of progress that each student is making and to discourage students from comparing themselves with each other in terms of the levels or scores that they have attained.

The research also underlines the value of involving students in self-assessment (Schunk, 1996) and in decisions about tests (Leonard and Davey, 2001; Perry, 1998). Both of these necessitate helping students to understand the reasons for the tests and the learning that will be assessed, thus helping to promote goals as learning. These practices are more readily applied to those tests that teachers control rather than to external tests. However, there is abundant evidence that the majority by far of tests that students undergo are imposed by teachers, either as part of regular checking or in practising for external tests. Thus a key action that can be taken is to minimize the explicit preparation for external tests and use feedback from regular classwork to focus students on the skills and knowledge that will be tested.

If teachers are to take these actions, they need support at the school level in the form of an ethos and policy that promotes the use of assessment to help learning as well as serving summative purposes. There are implications for the management of schools in establishing effective communication about assessment and developing and maintaining collegiality through structures and expectations that enable teachers to avoid the negative impact of assessment on motivation for learning. These school procedures and policies have also to be communicated to parents.

Finally, there are of course implications for local and national assessment policies. The force driving teachers to spend so much time on direct preparation for tests derives from the high stakes attached to the results. The regular national or state-wide tests for all students throughout primary and secondary school have greater consequences for teachers and schools than for students. But whether the stakes are high for the student (as when the results are used for certification or selection) or for the teacher and school (as when aggregated student tests or examination results are used as a measure of teacher or school effectiveness), the consequence is that teaching and learning are focused on what is tested with all the consequences for motivation for learning that have been discussed here.

The irony is that, as an outcome of the high stakes use, the tests do not provide the valid information required for their purposes. In particular, tests taken by all students can only cover a narrow sample (and the most reliably marked sample) of student attainment; teaching how to pass tests means that students may be able to pass even when they do not have the skills and under-standing which the test is intended to measure (Gordon and Reese, 1997). Further, the reliability of the tests as useful indicators of students' attainment is undermined by the differential impact of the testing procedures on a significant proportion of students. Girls and lower achieving students are likely to have high levels of test anxiety that influence their measured performance (Evans and Engelberg, 1988; Benmansour, 1999; Reay and Wiliam, 1999). Older lower achieving students are likely to minimize effort and may even answer ran-domly since they expect to fail anyway (Paris et al., 1991). Thus results may be unreliable and may exaggerate the difference between the higher and lower achieving students.

To avoid these pitfalls, the Assessment Reform Group (ARG), as a result of consultation with policy makers and practitioners on the implications of the research, concluded that designers and users of assessment systems and tests should:

- Be more actively aware of the limited validity of the information about pupil attainment that is being obtained from current high stakes testing pro-grammes;
- Reduce the stakes of such summative assessments by using, at national and local levels, the performance indicators derived from them more selectively and more sensitively. They should take due account of the potential for those indicators to impact negatively on learning, on teaching and on the curricu-lum;
- Be more aware of the true costs of national systems of testing, in terms of teaching time, practice tests and marking. This in turn should lead policy makers to come to reasoned conclusions about the benefits and costs of each element in those systems;
- Consider that for tracking standards of attainment at national level it is worth testing a sample of pupils rather than a full age cohort. This would reduce both the negative impacts of high stakes tests on pupil motivation and the costs incurred;

- Use test development expertise to create forms of tests and assessments that will make it possible to assess all valued outcomes of education, including for example creativity and problem solving;
- Develop a broader range of indicators to evaluate the performance of schools. Indicators that are derived from summative assessments should therefore be seen as only one element in a more broadly-based judgment. This would diminish the likely impact of public judgments of school performance on those pupils whose motivation is most 'at risk' (ARG, 2002b: 11–12).

This chapter has discussed evidence that the way in which assessment is used both inside the classroom by teachers, and outside by others, has a profound impact on students' motivation for learning. It is evident that motivation has a key role in the kind of learning in which students engage; a central concern of this book.

It is natural for students and teachers to aim for high performance, but when this is measured by external tests and when the results are accompanied by penalties for low performance, the aim becomes to perform well in the tests and this is often not the same as to learn well. Moreover, when there are high stakes attached to the test results the tests are inevitably designed to have high reliability and focus on what can be tested in this way. Although the reliability of these tests may not be as high as assumed (see Chapter 7), the attempt to aspire to 'objectivity' is generally to the detriment of the validity of the test. The inevitable consequence, as the research shows, is to narrow the learning experiences of the students. However, the impact of high stakes testing may well have longer-term consequences than the narrowness of curriculum experience. Further learning and continued learning throughout life depend on how people view themselves as learners, whether they feel they can achieve success through effort, whether they gain satisfaction from learning; all aspects of motivation for learning.

The impact that assessment can have on students can be either positive, as discussed in Chapter 1, or negative as set out in this chapter. What happens depends on how the teacher mediates the impact of assessment on students. Chapter 3 showed that teachers' views of learning affect their pedagogy. When teachers see this role as helping students to pass tests, by whatever means, their teaching methods and the experiences of the students are distorted. The alignment of assessment, curriculum and pedagogy is most easily upset by changes in assessment and this has to be taken into account in designing assessment policy.

Chapter 5

Developing a Theory of Formative Assessment

Paul Black and Dylan Wiliam

A model for classroom transactions

Whilst previous chapters have described the development of formative assessment practices, and have explored various specific aspects of these and their operation, the aim in this chapter is both more holistic and more ambitious. We will attempt to set out a theory of formative assessment. Such a theory should help interrelate the discussion so far within a single comprehensive framework and thereby provide a basis for further exploration. It would be extravagant to claim that it achieves this purpose, not least because its limited basis is our findings from the King's-Medway-Oxfordshire Formative Assessment Project, the KMOFAP example as described in Chapter 1.

That project was designed to enhance learning through the development of formative assessment. The basic assumptions that informed the design of the work were in part pragmatic, arising from the evidence that formative assessment work did enhance students' performance, and in part theoretical. One theoretical basis was to bring together evidence about classroom questioning practices (for example research on optimal 'wait time') with the general principle that learning work must start from the learner's existing ideas. The other was provided by arguments from Sadler that self-assessment and peer assessment were essential to the effective operation of formative assessment, a view that was supported in some of the research evidence, notably the work of White and Frederiksen (1998).

However, these are too narrow a basis for making sense of our project's outcomes. The need to expand the theoretical base was signalled in the response made by Perrenoud to our review:

> This [feedback] no longer seems to me, however, to be the central issue. It would seem more important to concentrate on the theoretical models of learning and its regulation and their implementation. These constitute the real systems of thought and action, in which feedback is only one element. (1998: 86)

By 'regulation', he meant the whole process of planning, classroom implementation, and adaptation, by which teachers achieve their learning intentions for their students. In what follows, we will try to link the ideas

81

expressed in this statement with an expanded theoretical perspective. The principal aim is to provide a framework within which we can make sense of what it was that changed in those classrooms where teachers were developing their use of formative assessment

It is obvious that a diverse collection of issues is relevant to the understanding of classroom assessment and so it follows that, if there is to be a unifying framework, it will have to be eclectic yet selective in eliciting mutually consistent messages from different perspectives. As one study expresses it:

> ... an attempt to understand formative assessment must involve a critical combination and co-ordination of insights derived from a number of psychological and sociological standpoints, none of which by themselves provide a sufficient basis for analysis. (Torrance and Pryor, 1998: 105)

However, if such a framework is to be more than a mere collection, it will have to serve to interrelate the collection in a way that illuminates and enriches its components. It should also suggest new interpretations of evidence from classrooms, and new ideas for further research and development work.

In what follows, we will develop our theory on the basis of the work described in Chapter 1. However, other approaches are mentioned throughout, and near the end we shall use the framework to make comparisons between this and other projects which were also designed to study or change teaching and learning in classrooms.

Starting points

We will begin by considering the classroom as a 'community of practice' (Lave and Wenger, 1991; Wenger, 1998) or as a 'figured world' (Holland et al., 1998). In both these perspectives, the focus is not so much on 'what is' but rather on what the various actors involved take things to be:

> By 'figured world', then, we mean a socially and culturally constructed realm of interpretation in which particular characters and actors are recognized, significance is attached to certain acts, and particular outcomes are valued over others. Each is a simplified world populated by a set of agents ... who engage in a limited range of meaningful acts or changes of state ... as moved by a specific set of forces. (Wenger, 1998: 52)

The focus of the approach is a careful delineation of the constraints and affordances (Gibson, 1979) provided by the 'community of practice' or 'figured world' combined with a consideration of how the actors or agents, in this case the teacher and the students, exercise agency within these constraints and affordances. Their actions are to be interpreted in terms of their perceptions of the structure in which they have to operate, in particular the significance they attach to beliefs or actions through which they engage, that is, the ways in which they as agents interact with the other agents and forces. These ways serve to define the roles that they adopt. Many of the changes arising in our project can be interpreted as changes in the roles adopted, both by teachers and students. However, these perspectives proved inadequate as explanatory or illuminative mechanisms.

This was because although the notions of communities of practice and figured worlds accounted well for the ways in which the actions of agents are structured (and that of the figured world in particular accounts for the differing degrees of agency exhibited), neither conceptual framework provides for the activities of agents to change the structure. In Wenger's example people learn to become claims processors, and are changed in the process, but the world of claims processing is hardly changed at all by the enculturation of a new individual. Similarly, in the examples used by Holland et al., agents develop their identities by exercising agency within the figured worlds of, for example, college sororities, or of Alcoholics Anonymous, but the figured worlds remain substantially unaltered. In contrast, the agency of teachers and students, both as individuals and as groups within the classroom can have a substantial impact on what the 'world of that classroom' looks like. Furthermore, our particular interest here is more in the changes that occurred in teachers' practices, and in their classrooms, than in the continuities and stabilities.

For this reason, we have found it more productive to think of the subject classroom as an 'activity system' (Engeström, 1987). Unlike communities of practice and figured worlds, which emphasize continuity and stability, ' ... activity systems are best viewed as complex formations in which equilibrium is an exception and tensions, disturbances and local innovations are the rule and the engine of change' (Salomon, 1993: 8–9).

For Engeström the key elements of an activity system are defined as follows:

The subject refers to the individual or subgroup whose agency is chosen as the point of view in the analysis. The object refers to the 'raw material' or 'problem space' at which the activity is directed and which is moulded or transformed into outcomes with the help of physical and symbolic, external and internal tools (mediating instruments and signs). The community comprises multiple individuals and/or subgroups who share the same object. The division of labour refers to both the horizontal division of tasks between the members of the community and to the vertical division of power and status. Finally the rules refer to the explicit and implicit regulations, norms and conventions that constrain actions and interactions within the activity system. (Engeström, 1993: 67)

These elements form two interconnected groups. The first group constitutes the *sphere of production* – the visible actions undertaken within the system directed towards achieving the desired goals – but these are merely the 'tip of the iceberg'. Underlying these elements are the *social, cultural* and *historic conditions* within which the goals are sought, and these two groups of elements and the dialectic between them together constitute an activity system.

As noted above, we believe that the most useful starting point for analysis is to analyse the classroom as an activity system. It would, of course, be possible to consider the whole school or even the wider community as an activity system, but such an analysis would necessarily ignore the particularities of the features of individual classrooms that would in our view paint too simplistic a picture. At the other extreme, we could view small groups of students in classrooms as an activity system, with the classroom as the wider context in which they act, but such groups are not well defined in most of the classrooms we observed and thus would be rather artificial. Adopting the classroom as the activity system allows other sources of influence to be taken into account. The students' motivations and beliefs are strongly shaped by their lives outside the school, whilst the classroom is itself embedded in the context of a particular school

How teachers act, and how their students participate, in classrooms studying particular subjects will be influenced by their experiences in other subject classrooms, by the ethos of the school and by the wider community. Therefore, we believe that it is important that the activity system is the *subject* classroom. There are important differences between a group of students and a teacher gathering in a particular place for the learning of mathematics and those meeting to learn science or English. Whilst this view derives in part from the initial emphasis of our work on classrooms in secondary/high schools, our more recent experiences with primary schools also suggest that, in primary classrooms also, the subject being taught at the time exerts a strong influence on the way that formative practices are implemented.

Before considering the implications of treating the subject classroom as an activity system, we need to discuss in more detail the changes in the practice of the KMOFAP teachers. We shall do this in terms of four key aspects, which we will suggest provide the minimal elements of a theory of formative assessment. First, we discuss changes in the relationship between the teacher's role and the nature of the subject discipline. Second, we discuss changes in the teachers' beliefs about their role in the regulation of the learning process (derived from their implicit theories of learning). Third, we discuss the student-teacher interaction focusing specifically on the role of feedback in this process, which involves discussion of the levels of feedback, the 'fine-grain of feedback', and a brief discussion of the relevance of Vygotsky's notion of the 'zone of proximal development' (ZPD) to the regulation of learning. The fourth element of the model is the role of the student.

While a theory that focuses on these four components and the way that they play out in the classroom may not have sufficient explanatory power to be useful, we do not believe that any attempt to understand the phenomena that we are studying without taking these factors into account is likely to be successful. We have formulated these components because we believe, on the basis of the data available to us, that they form key inputs for the formulation of any theory. Our intention is also to show that these four components form a framework which can be incorporated in, and illuminated by, a treatment of the subject classroom as an activity system.

First component: teachers, learners and the subject discipline

As the project teachers became more thoughtful about the quality, both of the questions they asked and of their responses to students' answers, it became evident that the achievement of this quality depended both on the relevance of questions and responses in relation to the conceptual structure of the subject matter, and on their efficacy in relation to the learning capacities of the recipients. Thus there was a need to analyse the interplay between teachers' views of the nature of the subject matter particularly of appropriate epistemology and ontology, and the selection and articulation of goals and subject matter that followed on the one hand, and their models of cognition and of learning (new theories of cognition could well be central here – see Pellegrino et al., 1999) on the other. The types of classroom interaction entailed in the learning contexts of different subject matters will not necessarily have a great deal in common with one another.

Comparisons between our experiences of work with teachers of English, science and mathematics respectively have strengthened our view that the subject disciplines create strong differences between both the identities of teachers and the conduct of learning work in their classes (Grossman and Stodolsky, 1994; Hodgen and Marshall, 2005). One clear difference between the teaching of English and the teaching of mathematics and science is that in the latter there is a body of subject matter that teachers tend to regard as giving the subject unique and objectively defined aims. It is possible to 'deliver' the subject matter rather than to help students to learn it with understanding, and even where help with understanding is given priority, this is often simply designed to ensure that every student achieves the 'correct' conceptual goal.

In the teaching of writing, there is little by way of explicit subject matter to 'deliver', except in the case of those teachers who focus only on the mechanics of grammar, spelling and punctuation. So there is no single goal appropriate for all. Thus most teachers of this subject are naturally more accustomed to giving individual feedback to help all students to improve the quality of their individual efforts at written communication. There is a vast range of types of quality writing – the goal can be any point across an entire horizon rather than one particular point. These inter-subject differences might be less defined if the aims of the teaching were to be changed. For example, open-ended investigations in mathematics or science, or critical study of the social and ethical consequences of scientific discoveries, are activities that have more in common with the production of personal writing or critical appreciation in English.

It is also relevant that many teachers of English, at least at high-school level, are themselves writers, and students have more direct interaction with the 'subject' through their own reading and writing than they do with (say) science. Nevertheless, whilst teachers of English might naturally engage more with use of feedback than many of their science colleagues, the quality of the feedback that they provide and the overall strategies in relation to the meta-cognitive quality of that feedback still need careful, often radical, development.

While much research into teacher education and teacher development has focused on the importance of teachers' subject knowledge, such research has rarely distinguished between abstract content knowledge and pedagogical content knowledge (Shulman, 1986). A study of elementary school teachers conducted for the UK's Teacher Training Agency in 1995–1996 (Askew et al., 1997) found no relationship between learners' progress in mathematics and their teachers' level of qualification in mathematics, but a strong positive correlation existed regarding their pedagogical content knowledge. This would suggest that it is important to conceptualize the relationship between teacher and subject matter as a two-way relationship, in that the teacher's capacity to explore and reinterpret the subject matter is important for effective pedagogy.

What is less clear is the importance of change in the interaction between students and the subjects they are studying. In the main, most middle and high school students seem to identify a school subject with the subject teacher: this teacher generally mediates the student's relationship with the subject, and there cannot be said to be any direct subject-student interaction. However, one aim of the teacher could well be to enhance the learner's capacity to interact directly with the subject's productions, which would involve a gradual withdrawing from the role of mediator. The meaning to be attached to such a change, let alone the timing and tactics to achieve this end, will clearly be different between different subjects. In subjects that are even more clearly performance subjects, notably physical education and musical performance, feedback is even less problematic in that its purpose can be evident to both teacher and student, and it is clear that the learning is entirely dependent on it. The students-as-groups aspect may also emerge more clearly insofar as students work together to reproduce, or at least to simulate, the community practices of the subject areas, for example as actors in a stage drama, or as a team in a science investigation.

Second component: the teacher's role and the regulation of learning

The assessment initiatives of our project led many teachers to think about their teaching in new ways. Two of them described the changes as follows:

> I now think more about the content of the lesson. The influence has shifted from 'what am I going to teach and what are the pupils going to do?' towards 'how am I going to teach this and what are the pupils going to learn?'

and

> There was a definite transition at some point, from focusing on what I was putting into the process, to what the pupils were contributing. It became obvious that one way to make a significant sustainable change was to get the pupils doing more of the thinking. I then began to search for ways to make the learning process more transparent to the pupils. Indeed I now spend my time looking for ways to get pupils to take responsibility for their learning at the same time making the learning more collaborative. This inevitably leads to more interactive learning activities in the classroom.

These teachers' comments suggested a shift from the regulation of activity ('what are the students going to do?') to the regulation of learning ('what are the students going to learn?'). In considering such regulation, Perrenoud (1998) distinguishes two aspects of teacher action. The first involves the way a teacher plans and sets up any lesson. For this aspect, we found that a teacher's aim of improving formative assessment led them to change the ways in which they planned lessons with a shift towards creating 'didactic situations' – in other words, they specifically designed these questions and tasks so that they generated 'teachable moments' – occasions when a teacher could usefully intervene to further learning. The second involves teacher action during the implementation of such plans, determined by the fine detail of the way they interact with students. Here again teachers changed, using enhanced wait time and altering their roles from simply presentation to encouraging dialogue.

Overall, it is also clear from these two quotations that the teachers were engaged in 'interactive regulation' by their emphasis on the transfer to the students of responsibility for their learning. This transfer led teachers to give enhanced priority to the need to equip students with the cognitive strategies required to achieve transition to the new understandings and skills potentially accessible through the subject matter. This implied giving more emphasis to cognitive and meta-cognitive skills and strategies than is usually given in schools. Such changes were evident in the shifts in questioning, in the skilful use of comments on homework, and particularly in the new approach to the use of tests as part of the learning process. It is significant that, a few months into the project, the teachers asked the research team to give them a talk on theories of learning, a topic that we would have judged too theoretical at the start of the project.

Some teachers have seemed quite comfortable with this transfer of responsibility to the student, and the implications for change in the student's role and in the character of the teacher-student relationship are clear. However, some other teachers found such changes threatening rather than exciting. Detailed exploration of the trajectories of development for different teachers (see for example, Lee, 2000, and Black et al., 2003) showed that the changes have been seen as a loss of control of the learning, by some who were trying seriously to implement them. Although one can argue that, objectively, teacher control was going to be just as strong and just as essential, subjectively it did not feel like that to these particular teachers, in part because it implied a change in their conception of how learning is mediated by a teacher. Such a shift alters the whole basis of 'interactive regulation' which is discussed in more detail in the following section.

Third component: feedback and the student-teacher interaction

The complex detail of feedback

It emerges from the above discussion that in the four-component model that we would propose, the crucial interaction is that between teacher and student, and this is clearly a central feature in any study of formative assessment. As already pointed out, our starting position was based in part on the seminal paper by Sadler (1989) on formative assessment. One main feature of his model was an argument that the learner's task is to close the gap between the present state of understanding and the learning goal, that self-assessment is essential if the learner is to be able to do this. The teacher's role, then, is to communicate appropriate goals and to promote self-assessment as students work towards them. In this process, feedback in the classroom should operate both from teacher to students and from students to the teacher.

Perrenoud (1998) criticized the treatment of feedback in our 1998 review. Whilst we do not accept some of his interpretations of that paper, his plea that the concept of feedback be treated more broadly, as noted earlier, is a valuable comment. The features to which he drew attention were:

- The relationship of feedback to concepts of teaching and learning;
- The degree of individualization (or personalization of the feedback);
- The way the nature of the feedback affects the cognitive and the socio/affective perspectives of the pupils;
- The efficacy of the feedback in supporting the teachers' intentions for the pupils' learning;
- The synergies between feedback and the broader context of the culture of classroom and school, and the expectations of the pupils.

Some aspects of these points have already been alluded to above. However, a more detailed discussion is called for which will be set out here under three headings: the different levels of feedback; the fine-grained features of feedback; the relevance of Vygotsky's notion of the zone of proximal development (and in particular the importance of differentiation).

Levels of feedback

The enactment of a piece of teaching goes through a sequence of stages as follows:

a) A design with formative/feedback opportunities built in;
b) Implementation in which students' responses are evoked;
c) Reception and interpretation of these responses by a teacher (or by peers);
d) Further teaching action based on the interpretation of the responses;
e) Reception and interpretation of these responses by the student;
f) Moving on to the next part of the design.

This is set out to make clear that the students in (b) and (e) and the teachers in (c) and (d) are involved in feedback activities. Feedback can involve different lengths of loop, from the short-term loops (c) to (d) to (e) and back to (c), to longer-term loops around the whole sequence, that is, from (a) to (e) and then back again when the whole sequence may be redesigned. The concept of regulation involves all of these.

Two points made by Perrenoud are relevant here. One is to emphasize that the mere presence of feedback is insufficient in judging the guidance of learning (see Deci and Ryan, 1994). The other is that learning is guided by more than the practice of feedback. In particular, not all regulation of learning processes uses formative assessment. If, for example, the teaching develops metacognitive skills in the students, they can then regulate their own learning to a greater extent and thus become less dependent on feedback from others. More generally, it is important to look broadly at the 'regulation potential' of any given learning activity, noting however that this depends on the context, on what students bring, on the classroom culture that has been forged 'upstream' (that is, the procedures whereby a student comes to be placed in a context, a group, a situation), and on ways in which students invest themselves in the work. Several of the project teachers have commented that when they now take a class in substitution for an absent teacher, the interactive approaches that they have developed with their own classes cannot be made to work.

The fine-grain of feedback

Whilst the inclusion in our framework of models of learning, of teachers' perceptions of the subject matter and of their pedagogical content knowledge deals in principle with the necessary conditions for effective feedback, these are but bare bones and in particular may mislead in paying too little attention to the complexity of what is involved. The complexities are discussed in some detail by Perrenoud, and some of his main points are briefly summarized here.

The messages given in feedback are useless unless students are able to do something with them. So the teacher needs to understand the way students think and the way in which they take in new messages both at general (subject discipline) and specific (individual) levels. The problem is that this calls for a theory relating to the mental processes of students which does not yet exist (although some foundations have been laid: see Pellegrino, et al., 2001). Teachers use intuitive rudimentary theories, but even if good theory were to be available, applying it in any specific context would be a far from straightforward undertaking.

For both the teacher, and any observer or researcher, it follows that they can only draw conclusions from situations observed in the light of theoretical models. As Perrenoud argues:

> Without a theoretical model of the mediations through which an interactive situation influences cognition, and in particular the learning process, we can observe thousands of situations without being able to draw any conclusions. (1998: 95)

In framing and guiding classroom dialogue, judgments have to be grounded in activity but must achieve detachment from it (that is, to transcend it) in order to focus on the knowledge and the learning process. A teacher's intervention to regulate the learning activity has to involve:

> ... an incursion into the representation and thought processes of the pupil to accelerate a breakthrough in understanding, a new point of view or the shaping of a notion which can immediately become operative. (1998: 97)

89

Torrance and Pryor (1998) studied the fine grain of feedback through video recordings of episodes in primary school classrooms. Many of their findings echo those of our study, albeit as an analysis of the variations in practice between teachers rather than as part of an intervention. What they are keen to emphasize is the complexity of the social interaction in a classroom, which leads them to look closely at issues of power mainly as exercised by teachers at different levels, for example exerting *power over* students with closed questioning, or sharing *power with* students (Kreisberg, 1992) using more open questioning. Torrance and Pryor also give an example of how feedback, which does no more than guide the group discussion that a teacher is mainly trying to observe, transfers power. However, this is then unevenly distributed amongst the students.

The zone of proximal development and differentiation

Sadler's emphasis on a teacher's task in defining the gap between what the learner can achieve without help and what may be achieved with suitable help, and the fact that this lays emphasis on the social and language aspects of learning, might seem to connect directly with a common interpretation of Vygotsky's concept of a Zone of Proximal Development (Vygotsky, 1986). Also relevant are the concepts of *scaffolding* as developed by Wood et al. (1976), and Rogoff's (1990) broader notion of *guided participation*, which serve to emphasize and clarify the role of a teacher.

However, discussions of the ZPD are difficult to interpret without knowing precisely how the authors interpret the concept. Here we draw on the analysis of Chaiklin (2005), who points out that for Vygotsky the zone has to be defined in terms of a model of development. These different 'ages' of development are defined as a sequence of coherent structures for interacting intellectual functions. A learner will have achieved a particular 'age' of development, and possess immature but maturing functions which will lead to the next 'age'. In an interactive situation, one which may be aimed at diagnosis rather than for specific teaching purposes, the learner may be able to share, in collaboration, only the mature functions: 'the area of immature, but maturing, processes makes up the child's zone of proximal development' (Vygotsky, 1998: 202).

Teaching should then focus on those maturing functions which are needed to complete the transition to the next age period. Whilst the age periods are objectively defined, the ZPD of each learner will be subjectively defined. Interventions such as those by the thinking skills programmes (Shayer and Adey, 1993) may succeed because they focus on maturing processes of general importance. It follows that what is needed is those learning tasks in which a learner is involved in interaction with others, and these will serve to identify the particular areas of intellectual function which, in relation to achieving the next 'age' of development for that learner, are still immature. This has to be done in the light of a comprehensive model of 'ages' of intellectual development.

This is clearly a task of immense difficulty, one that is far more complex than that implied by the notion of a 'gap', which many see as implied by Sadler's analysis. It is probably true that less sophisticated notions of a 'gap', and of scaffolding interventions to close such, are of practical value. However, they cannot be identified with Vygotsky's concept of a ZPD, and they will not attend to the real complexity of the obstacles that learners encounter in advancing the maturity of their learning.

This argument serves to bring out the point that success in fostering and making use of enhanced teacher-student interactions must depend on the capacity to adapt to the different ZPDs in a class, that is, on the capacity of a teacher to handle differentiation at a rather subtle level of understanding of each learner. However, it does not follow that the problem reduces to a one-on-one versus whole class dichotomy, for social learning is a strong component of intellectual development and capacity to learn in interaction is an essential diagnostic tool. Self-assessment, peer assessment, peer teaching, and group learning in general have all been enhanced in our project's work, and the way that the need for differentiation is affected by these practices remains to be studied. The fact that in some research studies enhanced formative assessment has produced the greatest gains for those classified initially as 'low-achievers' may be relevant here.

The overall message seems to be that in order to understand the determinants of effective feedback, or broaden the perspective whilst detecting and interpreting indicators of effective regulation, we will need theoretical models that acknowledge the situated nature of learning (Greeno et al., 1998) and the operation of teaching situations. We have to understand the context of schemes of work by teachers and we have to study how they might plan for and interact on the spot to explore and meet the needs of different students. This sets a formidable task for any research study of formative work in the classroom.

Fourth component: the student's role in learning

The perceptions of our teachers, as reported above, are that their students have changed role from being passive recipients to being active learners who can take responsibility for and manage their own learning. Another teacher reported this as follows:

> They feel that the pressure to succeed in tests is being replaced by the need to understand the work that has been covered and the test is just an assessment along the way of what needs more work and what seems to be fine ... They have commented on the fact that they think I am more interested in the general way to get to an answer than a specific solution and when Clare [a researcher] interviewed them they decided this was so that they could apply their understanding in a wider sense.

Other, albeit very limited, interviews with students have also produced evidence that students saw a change in that their teacher seemed really interested in what they thought and not merely on whether they could produce the right answer. Indeed, one aspect of the project has been that students responded very positively to the opportunities and the stimulus to take more responsibility for their own learning.

These changes can be interpreted in terms of two aspects. One already mentioned in an earlier section is the development of meta-cognition, involving as it must some degree of reflection by the student about his or her own learning (Hacker et al., 1998). Of significance here also is the concept of self-regulated learning as developed by Schunk (1996) and Zimmerman and Schunk (1989), and the findings of the Melbourne Project for Enhanced Effective Learning (PEEL) summarized in Baird and Northfield (1992).

Analysis of our work may be taken further along these lines, by relating it to the literature on 'meta-learning' (Watkins et al., 2001). Many of the activities described in our first section could readily be classified as meta-cognitive, on the part of both teachers and their students. The distinction, emphasized by Watkins et al., between 'learning orientation' and 'performance orientation' (see Dweck, 1986, 1999) is also intrinsic to our approach. The achievement of meta-learning is less clear, for what would be required is that students would reflect on the new strategies in which they had been involved, and would seek to deploy these in new contexts. The practice of active revision in preparation for examinations, or the realization that one needs to seek clarity about aims if one is to be able to evaluate the quality of one's own work, may well be examples of meta-learning, but evidence about students' perceptions and responses to new challenges would be needed to support any claims about outcomes of this type.

A second aspect, involving conative and affective dimensions, is reflected in changes in the students' perceptions of their teacher's personal interest in them. Mention has been made above, in the report on the abandonment of giving marks or grades on written work, of Butler and Neuman's (1995) account of the importance of such a change. It is not merely that a numerical mark or grade is ineffective for learning because it does not tell you what to do; it also affects your self-perception. If the mark is high, you are pleased but have no impetus to do better. If it is low, it might confirm your belief that you are not able to learn the subject. Many other studies have explored the negative effects not only on learning but also on self-concept, self-efficacy and self-attribution of the classroom culture in which marks and grades come to be a dominant currency of classroom relationships (see for example, Ames, 1992; Cameron and Pierce, 1994; Butler and Winne, 1995; Vispoel and Austin, 1995). In particular, as long as students believe that efforts on their part cannot make much difference because of their lack of 'ability', efforts to enhance their capability as learners will have little effect.

The importance of such issues is emphasized by Cowie's (2004) study which explored students' reactions to formative assessment. One of her general findings was that students are in any activity balancing three goals simultaneously, namely, completion of work tasks, effective learning and social-relationship goals. When these conflict they tend to prioritize the social-relationship goals at the expense of learning goals; so, for example, many will limit disclosure of their ideas in the classroom for fear of harm to their feelings and reputation. The way in which the teacher deals with such disclosures is crucial. The respect shown them by a teacher and their trust in that teacher affect students' responses to any feedback – they need to feel safe if they are to risk exposure. Cowie also found that the students' responses to formative feedback cannot be assumed to be uniform. Some prioritize learning goals and so look for thoughtful suggestions, preferably in one-to-one exchanges, whilst others pursue performance goals and so want help to complete their work without the distraction of questions about their understanding. Sadly, many felt that the main responsibility for their learning rested with the teacher and not with themselves. In an activity theory representation, as exemplified later in this chapter (Figures 5.1 and 5.2), all of the issues raised by such work are represented by the element labelled 'community'; the connections of this element with the other elements of the diagram are both important and complex.

Much writing about classroom learning focuses on the learner as an individual or on learning as a social process. Our approach has been to treat the social-individual interaction as a central feature, drawing on the writings of Bredo (1994) and Bruner (1996). Thus, feedback to individuals and self-assessment has been emphasized, but so have peer assessment, peer support in learning and class discussion about learning.

For the work of students in groups, the emphasis by Sadler (1989, 1998) and others that peer assessment is a particularly valuable way of implementing formative assessment has been amply borne out in the work reported here. Theoretically, this perspective ought to be evaluated in the broader context of the application to classrooms and schools of analyses of the social and communal dimensions of learning as developed, for example, in Wenger's (1998) study of communities of practice. These points are illustrated by the following extract from an interview with a student in the KMOFAP, discussing peer marking of his investigation:

> *After a pupil marking my investigation, I can now acknowledge my mistakes easier. I hope that it is not just me who learnt from the investigation but the pupil who marked it did also.*
>
> *Next time I will have to make my explanations clearer, as they said 'It is hard to understand', so I must next time make my equation clearer. I will now explain my equation again so it is clear.*

This quotation also bears out Bruner's (1996) emphasis on the importance of externalizing one's thoughts by producing objects or *oeuvres* which, being public, are accessible to reflection and dialogue, leading to enrichment through communal interaction. He points out that awareness of one's own thinking, and a capacity to understand the thinking of others, provide an essential reasoned base for interpersonal negotiation that can enhance understanding.

The importance of peer assessment may be more fundamental than is apparent in accounts by teachers of their work. For self-assessment, each student has to interact mainly with text; interactions with the teacher, insofar as they are personal, must be brief. Discussing the work of Palincsar and Brown (1984) on children's reading, Wood states:

This work, motivated by Vygotsky's theory of development and by his writings on literacy, started from the assumption that some children fail to advance beyond the initial stages of reading because they do not know how to 'interact' with text, that is, they do not become actively engaged in attempts to interpret what they read. Briefly, the intervention techniques involved bringing into the open, making public and audible, ways of interacting with text that skilled readers usually undertake automatically and soundlessly. (1998: 220–1)

Thus if a student's interpretation of aims and of criteria of quality of performance is to be enriched, such enrichment may well require 'talk about text', and given that it is impracticable to achieve this through teacher-student interactions the interactions made possible through peer assessment may meet an essential need.

Overall, it is clear that these changes in a student's role as learner are a significant feature in the reform of classroom learning, that our formative assessment initiative has been effective in its impact on these features, and that changes in a student's own beliefs and implicit models of learning also underlie the developments involved.

Applying activity theory

In considering the interpretation of these four components in terms of a representation of the subject classroom as an activity system, we have concentrated mainly on the 'tip of the iceberg': subjects, objects and cultural resources, and the relationships between these three elements. As will be clear in our exposition of these ideas, the nature of these relations is strongly influenced by the other elements of activity systems, that is, rules, community, and division of labour. The discussion of these relationships will be brief; a full exploration would require a far longer treatment than is possible here.

In the activity system of the subject classroom, the *tools* or cultural resources that appear to be particularly important in the development of formative assessment are:

- Views and ideas about the nature of the subject, including pedagogical content knowledge;
- Methods for enhancing the formative aspects of interaction, such as rich questions, ideas about what makes feedback effective and techniques such as 'traffic lights' and so on;
- Views and ideas about the nature of learning.

The *subjects* are, as stated earlier, the teacher and the students, although it is important to acknowledge that it useful to distinguish between students as individuals and students in groups in the classroom (Ball and Bass, 2000).

The *object* in most of the subject classrooms we studied was increased student success, either in terms of better quality learning or simply better scores on state-mandated tests. Many teachers spoke of their interest in participating in the project because of the promise of better results. However, as well as this object which, as noted above, was secured by most of the participating teachers, the *outcomes* of the projects included changes in the expectations that teachers had of their students, and also changes in the kinds of assessments that these teachers used in their routines. The most important change in the teachers' own assessments was a shift towards using those that provided information for the teacher not only about who had learnt what, but also proferred some insights into why this was, in particular – when interpreted appropriately – those that gave some idea as to what to do about it. In other words, a shift towards assessments that could be formative *for the teacher*.

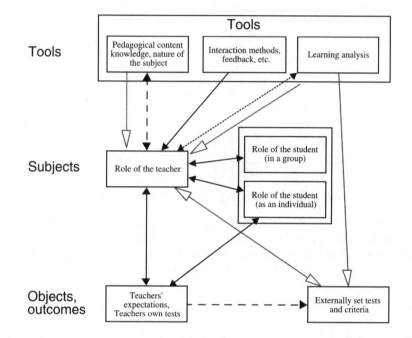

Figure 5.1: *Patterns of influence in the KMOFAP and BEAR projects (solid-headed arrows represent influences in KMOFAP; open-headed arrows represent influences in BEAR)*

Figure 5.1 uses the context of the KMOFAP and a US example, the Berkeley Evaluation and Assessment Research project (BEAR; see Wilson and Sloane, 2000), to illustrate the various components of the theoretical framework outlined above and their interrelationships. Components 1, 2 and 4 are represented as tools, while component 3 is represented in the links between the teacher and the students (both individually and in groups). Solid-headed arrows are used to represent the key influences in the KMOFAP project while the open-ended arrows represent influences in the BEAR project. Using this framework, the course of the KMOFAP can be seen as beginning with *tools* (in particular findings related to the nature of feedback and the importance of questions) which prompt changes in the relationship *between the subjects* (that is, in the relationship between the teacher and the students) which in turn prompt changes in the *subjects* themselves (that is, changes in the teacher's and students' roles). These changes then trigger further changes in other *tools* such as the nature of the subject and the view of learning. In particular, the changes prompted in the teacher classroom practices involved moving from simple associationist views of learning to embracing constructivism and taking responsibility for learning linked to self-regulation of learning, metacognition and social learning.

Figure 5.1 does not represent an activity system in the canonical way. This more common representation, using the nested triangles, is shown in Figure 5.2. Here the relationships are brought out more clearly by placing tools at the apex with subjects, and objects and outcomes on the base of the upper triangle. Thus it would be possible in principle to map Figure 5.1 into this part of Figure 5.2 but much of the detail would either be lost or appear confusingly complex.

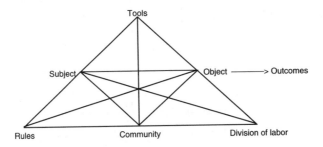

Figure 5.2: *Elements of activity systems (Engeström, 1987)*

However, what the canonical representation makes more explicit are the elements in the lowest row of Figure 5.2 and their links with the rest. Whilst the community, deemed as the subject classroom, is a given, both the *rules* and the *division of labour* are changed by a formative innovation. For the rules, if teachers cease to give grades or marks on homework in order to focus on feedback through comments, they may be in conflict with management rules and parental expectations for many schools. Yet in two of the KMOFAP schools such rules were eventually changed, the new rule being, for the whole school, that marks and grades were not to be given as feedback on written homework. The more pervasive 'rule' – that schools are under pressure to produce high grades in national tests – did limit some formative developments, and it is clear that synergy between teachers' formative practices and their responsibilities for summative assessments would be hard to achieve without some room for manoeuvre in relation to high-stakes testing.

The *division of labour* is a feature that is radically transformed, as made clear in the second component for changes in the teacher's role, and in the fourth component for changes in the student's role. One aspect of the transfer of power and responsibility that is involved here is that the students begin to share ownership of the tools, for example by involvement in summative testing processes, and by becoming less dependent on the teacher for their access to subject knowledge.

What is obvious from this discussion is that there are strong interactions between the various elements of the system. This suggests that any attempt to record and interpret the dynamics of change as an innovation, notably in formative assessment, could do well to adopt and adapt an activity theory approach along the lines sketched here.

Strategies for development

The KMOFAP and BEAR projects

It is useful at this point to contrast the approach adopted in our project with an alternative strategy, clearly exemplified in the BEAR project (Wilson and Sloane, 2000) and impressive in the evidence of learning gains associated with an emphasis on formative assessment. This differed from the work described in the first part of this paper in the following ways:

- It was part of a curriculum innovation into which were 'embedded' new formative assessment practices;
- An important aim was to secure and establish the reliability and validity of 'alternative' assessment practices so that assessment by teachers could withstand public scrutiny and claim equal status with the external standardized tests which have such negative effects on education in the USA;
- The aims were formulated as a profile of a few main components, with each component being set out as a sequence of levels to reflect the expected progression of learning within each;
- The assessment instruments were written tests provided externally, some to be used as short-term checks on progress, some of greater length to be used a medium-term checks;
- Whilst formative use was emphasized, there was very little account of the ways in which feedback was deployed or received by students.

To over-simplify, it could be said that the apparent weakness of the BEAR project lies in those aspects in which our project was strong. At the same time its strengths, in the quality of the assessment instruments and the rigour in their use and interpretation, throw into sharp relief the weakness of our project, for the cognitive quality of the questions used by our teachers and of their feedback comments whether oral or written still needs further attention. Whilst the two approaches may be seen as complementary, and each may have been the optimum approach for the particular context and culture in which it was designed to operate, there remains the issue of whether some aspects of either could be incorporated, albeit at a later stage in implementation, in the other.

In terms of our model, the BEAR project imports theories of the subject and of learning and requires teachers to work to these models, but is not explicit on the nature of the teacher-student interactions or the change in roles of either teachers or students. Thus the project does not seem to have affected the classroom community through any significant shift in the division of labour. Similar, although not identical, contrasts could be drawn by analysis of many of the research initiatives described in the 1998 review by Black and Wiliam. The

97

contrast between our work and that of the BEAR project is brought out clearly in Figure 5.1, which shows the patterns of influence in the two projects.

This comparison can help to draw attention to the options available in any programme of teacher development. The partial successes of our own approach have a peculiar significance in that they have led to changes transcending the boundaries envisaged by our initial concentration on formative assessment. This expansion may in part have arisen because of our emphasis on the responsibility of the teachers as partners with us, sharing responsibility for the direction of change. It might have been predictable that their initiatives would broaden the scope, because their work has to marry into the full reality of classroom work and cannot be limited to one theoretically abstracted feature. Indeed we have come to think of formative assessment as a 'Trojan Horse' for more general innovation in pedagogy – a point to which we shall return in the concluding section below.

Other related research and development studies

The BEAR study was similar in many respects to our own, so it is particularly interesting to explore the comparison in detail. However, we have developed the view that what is at issue is a theory of classroom pedagogy, and from this perspective the number of relevant studies becomes far too great for any synthesis to be attempted here.

Three examples of related studies may suffice to indicate possibilities. The first is the cognitive acceleration work associated with Shayer (1999). In comparison with the cognitive acceleration initiative, our formative intervention did not target specific reasoning skills and so does not call for ad hoc teaching, although within the set piece lessons of that initiative many of the practices have much in common with the formative practices. In terms of the scheme of Figure 5.1, the work involves very specific tools and is characterized by a more explicit – and thereby less eclectic – *learning analysis* which impacts directly on *the role of the teacher*. It resembles the BEAR project in these respects, but it does not resemble it in respect of the direct link to *externally set tests and criteria*.

A second example is the work on 'Talk Lessons' developed by Neil Mercer and his colleagues (Mercer, 2000; Mercer et al., 2004). These lessons could indeed be seen as a powerful way of strengthening the development of peer assessment practices in enhancing students' capacity to learn. This initiative develops different specific tools but it also, in terms of Figure 5.1, works to direct links between *the learning analysis, the interaction methods* and the division of labour by focusing its effort on *the role of the student in a group*.

The third example is related to the second, but is the broader field summarized in Alexander's (2004) booklet *Towards Dialogic Teaching*, which draws on a range of studies of classroom dialogue. The main argument here starts from the several studies that have shown that classroom dialogue fails to develop students' active participation, reducing dialogue to a ritual of superficial questions in a context of 'delivery' teaching whereby thoughtful participation cannot develop. His arguments call for an emphasis on all three of the *tools* areas in Figure 5.1, and puts extra emphasis on the community element represented directly in Figure 5.2 but only indirectly in the connecting arrows between teacher role and student roles in Figure 5.1.

Conclusions and implications

We have focused the discussion in this chapter on our own study, in part because our approach to theory was grounded in that work, in part because we do not know of any other study which is grounded in a comparably comprehensive and sustained development with a group of teachers. Whilst we regard the theory as a promising start, there is clearly further work to be done in both developing it and relating empirical evidence to it.

If we consider the potential value of the four component model that we have explored and discussed, an obvious outcome is that it could be used to suggest many questions which could form the starting point for further empirical research, many of which would requiring fine-grained studies of teacher-student interactions (see for example, Torrance and Pryor, 1998; Cowie, 2004). However, the more ambitious target for this chapter is more fundamental – to help guide the direction and interpretation of further research through the the-oretical framework that is proposed.

We have explored above, very briefly, the possibility for developing the theory through attempting new interpretations of initiatives already published. This exploration, which involves attempting to embed the formative aspect in a broader view of pedagogy, reflects the point made by Perrenoud quoted at the beginning of this chapter that it is necessary to consider formative feedback in the wider context of 'models of learning and its regulation and their imple-mentation'. This may seem to be over-ambitious in attempting a complete theory of pedagogy rather than only that particular aspect of pedagogy which is labelled 'formative assessment'. However, such an attempt seems inevitable given our experience of the initially limited aim of developing formative assess-ment leading to much more radical changes.

One function of a theoretical framework should be to guide the optimum choice of strategies to improve pedagogy, by identifying those key determi-nants that have to be evaluated in making such choices and in learning lessons from experiences in other contexts. It follows that the framework might be used to evaluate, retrospectively or prospectively, the design of any initiative in teaching and learning. In the case of the KMOFAP initiative, it should help answer the question of whether it was the optimum way of devoting effort and resources towards the improvement of classroom pedagogy. This would seem a very difficult question to answer in the face of the potential complexity of a comprehensive theory of pedagogy that might provide the basis for an answer. However, some significant insight could be distilled in a way that would at least help resolve the puzzle of the project's unexpected success, represented by the metaphor of the Trojan Horse mentioned in the previous section.

The argument starts by pointing out that the examples of change which the teachers described seemed to confirm that working to improve the teacher-student interaction through formative assessment could serve to catalyse changes in both the teacher's role and those adopted by that teacher's students. The changes motivate, perhaps demand, an alteration in the various interactions of both students and teachers with their theories of learning, and with the ways in which they perceive and relate to the subject matter that they are teaching. Thus whilst we cannot argue that development of formative assessment is the only way, or even the best way, to open up a broader range of desirable changes in classroom learning, we can see that it may be peculiarly effective, in part because the quality of interactive feedback is a critical feature in determining the quality of learning activity, and is therefore a central feature of pedagogy.

We might also speculate that a focus on innovation in formative assessment may be productive because many teachers, regardless of their perceptions of their teaching role and of the learning roles of their students, can see the importance of working on particular and limited aspects of feedback but might then have their perspectives shifted as they undertake such work. In the project, the tools provided led teachers to think more deeply – about their pedagogical content knowledge, about their assumptions on learning and about interactions with their students; hence activating all of the components of our framework for them.

Given that a development of formative assessment has this peculiar potential to catalyse more radical change, a theory that helps design and track such change would be an important resource. The approach sketched out here may help such tracking, inasmuch that the components of our model interpreted in terms of an activity system framework do seem to interact strongly and dynamically, and would help in interpreting any change process. A central feature may be that inconsistencies between the various elements of the classroom system are hard for the actors to tolerate. The interaction lines in the frameworks of Figures 5.1 and 5.2 are all-important for they signal that any innovation that succeeds in changing one element might well destabilize the existing equilibrium, so that the whole pattern of pedagogy is affected to achieve a new equilibrium.

Acknowledgements

We would acknowledge the support given by the Nuffield Foundation in funding the first phase of the KMOFAP, and by the National Science Foundation for funding the subsequent phase through their support of our partnership with the Stanford CAPITAL project (NSF Grant REC-9909370). This present paper reports the findings of our work in England to date: comparative and synthesized findings with the Stanford partners will be subjects for later study.

We are grateful to Sue Swaffield from Medway and Dorothy Kavanagh from Oxfordshire who, on behalf of their authorities, helped to create and nurture our links with their respective schools. The teachers in this project have been the main agents of its success. Their willingness to take risks with our ideas was essential, and their voices are an important basis for the main message of this paper.

Part III Formative and Summative Issues

Chapter 6

On the Relationship Between Assessment for Formative and Summative Purposes

Wynne Harlen

This chapter considers the relationship between assessment for two of its main purposes – to help learning and to summarize what has been learned. Both purposes are central to effective educational practice, but there are issues relating to whether it is useful to consider them as conceptually or pragmatically distinct. As a basis for this discussion the first part of the chapter suggests a representation of the distinction using models of assessment for learning and assessment of learning. The second and third sections address questions as to whether evidence gathered for one purpose can be used for the other. The fourth part considers whether there is a dimension of purposes rather than a dichotomy and whether the distinction between formative and summative assessment is useful or redundant. At a time when practice is only beginning to catch up with theory in relation to formative assessment, it is inevitable that this chapter raises more questions than it finds answers for. It ends by concluding that at present the distinction between formative and summative purposes of assessment should be maintained whilst assessment systems should include the provisions that make it possible for information gathered by teachers to be used for both purposes. It should be noted that the terms 'formative assessment' and 'summative assessment', and 'assessment for learning' and 'assessment of learning' are used interchangeably in this chapter.

A view of how assessment serves formative and summative purposes

It is generally agreed that assessment in the context of education involves deciding, collecting and making judgements about evidence relating to the goals of the learning being assessed. This makes no reference to the use of the evidence, who uses it and how. These are matters at the heart of the distinction between formative and summative assessment. What we now identify as summative assessment (assessment of learning) has been part of education for centuries. Some would argue that formative assessment (assessment for learning) has an equally long pedigree, with Rousseau's 1762 exhortation to 'Begin by making a more careful study of the scholars, for it is clear that you know nothing about them', (Preface: 1). However the identification of formative assessment as a distinct purpose of assessment, requiring precise definition, is more recent.

Identifying assessment in terms of its purposes, although not new, became widespread when the Task Group on Assessment and Testing (TGAT) report of 1988 distinguished between assessment for four different purposes: formative, diagnostic, summative and evaluative (DES/WO, 1988a). The word 'formative' was used to identify assessment that promotes learning by using evidence about where students have reached, in relation to the goals of their learning, to plan the next steps in their learning and know how to take them. To all intents and purposes the term 'formative assessment' includes diagnostic assessment, which is often taken to concern difficulties in learning since formative is concerned with both difficulties and positive achievements. 'Summative assessment' provides, as the term suggests, a summary of achievements at a particular point. It is a necessary part of an assessment system as it provides information to those with an interest in students' achievements: mainly parents, other teachers, employers, further and higher education institutions and the students themselves. Assessment serves an evaluative purpose when the performance of groups of students is used to report on the work of a class, a teacher, a school or another part of an educational system. The information about students that is used for this purpose is necessarily based on summative assessment. It is widely agreed, however, that the evaluation of education provision must use a good deal of information other than that which derives from the assessment of students.

Where individual students are concerned, the important distinction is between assessment for formative and summative purposes. Using the terms 'formative assessment' and 'summative assessment' can give the impression that these are different *kinds* of assessment or are linked to different methods of gathering evidence. This is not the case; what matters is how the information is used. It is for this reason that the terms 'assessment for learning' and 'assessment of learning' are sometimes preferred. The essential distinction is that assessment for learning is used in making decisions that affect teaching and learning in the short-term future, whereas assessment of learning is used to record and report what has been learned in the past. The difference is reflected in Figures 6.1 and 6.2.

Figure 6.1 represents formative assessment as a cycle of events. Evidence is gathered during activity A and interpreted in terms of progress towards the lesson goals. Some notion of progression in relation to the goal is needed for this interpretation, so that where students are can be used to indicate what next step is appropriate. Helping the students to take this next step, leading to activity B, is the way in which the evidence of current learning is fed back into teaching and learning. This feedback helps to regulate teaching so that the pace of moving toward a learning goal is adjusted to ensure the active participation of the students. As with all regulated processes, feedback into the system is the important mechanism for ensuring effective operation. Just as feedback from the thermostat of a heating or cooling system allows the temperature of a room to be maintained within a particular range, so feedback of information about learning helps ensure that new experiences are not too difficult nor too easy for students.

In the case of teaching, the feedback is both to the teacher and to the students. Feedback to teachers is needed so that they can consider appropriate next steps and the action that will help the students to take them. Feedback to students is most effective in promoting learning if it involves them in the process of deciding what the next steps should be, so they are not passive recipients of the teacher's judgments of their work. Thus the students are at the centre of the process and the two-headed arrows in Figure 6.1 indicate that they have a role in the collection, interpretation and use of the evidence of their learning.

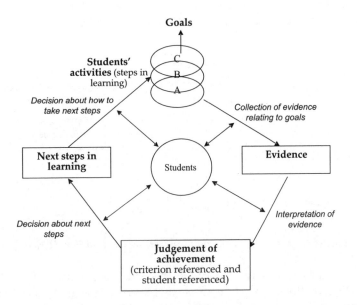

Figure 6.1: *Assessment for learning as a cycle of events (adapted from Harlen, 2000)*

The actions indicated by the boxes in Figure 6.1 are not 'stages' in a lesson or necessarily conscious decisions made by the teacher. They represent a framework for thinking about what is involved when focusing on what and how students are learning, and are using this to help further learning. In some cases it may be possible for teachers and students together to decide on immediate action. For example, if a teacher finds some students' ideas about an event they are investigating in science are not consistent with the scientific explanation, it may be possible for them to help the students to set up a test of their ideas and so see for themselves the need to consider alternative explanations. In other cases, a teacher may take note of what is needed and provide it at a later time. Implementing formative assessment means that not everything in a lesson can be planned in advance. By definition, if students' current learning is to be taken into account, some decisions will depend on what this learning is. Some ideas can be anticipated from teachers' experience but not all. What a teacher needs is not a prescribed lesson content but a set of strategies to deploy according to what is found to be appropriate on a particular occasion.

Figure 6.2, when compared with Figure 6.1, shows the essential difference between assessment for learning and assessment used to report on achievement. In Figure 6.2, evidence relating to the goals of learning may be gathered from regular activities or from special assessment tasks or tests. The interpretation is in terms of achievement of certain skills, understandings and attitudes as a result of a number of activities. It will be criterion-referenced, using the same criteria for all students because the purpose is to report achievement in a way that is comparable across students. There is no feedback into teaching – at least not in the same immediate way as in the assessment for learning cycle. In this model the students have no role in the assessment, although some argue that they can and should have a role (see for example, Frederiksen and White, 2004).

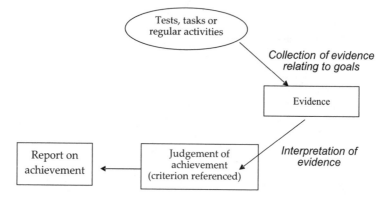

Figure 6.2: *Assessment of learning by teachers (adapted from Harlen, 2000)*

These models represent two conceptually different uses of evidence that enable clear distinctions to be made between assessment for learning and assessment of learning. But are these distinctions quite so sharp in practice? Can evidence collected to summarize learning be used to help learning? Can evidence collected for formative purposes also be used for summative purposes? If so, how is this done and what does it say about any real distinction between formative assessment and summative assessment? These are the questions addressed in the next two sections of this chapter, which draw upon some material from Harlen (2005).

Using summative assessment evidence to help learning

The question here is whether evidence gathered so that it efficiently and reliably serves a summative purpose can also serve to help learning. This evidence might be, for example, collected by tests or special tasks or a summation of coursework, in order to see to what extent certain skills or understandings have been acquired. Can the same evidence be used to help further learning? There are examples of practice provided by Maxwell (2004) and by Black et al. (2003) that would suggest a positive answer to this question.

Maxwell describes the approach to assessment used in the Senior Certificate in Queensland, in which evidence is collected over time in a student portfolio as 'progressive assessment'. He states that:

All progressive assessment necessarily involves feedback to the student about the quality of their performance. This can be expressed in terms of the student's progress towards desired learning outcomes and suggested steps for further development and improvement ...

For this approach to work, it is necessary to express the learning expectations in terms of common dimensions of learning (criteria). Then there can be discussion about whether the student is on-target with respect to the learning expectations and what needs to be done to improve performance on future assessment where the same dimensions appear.

As the student builds up the portfolio of evidence of their performance, earlier assessment may be superseded by later assessment covering the same underlying dimensions of learning. The aim is to report 'where the student got to' in their learning journey, not where they started or where they were on the average across the whole course. (Maxwell, 2004: 2–3)

The identification of goals and assessment criteria in terms of a 'common dimension of learning' is central to this approach. Descriptions of these dimensions of learning need to be detailed to be capable of giving guidance, yet not so prescriptive as to infringe teachers' ownership of the curriculum. As the research reviewed by Harlen (2004) shows, the dependability of assessment is enhanced when teachers have a thorough understanding of the goals and of the nature of progression towards them. In Queensland, this is facilitated by schools being able to make decisions about their own work plan and by teachers' regular participation in the process of moderation. Time for this participation and respect for the professionalism of teachers (Cumming and Maxwell, 2004) are also important. Conditions that promote dependability are clearly essential when teachers' assessment has high stakes for individual students. However, a significant feature of the Queensland system is that the assessment of students in the Senior Certificate is detached from school and teacher accountability procedures.

Black et al. (2003) include the formative use of summative assessment as one of four practices that teachers found were effective ways of implementing formative assessment (the others being questioning, feedback by marking and student peer and self-assessment – see Chapter 1). These practices were all devised or elaborated by teachers as they strove, working with the researchers, to make changes in their classrooms so that assessment was used to help learning. In relation to the formative use of summative tests, the teachers devised three main ways of using classroom tests, beyond just assessing attainment, to develop students' understanding. The first of these involved helping students to prepare for tests by reviewing their work and screening past test questions to identify areas of insecure understanding. This reflection on their areas of weakness enabled them to focus their revision. The second innovation was to ask students to set test questions and devise marking schemes. This helped them 'both to understand the assessment process and to focus further efforts for improvement' (Black et al., 2003: 54). The third change was for the teachers to use the outcome of tests diagnostically and to involve students in marking each other's tests, in some cases after devising the mark scheme. This has some similarity to the approach reported by Carter (1997), which she called 'test analysis'. In this the teacher returned test papers to students after indicating where there were errors, but left the students to find and correct these errors. The students' final marks reflected their response to the test analysis as well as the initial answers. Carter described this as shifting the responsibility for learning to the students, who were encouraged to work together to identify and correct their errors.

Whilst there is clearly value in using tests in these ways, there are several limitations to these approaches. First, the extent to which this information could guide teachers in how to help students work towards particular lesson goals would depend on how often tests or special tasks were set. Moreover, if the tasks are designed to summarize learning related to general criteria, such as statements of attainment in national curricula, they will not have the detail that enables them to be diagnostic in the degree needed to help specific learning. Although it is possible to use some external tests and examinations in this way, by obtaining marked scripts and discussing them with students, in practice the approach is one that teachers can use principally in the context of classroom tests over which they have complete control. Black et al. (1993) noted that when external tests are involved, the process can move from developing understanding to 'teaching to the test'. More generally, the pressures exerted by current external testing and assessment requirements are not fully consistent with good formative practices (Black et al., 2003: 56). There would be a strong tendency to gather frequently what is essentially summative evidence as a substitute for evidence that can be used formatively. Whilst the teachers described by Black et al. (2003) used their creativity to graft formative value on to summative procedures, a more fundamental change is needed if assessment is to be designed to serve both purposes from the start.

The ten principles of assessment for learning (ARG, 2002a) provide a means of checking the extent to which evidence from a summative assessment can be truly formative. Before assuming that such evidence is capable of helping learning, a teacher might judge it against these principles by asking, for instance:

- Does it focus on how students learn?
- Is it sensitive and constructive?
- Does it foster motivation?
- Does it promote understanding of goals and criteria?
- Does it help learners to know how to improve?
- Does it develop the capacity for self-assessment?
- Does it recognize all educational achievements?

The Queensland portfolio system could be said to match most of these requirements quite well; indeed, it is designed to serve a formative purpose as well as a summative one. But the same cannot be said of using tests and examinations. These can make a contribution to helping identify further learning, but can never be sufficient to meet the requirement of assessment for learning, because:

- The collection of summative evidence does not occur sufficiently frequently;
- The information is not sufficiently detailed to be diagnostic;
- It only occurs in reality in relation to tasks chosen, administered and marked by teachers;

- There is a danger of mistaking frequently collected summative evidence for evidence that can be used formatively and therefore neglecting genuine assessment for learning;
- Using external tests in this way risks teaching to the tests;
- It rarely matches the principles of assessment for learning.

Using formative assessment information for summative assessment

The approaches discussed above are linked to summative assessment which is an occasional, if regular, event. In between classroom tests or summary grading of course work, there are other innumerable classroom events in which teachers and students gather evidence about the latter's on-going achievements. They do this by observing, questioning, listening to informal discussions among students, reviewing written work and by using students' self-assessment (Harlen and James, 1997). As noted earlier, when utilized to adapt teaching and learning this evidence may be used immediately to provide students with help or it may be considered later and used to plan subsequent learning opportunities.

Evidence gathered in this way is often inconclusive and may be contradictory, for what students can do is likely to be influenced by the particular context. This variation, which would be a problem for summative assessment (see Chapter 7), is useful information for formative purposes, suggesting the contexts in which students can be helped to develop their ideas and skills. By definition, since it is gathered in the course of teaching evidence at this level of detail relates to all aspects of students' learning. It is valuable in that it relates to the goals of specific lessons or activities and can be used in deciding next steps for individual learners or for groups. An important question is: can this rich but sometimes inconsistent evidence be used for summative assessment purposes as well as for formative assessment, for which it is so well suited? If not, then separate summative assessment will be necessary.

A positive answer to this question was given by Harlen and James (1997) who proposed that both formative and summative purposes can be served provided that a distinction is made between the *evidence* and the *interpretation of the evidence*. For formative assessment, the evidence is interpreted in relation to the progress of a student towards the goals of a particular piece of work, next steps being decided according to where a student has reached. The decision that is informed relates to what needs to be done to help further learning, not what level or grade a student has reached. There are two related but different matters to be considered in moving from using evidence in this way to using it to summarize what has been learned. These are the goals involved and the basis of judgment of the evidence.

Goals at different levels

First of all the goals of a lesson, shared with the students, will be specific to the subject matter of that lesson. Addressing these specific goals will contribute to the development of a more general understanding or improved skill, that is, to goals at a more generic level than the specific lesson goals. For example, the goals of a specific lesson might include an understanding of how the structure and form of a snail is suited to the places where snails are found. This will contribute to an understanding of how animals in general are suited to their habitats, but achieving this will depend on looking at a variety of animals which will be the subject of other lessons with their own specific goals. Similarly, skills such as planning a scientific investigation are developed not in one lesson but in different contexts in different lessons.

So, while teachers and students use evidence to help learning in relation to specific goals the evidence from several lessons can contribute to a more general learning outcome. For this purpose it is important for teachers to have a view of progression in relation to the understanding and skills they are aiming for their students to achieve through particular lessons. The course of progression can be usefully expressed in terms of indicators, which serve both the purpose of focusing attention on relevant aspects of students' behaviour and enable teachers to see where students are in development. An example of indicators for the development of planning scientific investigations in the context of science at the primary level is given in Box 6.1.

Box 6.1: Example of developmental indicators

Things students do that are indicators of planning scientific investigations:

- Suggest a useful approach to answering a question or testing a prediction by investigation, even if details are lacking or need further thought;
- Make suggestions about what might happen when certain changes are made;
- Identify the variable that has to be changed and the things which should be kept the same for a fair test;
- Identify what to look for or measure to obtain a result in an investigation;
- Select and use equipment and measuring devices suited to the task in hand;
- Succeed in planning a fair test using the support of a framework of questions or planning board;
- Spontaneously structure a plan so that variables are identified and steps taken to make results as accurate as possible. (Harlen, 2005)

These indicators have been developed from what is known about progression from research and practice, but they are not by any means definitive. It is not likely that there is an exact and invariable sequence that applies to every student, but is it helpful to have a rough idea. Examples of similar lists have been published in Australia (Masters and Forster, 1996) and developed in California (as the Berkeley Evaluation and Assessment Research (BEAR) system (Wilson, 1990; Wilson et al., 2004). In these lists, the earlier statements indicate understanding, skills or attitudes that are likely to be developed before those following later in the list. There is no need for 'levels', grades or stages to be suggested; just a sequence expected for students in a particular age range (in the example, in primary and early secondary school years). For formative assessment it is not necessary to tie indicators to grade level expectation; all that is required is to see where students are and what is the next step in their further progress. This is consistent with the form of feedback for students in formative assessment, which should be non-judgemental and focused on the next steps in learning (see Chapters 1 and 4).

Teachers need thoroughly to understand, internalize and own these indicators if they are to be useful in their everyday work with students. This raises a potential problem relating to ensuring that they are carefully and rigorously defined to ensure validity, and at the same time understood and owned by teachers. It is not realistic for teachers alone to create such indicators for themselves, nor would it lead to valid outcomes; it requires input from researchers and developers with expertise in students' development as well as classroom experience. But somehow it is necessary to avoid a top-down imposition of a set of indicators which could turn their use into a mechanistic process. Research suggests that this can be avoided and ownership encouraged by training that includes experience of devising some indicators without having to cover the full set with the thoroughness required for use by all teachers in a range of circumstances.

As for reporting attainment there is another step to be taken, since the progressive criteria are too detailed for most summative purposes. What is required for summary reporting is, at most, an overall judgement about what has been achieved in terms of, for instance, 'knowledge and understanding of life processes and living things' or 'scientific enquiry skills'. A further aggregation of evidence is needed across the range of ideas and processes that are included in these global terms. To take the example of science enquiry skills, evidence from several lessons in which the goal is to help students plan scientific investigations will lead to identifying where students are in planning investigations. This skill, in turn, is part of a broader aim of developing enquiry skills, a target of the national curriculum on which teachers provide a summary end-of-year or key stage report. Thus there is a three-step process, depicted in Figure 6.3, of using information from individual lessons to produce a summary relating to reporting categories. But this is not a straightforward aggregation, as we see in relation to the second matter to be considered in summarizing the evidence; the basis of judgment.

Changing the basis of judgement of the evidence

As noted earlier, when evidence is gathered in a lesson (A, B, C, and so on in Figure 6.3) it may be used on the spot or later to help students or groups achieve the lesson goals. In doing this a teacher will interpret the evidence in relation to the progress of the individuals involved, so the judgment will be student-referenced (or ipsative) as well as being related to the criteria. However, if the evidence is also used to report on achievement of broader aspects of skills or knowledge, moving from left to right across Figure 6.3, then it must be evaluated according to the criteria only. Thus the evidence can be used for two purposes providing it is reinterpreted against criteria that are the same for all students. This means that if the information already gathered and used formatively is to be used for summative assessment it must be reviewed against the broader criteria that define levels or grades. This involves finding the 'best fit' between the evidence gathered about each student and one of the reporting levels. In this process the change over time can be taken into account so that, as in the Queensland portfolio assessment, preference is given to evidence that shows progress during the period covered by the summative assessment.

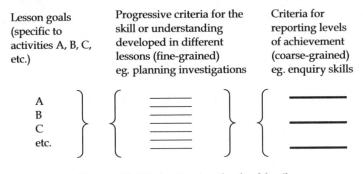

| Lesson goals (specific to activities A, B, C, etc.) | Progressive criteria for the skill or understanding developed in different lessons (fine-grained) eg. planning investigations | Criteria for reporting levels of achievement (coarse-grained) eg. enquiry skills |

Figure 6.3: *Goals at various levels of detail*

These considerations show that it is quite possible to use evidence gathered as part of teaching both to help learning and for reporting purposes. But, as with the use of summative data for formative purposes, there are limitations to the process. By definition, in this context, the judgement is made by the teacher and for summative purposes there needs to be some assurance of dependability. Thus some quality assurance procedures need to be in place. The more weight that is given to the summative judgement, the more stringent the quality assurance needs to be, possibly including some inter-school as well as intra-school moderation in judgements of evidence. This is difficult in relation to outcomes where the evidence is ephemeral and a consequence of this can be that the end-use of the evidence influences what evidence is gathered and how. It could result in a tick-list approach to gathering evidence or a series of special tasks that give concrete evidence, making formative assessment into a succession of summative assessments.

A further limitation is that if summative assessment is based solely on evidence gathered within the context of regular classroom activities, this evidence will be limited by the range and richness of the educational provision and the efficiency of the teachers in collecting evidence. In some circumstances the evidence required to summarize learning may need to be supplemented by introducing special tasks if, for instance, a teacher has been unable for one reason or another to collect all that is necessary to make judgements about all the students. For formative purposes it is often appropriate to consider the progress of groups rather than of individual students. Additional evidence may then be needed when making a report on the achievement of individual students.

In summary, limitations on using evidence gathered for formative assessment, if it is to meet the requirements of summative assessment, are:

- It is essential to reinterpret the evidence in relation to the same criteria for each student;
- It is important for teachers to be very clear about when level-based criteria are appropriate and not to use them for grading students when the purpose of the assessment is formative;
- Since the formative use of evidence depends on teachers' judgments, additional quality assurance procedures will be needed when the information is used for a different purpose;
- Teachers may need to supplement evidence from regular classroom events with special tasks to ensure that all necessary evidence is collected for all students;
- The difficulty of dealing with ephemeral evidence could lead to a tick-list approach or a series of summative tasks;
- This may well change the nature of formative assessment, making it more formal.

Revisiting the relationship

A dichotomy or a dimension?

The discussion in the previous two parts of this chapter indicates that there is no sharp discontinuity between assessment for learning and assessment to report learning. In particular, it is possible to view the judgements of evidence against the progressive criteria in the middle column of Figure 6.3 both as formative, in helping decisions about next steps, and as summative in indicating where students have reached. This suggests that the relationship between formative and summative assessment might be described as a 'dimension' rather than a 'dichotomy'. Some points along the dimension are indicated in Figure 6.4 (derived from Harlen, 1998).

At the extremes are the practices and uses that most typify assessment for learning and assessment of learning. At the purely formative end is assessment that is integral to student-teacher interaction and is also part of the student's role. The teacher and student consider work in relation to the goals that are appropriate for the particular learner and so the judgements are essentially student-referenced. The central purpose is to enable teacher and students to identify the next steps in learning and to know how to take these. At the purely summative end of the dimension the purpose is to give an account of what has been achieved at certain points. For this purpose, the assessment should result in a dependable report on the achievements of each individual student. Although self-assessment may be part of the process, the ultimate responsibility for giving a fair account of how each student's learning compares with the criteria or standards rests with the teacher.

Between these ends it is possible to identify a range of procedures having various roles in teaching and learning. For instance, many teachers would begin a new topic by finding out what the students already know, the purpose being to inform the teaching plans rather than to identify the point of development of each individual. Similarly, at the end of a section of work teachers often give an informal test (or use 'traffic-lighting' – see Chapter 1) to assess whether new ideas have been grasped or need consolidation.

	Formative←		→Summative	
	Informal formative	Formal formative	Informal summative	Formal summative
Major focus	What are the next steps in learning?		What has been achieved to date?	
Purpose	To inform next steps in learning	To inform next steps in teaching	To monitor progress against plans	To record achievements of individuals
How is evidence collected?	As normal part of class work	Introduced into normal class work	Introduced into normal class work	Separate task or test
Basis of judgement	Student referenced	Student and criterion referenced	Criterion referenced	Criterion referenced
Judged by	Student and teacher	Teacher	Teacher	Teacher or external marker
Action taken	Feedback to students and teacher	Feedback into teaching plans	Feedback into teaching plans	Report to student, parent, other teachers, etc.
Epithet	Assessment for learning	Matching	Dip stick	Assessment of learning

Figure 6.4: *A possible dimension of assessment purposes and practices*

There is some parallel here with intermediate purposes for assessment identified by others. Cowie and Bell (1999) interpreted their observation of the assessment practices of ten teachers in New Zealand as indicating two forms of formative assessment: planned and interactive. Planned formative assessment concerns the whole class and the teacher's purpose is to find out how far the learning has progressed in relation to what is expected in the standards or curriculum. Information gathering, perhaps by giving a brief class test or special task, is planned and prepared ahead; the findings are fed back into teaching. This is similar to 'informal summative'. Interactive formative assessment is not planned ahead in this way; it arises from the learning activity. Its function is to help the learning of individuals and it extends beyond cognitive aspects of learning to social and personal learning; feedback is both to the teacher and the learners and is immediate. It has the attributes of 'informal formative'.

Cowie and Bell's interactive formative assessment is similar to the classroom assessment that Glover and Thomas (1999) describe as 'dynamic'. Like Black and Wiliam (1998b), they emphasize the involvement of students in learning and indeed speak of 'devolving power to the learners' and suggest that without this, dynamic assessment is not possible. Unlike Cowie and Bell, however, they claim that all assessment must be planned.

There are also different degrees of formality towards the summative end. What is described as 'informal summative' may involve similar practice to 'formal formative', as is illustrated in Figure 6.4. However, the essential difference is the use made of the evidence. If the cycle is closed, as in Figure 6.1, and the evidence is used in adapting teaching, then it is formal formative. If there is no feedback into teaching, as in Figure 6.2, then it falls into the category of 'informal summative', even though the evidence may be the same classroom test.

Yet rather than trying to make even more distinctions among assessment procedures, this analysis perhaps ought to be taken as indicating no more than that there are different ways of practising and using formative assessment and summative assessment. If this is so, do we then need the distinction at all?

Is there formative and summative assessment or just good assessment?

Some of those involved in developing assessment have argued that the formative/summative distinction itself is not helpful and that we should simply strive for 'good assessment'. Good formative assessment will support good judgements by teachers about student progress and levels of attainment and good summative assessment will provide feedback that can be used to help learning. Maxwell (2004) describes progressive assessment as blurring the boundary between formative and summative assessment.

The discussion of Figure 6.4 certainly indicates a blurred boundary. Added to this, the recognition of how evidence can be used for both purposes would at first sight seem to add to the case against retaining the distinction between formative and summative assessment. In both cases there are limitations in the dual use of the evidence, but on closer inspection these are seen to be of rather different kinds. The limitation of using evidence which has initially been gathered for a summative purpose to help learning bears on the validity of the evidence; it is just not sufficiently rich and readily available to be adequate for formative use. The limitation of using evidence which has initially been gathered to help learning to report on learning, bears on the reliability of the evidence. In this case there are steps that can be taken to address limitation and increase reliability: training can ensure that teachers collect evidence systematically and with integrity whilst moderation can optimize comparability.

When procedures are in place to assure quality in this way, then evidence gathered by teachers at a level of detail suitable for helping learning can also be used for dependable assessment of learning. This is what happens in the Queensland Senior Certificate, where all the information needed to grade students comes from evidence collected and judged by teachers. However, the reverse situation cannot be found; there are no examples of all the needs of assessment for learning being provided from evidence collected for summative purposes. Of course, it is not logical that this could be so.

This asymmetry in dual use seems to be a strong argument for maintaining the distinction in purposes. We need to know for what purpose the evidence was gathered and for what purpose it is used. Only then can we evaluate whether it is 'good' or not. One can conduct the same assessment and use it for different purposes just as one can travel between two places for different purposes. As the purpose is the basis for evaluating the success of the journey, so the purpose of assessment enables us to evaluate whether the purpose has been achieved. If we fuse or confuse formative and summative purposes, experience strongly suggests that 'good assessment' will mean good assessment of learning, not for learning.

Conclusion

The notion of progression is one of two key elements in the discussion in this chapter. To develop students' understanding and skills teachers need to have in mind some developmental criteria in order to see how the goals of specific lessons are linked to the progression of more general concepts and skills. For formative purposes, these criteria do not need to be linked to levels; they just provide a guide to the next steps in learning. For summative assessment purposes, where a summary is required, the use of levels, standards or grades is a way of communicating what a student has achieved in terms of the criteria represented by the levels, standards or grades. This process condenses evidence and necessarily means a loss of detail. The uses to which summative information is put require that the levels and their like mean the same for all students. That is, putting aside for the moment the possibility of mis-grading discussed in Chapter 7, a level or grade X for student A means this student has achieved roughly the same as student B who also achieved a level or grade X. It is only for convenience that we use levels; in theory we could report performance in terms of a profile across a succession of progressive criteria, but this would probably provide far too much detail for most purposes where a concise summary is required.

It is the different purposes of the information, the second key feature of this chapter, that create a distinction between formative and summative assessment. We have argued that evidence gathered as part of teaching and learning can be used for both formative and summative purposes. It is used to help learning when interpreted in terms of individuals' progress towards lesson goals. The same evidence can also be interpreted against the general criteria used in reporting achievement in terms of levels or grades. However, we have noted that evidence gathered in a form that is already a summary, as from a test or examination, generally lacks the detail needed to identify and inform next steps in learning. This means that we cannot use any evidence for just any purpose. It argues for maintaining a clear distinction between formative and summative in terms of the use made of the evidence.

Although there are shades of formality in the ways of conducting formative assessment and summative assessment, as indicated in Figure 6.4, the difference in purpose remains. We cannot make an assumption that the way in which evidence is gathered will determine its use in learning; a classroom test can be used to inform teaching without any reference to levels or it can be used to provide a grade or level for end of stage reporting. The asymmetrical relationship – that evidence collected for formative assessment can be used for summative assessment but not vice versa – means that removing the labels and referring only to 'assessment' would inevitably favour summative purposes.

It is both a weakness and a strength that summative assessment derived by reinterpreting formative evidence means that both are in the hands of the teacher. The weakness arises from the known bias and errors that occur in teachers' judgements. All assessment involves judgement and will therefore be subject to some error and bias. While this aspect has been given attention in the context of teachers' assessment for summative uses, it no doubt exists in teachers' assessment for formative purposes. Although it is not necessary to be over-concerned about the reliability of assessment for this purpose (because it occurs regularly and the teacher will be able to use feedback to correct for a mistaken judgment), the more carefully any assessment is made the more value it will have in helping learning. The strength, therefore, is that the procedures for ensuring more dependable summative assessment, which need to be in place in a system using teachers' judgements, will benefit the formative use, the teacher's understanding of the learning goals and the nature of progression in achieving them. Experience shows that moderation of teachers' judgements, necessary for external uses of summative assessment, can be conducted so that this not only serves a quality control function but also has a quality assurance function, with an impact on the process of assessment by teachers (ASF, 2004). This will improve the collection and use of evidence for a formative as well as a summative purpose.

This chapter has sought to explore the relationship between formative assessment and summative assessment with a view to using the same evidence for both purposes. We have seen that there are potential dangers for formative assessment in assuming that evidence gathered for summative assessment can serve formative purposes. Similarly, additional measures need to be put in place if summative assessment based on evidence gathered and used for formative assessment is to be adequately reliable. These issues are key to protecting the integrity of assessment and particular to protecting the integrity of formative assessment so that assessment has a positive impact on learning, which is the central concern of this book.

Chapter 7

The Reliability of Assessments

Paul Black and Dylan Wiliam

The discussion at the end of the previous chapter raises the question of the part that teachers play in the summative assessment of their students. For many of the decisions made within schools, summative assessments made by teachers play an important role and affect the progress of students. For summative assessments that are used outside the school, whether for progress to employment, further stages of education or for accountability purposes, the stakes are even higher. The question of the extent to which such assessments should be entrusted to teachers and schools is a key issue in assessment policy.

Any assessments should be so designed that the users of the results, be they the students, their parents, their teachers or the gatekeepers for further stages of education or employment, can have confidence in the results. There are two main criteria of quality of an examination result that should be a basis for such confidence: reliability and validity. This chapter is concerned only with the first of these, although there are areas of overlap between them. The term 'dependability' is used to signify the overall judgement of quality for an assessment which may be influenced by both reliability and validity, and by other features also.

It is not possible to optimize the systems for producing summative assessments, either for use within schools or for more general public use, unless both the reliability and the validity of the various methods available are carefully appraised. Both qualities are essential. However, the public in general and policy makers in particular do not understand or pay attention to reliability. They appear to have faith in the dependability of the results of short tests when they are in fact ignorant of the sizes of the inescapable errors that accompany this and any other measure. This is a serious failing. Decisions which will have an important effect on a student's future may be taken by placing more trust in a test-score than in other evidence about that student, when such trust is not justified.

In this chapter, the first section discusses what is meant by the reliability of the score obtained from a summative test and the second examines published evidence about test reliabilities. The third section then looks at decision consistency, that is, the effects of limited reliability on the errors that ensue in assigning candidates to specific grades or levels on the basis of test scores. The scope of the considerations then broadens in the next three sections, which discuss in turn the overlap between reliability and validity, the reliability of formative assessments and the broader issue of dependability. The leading issues are then highlighted in a closing summary.

Threats to reliability

No test is perfectly reliable. It is highly unlikely that the score that someone gets on one occasion would be exactly the same as on another occasion, even on the same test. However, if they took the same or similar tests on a number of occasions then the average of all those scores would, in general, be a good indicator of their capability on whatever it was that the test was measuring. This average is sometimes called the 'true score'. Thus, the starting point for estimating the reliability of a test is to hypothesize that each student has a 'true score' on a particular test – this does not mean that we believe that a student has a true 'ability' in (say) reading, nor that the reading score is in any sense fixed.

The main sources of error that can threaten the reliability of an examination result are:

- Any particular student may perform better or worse depending on the actual questions chosen for the particular administration of the test;
- The same student may perform better or worse from day-to-day;
- Different markers may give different marks for the same piece of work. (Black and Wiliam, 2002)

The first of these three is a problem of question sampling. On any syllabus, there will be a very large number of questions that can be set. Questions can differ both in their content (for example, force, light, electricity in physics) and in the type of attainment that they test (for example, knowledge of definitions, solution of routine short problems, design of an experiment to test a hypothesis). Those who set the UK General Certificate of Secondary Education (GCSE) and Advanced-level examinations usually work with a two-dimensional grid with (say) content topics as the rows and types of attainment as the columns. The relative weights to be given to the cells of this grid are usually prescribed in the syllabus (but they can vary between one syllabus and another); so across any one examination, the examiners must reflect this in the distribution of the questions (for example, one on the definition of force, two on applying the concept in simple quantitative problems, and so on). In addition, they may deploy different types of questions, for example using a set of 40 multiple-choice questions to test knowledge and simple applications so as to cover many cells, and then having a small number of longer problems to test application of concepts and synthesis of ideas (for example, design of an experiment involving detection of light with devices which give out electrical signals).

What the examples here demonstrate is that the composition of an examination is a delicate balancing act. There is a huge number of possible questions that can be set on any one syllabus: the examiners have to select a tiny proportion and try to make their selection a fair sample of the whole.[1] If the time allowed for the test or tests is very short, the sample will be very small. The smaller the sample, the less confidence one can have that the result for any one candidate would be the same as that which would be given on another sample composed in the same way. Thus, any examination can become more reliable if it can be given a longer time.

120

No examination can produce a perfect, error-free result. The size of the errors due to the first of the sources of error listed above can be estimated from the internal consistency of a test's results. If, for a test composed of several items, candidates are divided according to their overall score on the test, then one can look at each component question (or item) to see whether those with a high overall score have high scores on this question, and those with low overall scores have low scores on this question. If this turns out to be the case, then the question is said to have 'high discrimination'. If most of the questions have high discrimination, then they are consistent with one another in putting the candidates in more or less the same order. The reliability-coefficient that is often quoted for a test is a measure of the internal consistency between the different questions that make up the test. Its value will be a number between zero and one. The measures usually employed are the Kuder-Richardson coefficient (for multiple-choice tests) or Cronbach's alpha (for other types of test); the principle underlying these two is the same.

If this internal consistency is high, then it is likely that a much longer test sampling more of the syllabus will give approximately the same result. However, if checks on internal consistency reveal (say) that the reliability of a test is at the level of 0.85, then in order to increase it to 0.95 with questions of the same type, it would be necessary to more than triple the length of the test. Reliability could be increased in another way – by removing from the test all those questions which had low discrimination and replacing them with questions with high discrimination. This can only be done if questions are pre-tested, and might have the effect of narrowing the diversity of issues represented in the test in order to homogenize it.

Indices based on such checks are often claimed to give the reliability of an examination result. Such a claim is not justified, however, for it takes no account of other possible sources of error. For example, a second source of error means that the actual score achieved by a candidate on a given day could vary substantially from day to day. Again, this figure could be improved, but only by setting the test in sections with each taken on different days. Data on this source are hard to find so it is usually not possible to estimate its effect. It would seem hard to claim a priori that it is negligible.

The third source – marker error – is dealt with in part by careful selection and training of markers, in part by rigorous rules of procedure laid down for markers to follow and in part by careful checks on samples of marked work. Whilst errors due to this source could be reduced by double marking of every script, this would also lead to very large increases both in the cost of examinations and in the time taken to determine results. Particular cases of marker error justifiably attract public concern, yet overall the errors due to this source are probably small in comparison with the effects of the other sources listed here.

It is important to note, therefore, that the main limitations on the accuracy of examination results are not the fault of testing agencies. All of the sources could be tackled, but only if increases in costs, examining times and times taken to produce results were to be accepted by the educational system. Such acceptance seems most unlikely; in this, as in many other situations, the public gets what it is prepared to pay for.

Evidence about reliability

Because there are few published studies relating to the reliability of public examinations, the proportions of candidates awarded the 'wrong' grade on any one occasion are not known. It is very surprising that there are no serious attempts to research the effects of error in public examinations, let alone publish the results.

The crucial criterion is therefore how close the score we get on a particular testing occasion is to the 'true score', and given possible error in a final mark, there follows the possibility that a candidate's grade, which is based on an interpretation of that mark, will also be in error.

Thus this criterion is concerned with the inevitable chance of error in any examination result. Four studies serve to illustrate the importance of this criterion. The first is a study by Rogosa (1999) of standardized tests used in the state of California. This shows that even for tests with apparently high indices of reliability, the chances of a candidate being mis-classified are high enough to lead to serious consequences for many candidates. His results were expressed in terms of percentiles, a measure of position in the rank order of all candidates. If a candidate is on (say) the 40th percentile this means that 40 per cent of all candidates have marks at or below the mark achieved by that candidate. His results showed, for example, that in grade 9 mathematics there is only a 57 per cent probability that candidates whose 'true score' would put them in the middle of the rank order of candidates, that is, on the 50th percentile, will actually be classified as somewhere within the range 40th to 60th percentile, so that the other 43 per cent of candidates will be mis-classified by over ten percentile points. For those under-classified, this could lead to a requirement to repeat a grade or to attend a summer school. It could also result in assignment to a lower track in school, which would probably prejudice future achievement. Of the three sources of error listed above, this study explored the effects of the first only, that is, error due to the limited sample of all possible questions.

The second is a report by Black (1963) of the use of two parallel forms of tests for first-year physics undergraduates, the two being taken within a few days of one another and marked by the same markers to common criteria. The tests were designed to decide who should proceed to honours study. Out of 100 candidates, 26 failed the first paper and 26 failed the second, but only 13 failed both. Half of those who would be denied further access to the honours course on the one paper would have passed on the second, and vice versa. Until that year decisions about proceeding to different courses had been taken on the results of a single paper. The effects illustrated by this study could have arisen from the first two sources of error listed above.

The third study has provided results which are more detailed and comprehensive. Gardner and Cowan (2000) report an analysis of the 11-plus selection examination in Northern Ireland, where each candidate sits two parallel forms of test with each covering English, mathematics and science. They were able to examine both the internal consistency of each test and the consistency between them. Results are reported on a six-grade scale and each selective (grammar) school admits its applicants on the basis of their grade, starting with the highest, and working down the grades until all the places are filled. Their analysis shows that if one expects to infer a candidate's true grade from the reported grade and one wants to be correct in this inference 95 per cent of the time, then for a candidate in a middle grade one can say only that the true score lies somewhere between the highest and the lowest grades (the '95 per cent confidence interval' thus ranges from the lowest to the highest grade). For a candidate just in the highest grade the true score may be anywhere within the top four grades; given that this is the 95 per cent confidence interval, 5 per cent of students will be mis-classified by an even greater margin. Of course, for students close to the threshold, even a small mis-classification might lead to the wrong decision. Given that 6–7000 candidates secure selective places, it is likely that around 3000 will be mis-classified to the extent that either secures or denies acceptance of their entry to grammar school due to the unreliability of the test. This study reflects the effects of all three possible sources of error.

The fourth source of evidence was provided by an analysis carried out by Wiliam (2001) of the key stage tests used in England at ages 7, 11 and 14 respectively. He concluded that the chances of a student's level result being wrong by one level were around 20–30 per cent – this being an underestimate as it was based only on the variability revealed by the internal consistency of performances on the single test occasion. This example is discussed in more detail below. This study is similar to that by Rogosa quoted above, in that it explores only the effects of errors due to the limited sample of all possible questions.

One can note that three of the reliability studies quoted above were carried out by critics outside the systems criticized. There have been no formal attempts by governments or their agencies to conduct thorough research to establish the reliabilities of high-stakes examinations. If this were to be done, it seems likely that the resulting probabilities of mis-grading would be large enough to cause some public concern. Thus it is essential that such research be undertaken and the data made public. The following conclusion of Gardner and Cowan about the Northern Ireland test applies with equal force to all of our public testing:

> The published information on the Test does not meet the requirements of the international standards on educational testing, both generally in the provision of standard reliability and validity information and particularly, for example, in the validation of the Test outcomes in relation to its predictive power (for example, 'potential to benefit from a grammar school education'), establishing norms, providing information on potential mis-classification, and accommodating disability. (2000: 9)

Estimating the consequences: decision consistency

As noted above, an individual's true score on a test is simply the average score that the individual would get over repeated takings of the same or a very similar test. The issue to be explored in this section is the possible effect of errors in their actual test scores on decisions taken about the classification of candidates in grades or levels (for the examples quoted in the previous section it was these consequences which were the focus of attention).

Knowing a student's mark on a test is not very informative unless we know how difficult the test is. Because calibrating the difficulty of tests is complex the results of many standardized tests are reported on a standard scale, which allows the performance of individuals to be compared with the performance of a representative group of students who took the test at some point in the past. When this is done, it is conventional to scale the scores so that the average score is 100 and the standard deviation of the scores is 15. This means that:

- 68 per cent (that is, roughly two-thirds) of the population score between 85 and 115;
- For the other 32 per cent, 16 per cent score below 85 and 16 per cent score above 115;
- 96 per cent score between 70 and 130.

So we can say that the level of performance of someone who scores 115 on a reading test would be achieved or surpassed by 16 per cent of the population, or that this level of performance is at the 84th percentile.

From this it would be tempting to conclude that someone who scored 115 on the test really is in the top 16 per cent of the population, but this may not be the case because of the unreliability of the test. To explore the consequences of error in the score of any candidate, the first step is to examine the internal consistencies amongst the test's scores. This can be used to calculate the conventional measure known as the 'reliability coefficient'. A value for this coefficient of 1.0 means that the errors are zero, so there is no error and the test is perfectly reliable. A coefficient of 0.0 means that the errors are very variable and the spread in their likely values is the same as that of the observed scores, that is, the scores obtained by the individuals are all error so there is no information about the individuals at all! When a test has a reliability of zero the result of the test is completely random.

The reliability of tests produced in schools is typically around 0.7 to 0.8 while that for commercially produced educational tests range from 0.8 to 0.9, and can be over 0.9 for specialist psychological tests (a reputable standardized test will provide details of the reliability and how it was calculated). To see what this means in practice, it is useful to look at some specific kinds of tests.

If we assume a value for the reliability of a test, then we can estimate how far the observed score is likely to be from the true score. For example, if the reliability of a test is 0.75, then the standard deviation (SD) of the errors (a measure of the spread in the errors) turns out to be 7.5.[2] The consequences of this for the standardized test will be that:

- For 68 per cent of the candidates their actual scores will be within 7.5 (that is, one SD) of their true scores;
- For 96 per cent of the candidates their actual scores will be within 15 (that is, two SDs) of their true scores;

- For 4 per cent of the candidates their actual scores will be at least 15 away from their true score.

For most students in a class of 30, their actual score will be close to their true score (that is, what they 'should' have got), but it is likely that for at least one the score will be 'wrong' by 15 points (but of course we do not know who this student is, nor whether the score they got was higher or lower than their true score). For a test with a reliability of 0.75, this means that someone who scores 115 (who we might think is in the top sixth of the population) might on another occasion score just 100 making them appear average, or as high as 130, putting them in the top 2 per cent (often used as the threshold for considering a student 'gifted'). If the reliability were higher then this spread in the errors would be smaller – for a reliability of 0.85, the above value of 7.5 for the SD would be replaced by a value of 6.

Because the effects of unreliability operate randomly the averages across groups of students, however, are quite accurate. For every student whose actual score is lower than their true score there is likely to be one whose actual score is higher than their true score, so the average observed score across a class of students will be very close to the average true score. But just as the person with one foot in boiling water and one foot in ice is quite comfortable 'on average' we must be aware that the results of even the best tests can be wildly inaccurate for a few individual students, and therefore high-stakes decisions should never be based solely on the results of single tests.

Making sense of reliability for the key stage tests used in England is harder because these are used to assign levels rather than marks, for good reason. It is tempting to regard someone who gets 75 per cent in a test as being better than someone who gets 74 per cent, even though the second person might actually have a higher true score. In order to avoid unwarranted precision, therefore, we often just report levels. The danger, however, is that in avoiding unwarranted precision we end up falling victim to unwarranted accuracy – while we can see that a mark of 75 per cent is only a little better than 74 per cent, it is tempting to conclude that level 2 is somehow qualitatively better than level 1. Firstly, the difference in performance between someone who scored level 2 and someone who scored level 1 might be only a single mark, and secondly, because of the unreliability of the test, the person scoring level 1 might actually have had a higher true score.

Only limited data have been published about the reliability of national curriculum tests, although it is likely that the reliability of national curriculum tests is around 0.80 – perhaps slightly higher for mathematics and science. Assuming this reliability value, it is possible to calculate the proportion of students who would be awarded the 'wrong' levels at each key stage of the national curriculum. The proportion varies as a result of the unreliability of the tests as shown in Table 7.1.

It is clear that the greater the precision (that is, the more different levels into which students are to be classified as they move from KS1 to KS3) the lower the accuracy. What is also clear is that although the proportion of mis-classifications declines steadily as the reliability of a test increases, the improvement is very slow.

Table 7.1: *Variation in proportion of misclassifications in national curriculum tests with reliability*

	Reliability of Test							
	0.60	0.65	0.70	0.75	0.80	0.85	0.90	0.95
Key Stage	Percentage (%) of Students Misclassified at Each Key Stage							
KS1	27	25	23	21	19	17	14	10
KS2	44	42	40	36	32	27	23	16
KS3	55	53	50	46	43	38	32	24

We can make tests more reliable by improving the items included in the tests and by making the marking more consistent, but in general the effect of such changes is small. There are only two ways of achieving a significant increase in the reliability of a test: make the scope of the test narrower so you ask more questions on fewer topics, or make the test longer so you ask more questions on all of the topics.

It turns out that[3] if we have a test with a reliability of 0.75, and we want to make it into a test with a reliability of 0.85, we would need a test 1.9 times as long. In other words, doubling the length of the test would reduce the proportion of students mis-classified by only 8 per cent at Key Stage 1, by 9 per cent at Key Stage 2 and by 4 per cent at Key Stage 3. It is clear that increasing the reliability of the test has only a small effect on the accuracy of the levels. In fact, if we wanted to improve the reliability of Key Stage 2 tests so that only 10 per cent of students were awarded the incorrect level, we should need to increase the length of the tests in each subject to over 30 hours.[4]

Now it seems unlikely that even the most radical proponents of schools tests would countenance 30 hours of testing for each subject. In survey tests, which use only limited samples of students to obtain an overall evaluation of students' achievement, it is possible by giving different tests to different sub-samples to use 30 hours of testing (see for example, the UK Assessment of Performance Unit surveys – Black, 1990). However, the reliability of the overall test performance of a group will be far higher than that for any one individual, so that in optimizing the design of any such survey the extra testing time available has been used mainly to increase the variety of performance outcomes assessed, that is, to enhance validity.

Fortunately, there is another way of increasing the effective length of a test, without increasing testing time, and that is through the use of teacher assessment. By doing this we would, in effect, be using assessments conducted over tens if not hundreds of hours for each student so that there would be the potential to achieve a degree of reliability that has never been achieved in any system of timed written examinations. This possibility has to be explored in the light of evidence about the potential reliability of teachers' summative assessments. A review of such evidence (see Harlen, 2004; ASF, 2004) does show that it is possible to achieve high reliability if the procedures by which teachers arrive at summative judgments are carefully designed and monitored.

The overlap between reliability and validity

There are several issues affecting the interpretation of assessment results that involve overlap between the concepts of reliability and validity. One such issue bears on whether or not questions have been so composed and presented that the student's response will give an authentic picture of the capability being tested – a feature which may be called the 'disclosure of a question' (Wiliam, 1992). Good disclosure is not easy to attain. For example, several research studies have established that in multiple-choice tests in science many of those making a correct choice among the alternatives had made their selection on the basis of incorrect reasoning, whilst others had been led to a wrong choice by legitimate reasoning combined with unexpected interpretations of the question. It would seem that in such tests approximately one third of students are incorrectly evaluated on any one question (Tamir, 1990; Towns and Robinson, 1993; Yarroch, 1991). It has also been shown, for open-ended questions, that misinterpretation frequently leads candidates to fail to display what they know and understand (Gauld, 1980). This source of error might arise from a random source, for example careless reading by the student, and might have less impact if the student were to attempt a larger number of questions; it would then become a reliability issue. However, it might reflect a systematic weakness in the reading and/or interpretation of questions, which is not relevant to the performance that the test is designed to measure; it would then be a validity issue.

A similar ambiguity of overlap arises in considering the use of tests for prediction. For example, we might like most secondary schools in the UK want to use the results of IQ or aptitude tests taken at the age of 11 to predict scores on GCSE examinations taken at 16, or use such tests at the end of high school to predict performance in tertiary level work (Choppin and Orr, 1976). What we would need to do would be to compare the GCSE scores obtained by students at age 16 with those scores which the same students obtained on the IQ tests five years earlier, when they were 11. In general we would find that those who got high scores in the IQ tests at 11 get high grades in GCSE, and low scorers get lower grades. However, there will also be some students getting high scores on the IQ tests who do not go on to do well at GCSE and vice versa. How good the prediction is – often called the 'predictive validity of the test' – is usually expressed as a correlation coefficient. A correlation of one means the correlation is perfect, while a correlation of zero would mean that the predictor tells us nothing at all about the criterion. Generally, in educational testing, a correlation of 0.7 between predictor and criterion is regarded as good.

In interpreting these coefficients, care is often needed because they are frequently reported after 'correction for unreliability'. The validity of IQ scores as predictors of GCSE is usually taken to mean the correlation between true scores on the predictor and true scores on the criterion. However, as we have seen, we never know the true scores – all we have are the observed scores and these are affected by the unreliability of the tests. When someone reports a validity coefficient as being corrected for unreliability, they are quoting the correlation between the true scores on the predictor and criterion by applying a statistical adjustment to the correlation between the observed scores, which will appear to be much better than we can actually do in practice because the effects of unreliability are inescapable. For example, if the correlation between the true scores on a predictor and a criterion – that is, the validity 'corrected for unreliability' – is 0.7, but each of these is measured with tests of reliability 0.9, the correlation between the actual values on the predictor and the criterion will be less than 0.6. A decline from 0.7 to 0.6 might seem small, but it should be pointed out that the proportion of the common variance in the results depends on the square of the correlation coefficient, so that in this case there will be a decrease from 49 per cent to 35 per cent in the variance in the scores that is common to the two tests.

A similar issue arises in the common practice of using test results to select individuals. If we use a test to group a cohort of 100 students into four sets for mathematics, with, say, 35 in the top set, 30 in set 2, 20 in set 3 and 15 in set 4, how accurate will our setting be? If we assume that our selection test has a predictive validity of 0.7 and a reliability of 0.9, then of the 35 students that we place in the top set, only 23 should actually be there – the other 12 should be in sets 2 or 3. Perhaps more importantly, given the rationale used for setting, 12 students who should be in set 1 will actually be placed in set 2 or even set 3. Only 12 of the 30 students in set 2 will be correctly placed there – nine should have been in set 1 and nine should have been in sets 3 and 4. The complete situation is shown in Table 7.2.

Table 7. 2: *Accuracy of setting with a test of validity of 0.7*

		Number of Students that Should be Placed in Each Set			
		Set 1	Set 2	Set 3	Set 4
		35	30	20	15
Sets in which Students Are Actually Placed	Set 1	23	9	3	
	Set 2	9	12	6	3
	Set 3	3	6	7	4
	Set 4		3	4	8

In other words, because of the limitations in the reliability and validity of the test, only half of the students are placed where they 'should' be. Again, it is worth noting that these are not weaknesses in the quality of the tests but fundamental limitations of what tests can do. If anything, the assumptions made here are rather conservative – reliabilities of 0.9 and predictive validities of 0.7 are at the limit of what we can achieve with current methods. As with national curriculum testing, the key to improved reliability lies with increased use of teacher assessment, standardized and moderated to minimize the potential for bias.

A different issue in the relationship between reliability and validity is the 'trade-off' whereby one may be enhanced at the expense of the other. An example here is the different structures in the UK GCSE[5] papers for different subjects. A typical 90-minute paper in science includes approximately 12 structured questions giving a total of about 50 sub-sections. For each of these, the space allowed on the examination paper for the response is rarely more than four lines. The large number of issues so covered, and the homogeneity in the type of response demanded, help to enhance reliability but at the expense of validity, because there is no opportunity for candidates to offer a synthesis or comprehensive discussion in extended prose. By contrast, a paper in (say) a social science may require answers to only two or three questions. This makes the test valid in prioritizing modes of connected thinking and writing, but undermines reliability in that some candidates will be 'unlucky' because these particular questions, being a very small sample of the work studied, are based on topics that they have not studied thoroughly.

An extreme example of this trade-off is the situation where reliability is disregarded because validity is all important. A PhD examination is an obvious example; the candidate has to show the capability to conduct an in-depth exploration of a chosen problem. The inference that may be made is that someone who can do this is able to 'do research', that is, to do work of similarly good quality on other problems. This will be a judgment by the examiners: there is only a single task, and no possibility of looking for consistency of performance across many tasks, so that estimates of reliability are impossible. Here, validity does not depend on reliability. This is quite unlike the case of inferring that a GCSE candidate is competent in mathematics on the basis of an aggregate score over the several questions attempted in a written test. Here, reliability is a prior condition – necessary but not sufficient – for achieving validity. There are more complex intermediate cases, for example if a certificate examination is composed of marks on a written paper and an assessment of a single substantial project; in such a case, the automatic addition of a test paper score and a project score may be inappropriate.

Reliability for formative assessments

A different arena of overlap is involved in the consideration of formative assessment, given that all of the above discussion arises in relation to summative assessments. The issues here are very different from the summative issues. Any evidence here is collected and interpreted for the purpose of guiding learning on the particular task involved and generalization across a range of tasks to form an overall judgment is irrelevant. Furthermore, inadequate disclosure which introduces irrelevant variation in a test and thereby reduces reliability (as well as validity) is less important if the teacher can detect and correct for it in continuing interaction with the learner. However, some formative assessment takes place over longer time intervals than that of interactions in (say) classroom dialogue and involves action in response to a collection of several pieces of evidence. One example would be response to a class test, when a teacher has to decide how much time to give to remedial work in order to tackle weaknesses revealed by that test: here, both the reliability and validity of the test will be at issue, although if short-term interactions are to be part of any 'improvement' exercise any short-comings in the action taken should become evident fairly quickly and can be corrected immediately. This issue was expanded more fully in Wiliam and Black where the argument was summed up as follows:

> As noted above, summative and formative functions are, for the purpose of this discussion, characterized as the end of a continuum along which assessment can be located. At one extreme (the formative) the problems of creating shared meanings beyond the immediate setting are ignored; assessments are evaluated by the extent to which they provide a basis for successful action. At the other extreme (the summative) shared meanings are much more important, and the considerable distortions and undesirable consequences that arise are often justified by appeal to the need to create consistency of interpretation. Presenting this argument somewhat starkly, when formative functions are paramount, meanings are often validated by their consequences, and when summative functions are paramount, consequences are validated by meanings. (1996: 544)

Conclusion

This chapter ends with incomplete arguments because of the overlaps between reliability and validity. Of importance here is dependability, which is essentially an overall integrating concept in which both reliability and validity are subsumed. It follows that a comprehensive consideration of this overall issue belongs to the next chapter on validity.

However, the issues discussed here are clearly of great importance and ought to be understood by both designers of assessment systems and by users of test results. One arena, in which this has importance, is the use of assessment results within schools as guidance for students and decisions about them. The fact that teachers may be unaware of the limited reliability of their own tests is thus a serious issue. Where assessment results are used for decisions beyond schools, knowledge of reliability is also important. The fact that, at least for public examinations in the UK, reliability is neither researched nor discussed is a serious weakness. Data on reliability must be taken into account in designing test systems for optimum 'trade-off' between the various constraints and criteria that determine dependability. In the absence of such data, optimum design is hardly possible because it is not possible to evaluate fully alternative design possibilities. As emphasized at the beginning of this chapter, this absence is also serious because all users can be seriously misled. For example, decisions that have an important effect on a student's future may be taken by placing more trust in a test-score than in other evidence about that student, when such trust is clearly not justified.

Overall, one consequence of the absence of reliability data is that most teachers, the public in general, and policy makers in particular do not understand or attend to test reliability as an issue and some are indeed reluctant to promote research into reliability because of a fear that it will undermine public confidence in examinations. Of course, it may well do so to an unreasonable degree where the media and the public generally do not understand concepts of uncertainty and error in data. A debate that promotes the development of such understanding is long overdue.

Notes

1 In examination jargon, the whole collection of possible questions is called a 'domain', and the issue just discussed is called 'domain sampling'. In any subject, it is possible to split the subject domain (say physics) into several subdomains, either according to content or to types of attainment (say understanding of concepts, application in complex problems, design of experiments). One might then test each domain separately with its own set of questions and report on a student's attainment in each of these domains separately, so giving a profile of attainments instead of a single result. However, if this is done by splitting up but not increasing the total testing time, then each domain will be tested by a very small number of questions so that the score for each element of the profile will be far less reliable than the overall score.

2 Since the standard deviation of the scores is 15 for a reliability of 0.85, from our key formula we can say that the standard deviation of the errors is:

$$\sqrt{1 - 0.85} \times 15$$

which is just under 6. Similarly, for a reliability of 0.75, the same formula will give a value of 7.5.

3 In general if we have a test of reliability r and we want a reliability of R, then we need to lengthen the test by a factor of n given by:

$$n = \frac{R(1 - r)}{r(1 - R)}$$

4 The classification consistency increases broadly as the fourth root of the test length, so a doubling in classification consistency requires increasing the test length 16 times.

5 GCSE is the General Certificate of Secondary Education which comprises a set of subject examinations, from which most students in secondary schools in England, Wales and Northern Ireland at age 16, that is, at the end of compulsory education, choose to take a few (generally between 4 and 7) subjects.

Chapter 8

The Validity of Formative Assessment

Gordon Stobart

The deceptively simple claim of this chapter is that for formative assessment to be valid it must lead to further learning. The validity argument is therefore about the consequences of assessment. The assumption is that formative assessment generates information that enables this further learning to take place – the 'how to get there' of our working definition of assessment for learning (see the Introduction). One implication of this is that assessments may be formative in intention but are not so in practice because they do not generate further learning.

This 'consequential' approach differs from how the validity of summative assessments is generally judged. Here the emphasis is on the trustworthiness of the inferences drawn from the results. It is about the meaning attached to an assessment and will vary according to purpose. Reliability is more central to this because if the results are unreliable, then the inferences drawn from them will lack validity (see Chapter 6).

This chapter examines current understandings of validity in relation to both summative and formative assessment. It then explores the conditions that encourage assessment for learning and those which may undermine it. Two key factors in this are the context in which learning takes place and the quality of feedback. The learning context includes the socio-cultural and policy environment as well as what goes on in the classroom. Feedback is seen as a key element in the teaching and learning relationship. These factors relate directly to the treatment of 'making learning explicit' in Chapter 2, to motivation in Chapter 4 and the formative-summative relationship in Chapter 6. Reliability in formative assessment is discussed in Chapter 7.

Validity

Most of the theorizing about validity relates to testing and this will be used as the basis for looking at validity in formative assessment. In relation to testing, validity is no longer simply seen as a static property of an assessment, which is something a test has, but is based on the inferences drawn from the results of an assessment. This means that each time a test is given, the interpretation of the results is part of a 'validity argument'. For example, if a well-designed mathematics test is used as the sole selection instrument for admission to art school we may immediately judge it as an invalid assessment. If it is used to select for mathematics classes then it may be more valid. It is how the assessment information is understood and used that is critical. At the heart of current understandings of validity are assumptions that an assessment effectively samples the construct that it claims to assess. Is the assessment too restricted in what it covers or does it actually assess different skills or understandings to those intended? This is essentially about fitness-for-purpose. It is a property of the test scores rather than the test itself. The 1985 version of the American Educational Research Association's *Standards for Educational and Psychological Testing* was explicit on this: 'validity always refers to the degree to which ... evidence supports the inferences that are made from the scores' (1985: 9).

This approach was championed by Messick:

Validity is an integrated evaluative judgement of the degree to which empirical evidence and theoretical rationales support the adequacy and appropriateness of inferences and actions based on test scores or other modes of assessment. (1989: 13)

The validity of summative assessment is therefore essentially about trustworthiness, how well the construct has been assessed and the results interpreted. This brings into play both the interpretation of the construct and the reliability of the assessment. Any unreliability in an assessment weakens confidence in the inferences that can be drawn. If there is limited confidence in the results as a consequence of how the test was marked or how the final grade was decided, then its validity is threatened.

However, a test may be highly reliable yet sample only a small part of a construct. We can then have only limited confidence in what it tells us about a student's overall understanding. Take the example of a reading test. To be valid this test must assess competence in reading. But what do we mean by reading? Thirty years ago a widely used reading test in England was the Schonell's Graded Word Reading Test which required readers to pronounce correctly single decontextualized words of increasing difficulty (for example, tree – sidereal). The total of correctly read words, with the test stopping after ten consecutive failures, was then converted into a 'Reading Age'. By contrast, the current national curriculum English tests for 11-year-olds in England are based on a construct of reading that focuses on understanding of, and making inferences from, written text. Responses are written and there is no 'reading out loud' involved. Clearly a key element in considering validity is to agree the construct that is being assessed. Which of the above provides a more valid reading score or do both suffer from 'construct under-representation' (Messick, 1989)?

This approach links to the previous two chapters. Because the purpose of the assessment is a key element in validity – 'it does what it claims to do' – then the validity argument differs for formative and summative assessment (see Chapter 6). In formative assessment it is about consequences – has further learning taken place as a result of the assessment? In summative assessment it is the trustworthiness of the inferences that are drawn from the results – does our interpretation of students' results do justice to their understanding? On this basis much of what is discussed as reliability in Chapter 7 is subsumed into validity arguments.

Threats to validity

This chapter uses the idea of 'threats to validity' (Crooks et al., 1996) to explore where the validity argument may be most vulnerable. Crooks et al. use an approach which sees the validity process as a series of linked stages. The weakest link in the chain is the most serious threat to validity. If there is limited confidence in the results as a consequence of a highly inconsistent administration of a test, then this may be the most important threat to validity. Or it could be that a test was fairly marked and graded but the interpretation of the results, and the decisions made as a consequence, were misguided and therefore undermine its validity.

One of the key threats to validity in test-based summative assessment is that, in the quest for highly reliable assessment, only the more easily and reliably assessed parts of a construct are assessed. So speaking and listening may be left out of language tests because of reliability issues and writing may be assessed through multiple-choice tests. While reliability is necessary for validity, a highly reliable test may be less valid because it sampled only a small part of the construct – so we cannot make confident generalizations from the results. One of the strong arguments for summative teacher assessment is that it does allow a construct to be more fully, and repeatedly, sampled. So even if it may seem less reliable because it cannot be standardized as precisely as examination marking, it may be a more dependable assessment of the construct being measured (see Chapter 7).

A second major threat to validity is what Messick obscurely calls 'construct irrelevant variance'. If a test is intended to measure reasoning skills but students can do well on it by rote learning of prepared answers, then it is not doing what it claims it is doing; it therefore lacks validity. This is because success has come from performance irrelevant to the construct being assessed (Frederiksen and Collins, 1989).

This is important because it means that learning cannot simply be equated with performance on tests. Good scores do not necessarily mean that effective learning has taken place. This was evidenced by Gordon and Reese's conclusions on their study of the Texas Assessment of Academic Skills, which students were passing

> even though the students have never learned the concepts on which they are being tested. As teachers become more adept at this process, they can even teach students to correctly answer test items intended to measure students' ability to apply, or synthesize, even though the students have not developed application, analysis or synthesis skills. (1997: 364)

If increasing proportions of 11-year-olds reach level 4 on the national curriculum assessment in England, have educational standards risen? There is limited public recognition that there may be an 'improved test taking' factor that accounts for some of this and there may not be the same degree of improvement on other, similar, measures for which there has not been extensive preparation (Tymms, 2004; Linn, 2000).

This brief review of how validity is being interpreted in summative assessment provides a framework for considering the validity of formative assessments. Here validity arguments go beyond the focus on the inferences drawn from the results to consider the consequences of an assessment, a contested approach in relation to summative assessment (see Shepard, 1997; Popham, 1997).

Valid formative assessment

It is consequential validity which is the basis for validity claims in formative assessment. By definition, the purpose of formative assessment is to lead to further learning. If it fails in this then, while the intention was formative, the process was not (Wiliam and Black, 1996; Wiliam, 2000). This is a strict, and circular, definition which implies that validity is central to developing or practising formative assessment.

Validity in formative assessment hinges on how effectively this learning takes place. What gets in the way of this further learning can be treated as a threat to the validity of formative assessment. This parallels processes for investigating the validity of tests (Crooks et al.,1996) and of teacher-based performance assessments (Kane et al.,1999). In the following sections some of the key factors that may support or undermine formative assessment are briefly considered. The learning context in which formative assessment takes place is seen as critical. This includes what goes on outside the classroom, the social and political environment, as well as expectations about what and how teachers teach and learners learn within the classroom. At a more individual level, feedback has a key role in formative assessment. What we know about successful feedback is discussed, along with why some feedback practices may undermine learning.

The learning context

If validity is based on whether learning takes place as a consequence of an assessment, what can encourage or undermine this learning? Perrenoud (1998) has argued that formative assessment is affected by what goes on 'upstream' of specific teacher–learner interactions and that this context is often neglected, partly because it is so complex. Some of the cultural assumptions on which assessment for learning is based are a product largely of developed anglophone cultures (particularly Australia, New Zealand, the UK and the USA), with their 'whole child' approaches, individualism and attitude to motivation. It is therefore worth briefly considering how some different social and cultural factors may affect what goes on in the classroom, since these are likely to provide differing threats to effective formative assessment.

Outside the classroom

At the macro level, the role and status of education within a society will impact on students' motivation to learn and the scope for formative assessment. In a society where high value is placed on education, for example in Chinese education, student motivation to learn may be a 'given' (Watkins, 2000) rather than having to be fostered by schools as is often the assumption in many UK and North American schools (Hidi and Harackiewicz, 2000; ARG, 2002a). Similarly, the emphasis on feedback being task-related rather than self-related may sit · more comfortably in cultures which see the role of the teacher as to instruct (for example, France) rather than as to care for the 'whole child' (for example the UK, see Raveaud, 2004). There are also cultural differences around the extent to which education may be seen as a collective activity with group work as a natural expression of this, or as an individualistic activity in which peer assessment may seem alien (Watkins, 2000).

The curriculum and how it is assessed is another key 'outside' contextual factor. The opportunities for formative assessment, in a centralized curriculum with high-stakes national testing, will be different for those teachers who enjoy more autonomy over what they have to cover and how they assess it. In Chapter 6 the question is raised as to whether an outcomes-based/criterion-related curriculum, with its attempts to make learning goals and standards explicit, provides improved opportunities for formative assessment.

Inadequate training and resources are obvious threats to formative assessment. In many large and badly resourced classrooms, ideas of individual feedback or of regular groupwork are non-starters. In some countries very large classes may be taught by teachers with limited subject knowledge who are teaching an unfamiliar curriculum – all of which will limit potential (Meier, 2000).

The culture of schooling will also impact on the effectiveness of formative assessment. Entrenched views on teaching and learning may undermine or support formative assessment, as might deeply embedded assessment practices. For example, in a culture where the dominant model of teaching is didactic, moves towards peer and self-assessment by learners may involve radical, and managerially unpopular, changes to the classroom ethos (Carless, 2005; Black et al., 2003). Similarly, where continuous assessment by teachers is high stakes, determines progression and is well understood by parents, any move by a classroom teacher to provide feedback through comments rather than marks or grades is likely to meet resistance (Carless, 2005). This may come from both outside and inside the school – parents may see the teachers as not doing their jobs properly and the students may not co-operate because work that does not receive a mark does not count, and so is not worth doing.

These are just a few examples of the ways in which the social and educational context will shape and control what is possible inside the classroom and in individual teacher-student interactions. These social and cultural factors will condition how effective formative assessment in the classroom will be.

Inside the classroom: learning context and feedback

For formative assessment to lead to learning, the classroom context has to be supportive and the feedback to the learner productive. If the conditions militate against learning they become threats to validity.

Crooks (2001) has outlined what he considers are the key issues that influence the validity of formative assessment in the classroom. He groups these into four main factors: affective, task, structural and process. To reflect the themes of this book they can be organized in terms of trust and motivation; explicit learning; and the formative/summative relationship.

Trust and motivation

Chapter 4 demonstrates that learning involves trust and motivation. For Crooks, trust implies supportive classroom relationships and attitudes where the student feels safe to admit difficulties and the teacher is constructive and encouraging. Motivation involves both teacher commitment to the student's learning and the student's own wish to learn and improve. There may also be a strong contextual element in this, so that it will also fluctuate across different situations – I may be much more willing to learn in drama than I am in maths.

Crooks's approach to affective factors may reflect the cultural assumptions of English-speaking industrialized societies. In other cultures, motivation and trust may be differently expressed. For example, commentaries on Russian schooling suggest a very different attitude to praise and to building self-esteem. Alexander observes that while there was only a handful of praise descriptors in Russian, 'the vocabulary of disapproval is rich and varied' (2000: 375). Yet in this more critical climate, there is strong evidence of Russian students pursuing mastery goals and being willing to risk mistakes. Hufton and Elliott report from their comparative study that 'it was not unusual for students who did not understand something, to request to work in front of the class on the blackboard, so that teacher and peers could follow and correct their working' (2001: 10). Raveaud's (2004) account of French and English primary school classes offers some similar challenges to anglophone understandings of fostering trust and motivation.

It may be that we need a more robust view of trust to make sense of such findings. The Russian example of trust may be a lot less likely to occur in cultures in which teachers seek to minimize the risk of error and to protect learners' self-esteem. The trust seems to be based on the assumption that the teacher is there to help them learn but is not necessarily going to rescue them immediately from mistakes or misunderstandings. It is this kind of trust that makes the idiosyncratic and unplanned formative interactions in the classroom powerful; there is confidence in the teacher who has, in turn, confidence in the student's capacity to learn.

Explicit learning

An element of this trust is that the teacher knows what is to be learned. Explicit learning incorporates the teacher's knowledge and understanding of the task, the criteria and standards that are to be met and how effectively these are communicated to the learners. Clarke (2001, 2005) has continued to draw attention to the importance of being explicit about 'learning intentions'. The importance of subject knowledge may have been underplayed in some of the earlier writings on assessment for learning, though there is now an increased recognition of the importance of pedagogical content knowledge (see Chapter 2).

The reason for being more explicit about learning intentions is, in part, to engage the student in understanding what is required. One of the threats to validity is that students do not understand what they are supposed to be learning and what reaching the intended standard will involve. A recent survey of 13-year-olds in England (Stoll et al., 2003), which involved 2,000 students, asked 'what helps you learn in school?'. The largest group of responses involved the teacher making clear what was being learned:

> My science teacher and English teacher writes out the aims for the lesson, which helps me understand what we are going to do in the lesson. I don't like teachers who just give you a piece of work and expect us to know what to do, they have to explain the piece of work. (2003: 62–3)

Other work with students has also brought home how bewildered some are about what is being learned:

> It's not that I haven't learnt much. It's just that I don't really understand what I'm doing. (15-year-old student, Harris et al., 1995)

Understanding 'where they need to get to in their learning' is a key element in the definition of assessment for learning (ARG, 2002a). For Sadler (1989) it is this understanding of where they need to get to ('the standard') that is critical to successful feedback. When we are not sure what is needed, it is hard to make sense of feedback. At a more theoretical level this can be linked to construct validity – what is to be learned and how does this relate to the domain being studied?

Dilemmas in 'making explicit'

How explicit should learning intentions be? How do we strike a balance which encourages deep learning processes and mastery learning? If the intentions are too general the learner may not be able to appreciate what is required. If they are too specific this may lend itself to surface learning of 'knowledge in bits'.

The level descriptions used in the assessment of the national curriculum in England, and other comparable 'outcomes-based' approaches around the world, run the risk of being either too general or too 'dense' to be self-evident. They may need considerable further mediation by teachers in order for learners to grasp them. For example, this is the level description for the performance in writing expected of 11-year-olds in England:

Level 4 Writing
Pupils' writing in a range of forms is lively and thoughtful. Ideas are often sustained and developed in interesting ways and organized appropriately for the

purpose of the reader. Vocabulary choices are often adventurous and words are used for effect. Pupils are beginning to use grammatically complex sentences, extending meaning. Spelling, including that of polysyllabic words that conform to regular patterns, is generally accurate. Full stops, capital letters and question marks are used correctly, and pupils are beginning to use punctuation within the sentence. Handwriting style is fluent, joined and legible. (QCA, 2005)

While this may provide a good basis for explicit learning intentions, the practice of many schools to 'level' (that is, to award a level to) each piece of work is likely to be unproductive in terms of understanding the standard. This is especially so as the descriptions are used in a 'best fit' rather than in a criterion-referenced way, allowing the student to gain a level 4 without fully meeting all the requirements.

In a criterion-referenced system, in which the student must meet every statement at a level to gain that level, the threat is that the standard may become too detailed and mechanistic. This may encourage a surface learning approach in which discrete techniques are worked on in a way that may inhibit 'principled' understanding. For example, some of the occupational qualifications in England have been made so specific that 'learning' consists of meeting hundreds of competence statements, leading to a 'tick-box' approach in which students are 'hunters and gatherers of information without deep engagement in either content or process' (Ecclestone, 2002: 36). This approach is paralleled in highly detailed 'assessment objectives' in national tests and examinations which may encourage micro-teaching on how to gain an extra mark, rather than a broader understanding.

The formative/summative relationship

Crooks (2001) identifies 'connections' and 'purposes' as structural factors which influence the validity of formative assessment. His concern is the relationship of formative assessment to the end product and to its summative assessment (see Chapter 6). His assumption is that formative assessment is part of work-in-progress in the classroom. How does the final version benefit from formative assessment? While the salience of feedback on a draft version of a piece of in-class coursework may be obvious, it is less clear if the summative element is an external examination. The threat to validity in the preparing-for-tests classroom is that the emphasis may shift from learning to test-taking techniques, encouraging 'construct-irrelevant' teaching and learning.

When the work is strongly criterion-related, so that the standard of performance required to reach a certain level is specified, then this has implications for the teacher's role. The formative element in this process involves feedback on how the work relates to the criteria and how it can be improved to reach a particular standard. The summative judgement is whether, at a given point, the work meets the standard. The dilemma here for many teachers is how to play the roles of both facilitator and examiner. There is evidence from portfolio-based vocational qualifications that some teachers have found this problematical (Ecclestone, 2002).

In summary, within the classroom factors such as trust and motivation, clarity about what is being learned and the relationship of formative assessment to the summative goals will all affect the validity of formative assessments. This leads to the recognition that the possibilities for formative assessment are better in some learning contexts than others. The task is then to improve the learning context so as to increase the validity of formative assessment.

Validity and feedback

Feedback is one of the central components of assessment for learning. If feedback is defined in terms of 'closing the gap' between actual and desired performance then the key consequential validity issue is whether this has occurred. What the research evidence makes clear, however, is just how complex the process of feedback in learning is. While we can give feedback that is intended to help the learner to close the gap, this may not necessarily happen. It is not just that feedback does not improve learning, it may even interfere with it. Kluger and DeNisi conclude from their meta-analysis of the psychological research that:

> In over one third of the cases Feedback Interventions reduced performance ... we believe that researchers and practitioners alike confuse their feelings that feedback is desirable with the question of whether Feedback Intervention benefits performance. (1996: 275, 277)

For feedback in the classroom, the following play an important role in the establishment of valid feedback:

- It is clearly linked to the learning intention;
- The learner understands the success criteria/standard;
- It gives cues at appropriate levels on how to bridge the gap:
    a) self-regulatory/metacognitive
    b) process/deep learning
    c) task/surface learning;
- It focuses on the task rather than the learner (self/ego);
- It challenges, requires action, and is achievable.

The first two points refer back to the task factors and reinforce the relationship between clarity about what is being learned and those assessment criteria which relate directly to it.

'Cues at appropriate levels' is derived from psychological constructs used by Kluger and DeNisi and needs some decoding. The thrust of their argument is that if feedback is pitched at a particular level then the response to it is likely to be at that level. For example, if feedback is in terms of encouraging perseverance with a task ('self-regulation') the response will be in terms of more effort. While this in itself will not lead to new learning it may provide the context for seeking further feedback at the process or task level. Feedback is most power-

141

ful when it is provided at the process level and seeks to make connections and grasp underlying principles. Feedback at the task level is productive when it deals with incorrect or partial information, though less so when the task/concept is not understood.

This line of reasoning means that feedback at the self/ego level will focus attention at this level. The gap to be closed is then less about students' learning than their self-perception. Kluger and DeNisi discuss this in terms of reducing 'self-related discrepancy' which may involve switching to other tasks 'that would signal attainment of positive self-view'(1996: 266), a process which depletes the cognitive resources available for the task. If I am given feedback that my work has disappointed my teacher, who knows I could do better, I will seek ways of reconciling these judgements to my own self-understanding. I may attribute the quality of my work to lack of effort, protecting my view of myself as having the ability to do it (a favoured male technique?). However, if the teacher's judgement was on a task I had done my best on, I may begin to doubt my ability – a process which if continuously repeated may lead to a state of 'learned helplessness' (Dweck, 1999). In this I declare 'I am no good at this' and may avoid any further exposure, for example by dropping that subject and finding an easier one.

Research into classroom assessment (Gipps et al., 2000) has shown that even with expert teachers relatively little of this process or task-focused 'descriptive' feedback takes place. Rather, most feedback is 'evaluative' and takes the form of the teacher signalling approval or disapproval, with judgements about the effort made. While evaluative feedback may have a role in terms of motivation and effort, it is unlikely to lead directly to learning and so is not valid formative assessment.

Marks and grades as threats to valid formative assessment. Treating marks and grades as threats to valid formative assessment is one of the most provocative issues in assessment for learning. It is not a new claim. Thorndike, one of the founding fathers of behaviourism, claimed that grades can impede learning because as a feedback mechanism 'Its vice was its relativity [comparison to others] and indefiniteness [low level of specificity]' (1913: 286). Building on the work of Butler (1988), which showed significant student learning gains from comment-only marking when compared with marking which used grades and comments, there has been encouragement to move to 'comment-only' marking (Black et al., 2003; Clarke, 2001). The rationale for this is that grades, marks and levels do not provide information about how to move forward; any information is too deeply encoded. For many students they will have a negative effect because:

- Learning is likely to stop on the task when a summative grade is awarded for it (Kohn, 1993);
- The level of response may shift to a self/ego level in which the learners' energies go into reconciling the mark with their view of themselves as learners;
- They may encourage a performance orientation in which the focus is success in relation to others rather than learning. This in turn may have negative motivational and learning consequences for those who get low grades (ARG, 2002b; Reay and Wiliam, 1999).

For many this is an area in which social and political expectations make any such move problematic, as evidenced by the press furore when *Inside the Black Box* (Black and Wiliam, 1998b) was launched, with national newspaper headlines such as:

DON'T MARK HOMEWORK – *It upsets dunces says top education expert* (Daily Mirror *06/02/98);*

and

TWO OUT OF TEN – *For educationalists who want the world to be a different place* (The Times, *editorial, 06/02/98)*

Smith and Gorard (2005) also provide a cautionary example of where 'comment only' was introduced with some negative learning consequences. This was the result of teachers simply providing the evaluative comments they usually made alongside their marks ('try and improve'), rather than providing feedback on 'where ... to go and how best to get there'. For the students it meant they were confused about the standard they had achieved, as marks at least provide an indication of the relative merit of the work.

Praise as a threat to valid formative assessment. This is another highly sensitive area. The logic behind this claim is that praise is unable to directly improve learning. What it may do is motivate or encourage future learning, but this does not constitute formative assessment. The threat is that it may even get in the way of learning. Praise is essentially self, rather than task, focused (or will be treated that way by the recipient). Kluger and DeNisi (1996) suggest that while praise may help when a task is relatively simple, it impairs performance on cognitively demanding tasks, partly because it shifts attention away from the task.

What Gipps et al. (2001) have shown is that praise was one of the predominant forms of feedback in the classrooms they observed, with task focused feedback infrequent. While we might understand this as busy teachers keeping students motivated, with detailed feedback a luxury under normal classroom conditions, the teachers would probably consider that they were giving formative feedback. This is a misunderstanding that has regularly been noted (ARG, 1999). An unpublished study by Bates and Moller Boller (2000) has supported this. Their research involved examining, as part of a local authority review of schools' assessment policies, the marking comments over a seven month period across 12 subjects in one 11-year-old's work books. Over 40 per cent of the 114 written comments were praise unaccompanied by feedback. A further 25 per cent were presentational comments: 'don't squash up your work'; 'please take care – spelling'; 'very good – always write in pen'. The highly generalized nature of the feedback was borne out by it being impossible to determine to which subjects the majority of the feedback related. In only 23 per cent of the cases was there specific process level feedback, for example: 'what parts of her character do you like?'; 'why did you do 2 different tests?'; 'Why is this? What do you think you really learned?'.

Dweck (1999) and Kohn (1993) have cited the negative impact of praise and rewards on conceptions of learning. Dweck's experiments have shown how those receiving constant praise and rewards are likely to attribute their success to their ability. This is perceived as a fixed entity, as opposed to 'incrementalists' who take a more situational and effort-based view of successful learning. The consequence of this can be that 'straight A' students will do all they can to preserve their reputation, including taking easier courses and avoiding any risk of failure. The emphasis is then on performance – gaining good grades ('proving competence') – rather than on mastery with its attendant risks of set-backs and even failure ('improving competence'; Watkins et al., 2001). Dweck goes on to show the negative impact on 'top students' (particularly females) when they progress to colleges where success may be more elusive, who generate self-doubt about whether they really had the 'ability' they had been conditioned into thinking they possessed.

This approach raises questions about the use of merits, gold stars and smiley faces in the classroom. These are not about learning so much as motivation, and this form of motivation can undermine deep learning and encourage a performance motivation (see Chapter 2). Clarke has taken a practical look at some of the 'sticky issues' of external rewards (2001: 120) in relation to formative assessment in the primary classroom.

Valid feedback challenges, requires action and is achievable. Clarke (2001) has also observed that one problem area of classroom feedback is that while students are given feedback on a piece of work they are often not required to do anything active with it; in effect it is ignored. This is particularly unproductive when the comment is made repeatedly (for example, 'you must improve your presentation'). Research from the LEARN project (Weeden et al., 2002) found that written feedback was sometimes undermined by teachers being unclear, both because the handwriting was hard to read and because the language used was difficult to understand.

While too little challenge in feedback does not directly encourage learning, too much can make the gap seem impossible to bridge. Most of us will have experienced 'killer feedback' which makes such huge, or numerous, demands that we decide it is not worth the effort.

A further, and salutary, factor in feedback not leading to learning is that the learner has a choice as to what to do with the feedback. If 'learners must ultimately be responsible for their learning since no-one else can do it for them' (ARG, 1999: 7) then the manner in which they use feedback is part of this. The risk of only making limited use increases when feedback is given in the form of a 'gift' – handed over by the giver to the recipient – rather than as part of a dialogue (Askew and Lodge, 2000). Kluger and DeNisi (1996) also show how the learner has options when faced with feedback, and can choose to:

- Increase their effort rather than lower the standard;
- Modify the standard;
- Abandon the standard ('retire hurt');
- Reject the feedback/messenger.

The first response is more likely when 'the goal is clear, when high commitment is secured for it and when belief in eventual success is high' (1996: 260). We see the other three options being exercised (and exercise them ourselves) when students settle for 'all I want to do is pass', having started with more ambitious goals; when they declare they are 'rubbish at … ' and make no further effort and when, to punish a teacher they do not like, they deliberately make no effort in that subject.

Other sources of feedback

Feedback in this chapter has been treated largely in terms of the teacher-learner relationship. It can, however, come from a variety of sources. What is increasingly being recognized is that peer and self-assessment have a significant role to play in valid formative assessment. The logic of this is that, for these forms of assessment to be effective, students have to be actively aware of the learning intention and the standard that has to be met. Sadler argued that the ultimate aim of formative assessment is:

> to download that evaluative [assessment] knowledge so that students eventually become independent of the teacher and intelligently engage in and monitor their own development. If anything, the guild knowledge of teachers should consist less in knowing how to evaluate student work and more in knowing ways to download evaluative knowledge to students. (1989: 141)

While the aim of feedback is to reduce trial and error in the learning process, it is not intended to completely exclude them. Kluger and DeNisi make the point that 'even when FI [feedback intervention] is accompanied by useful cues, they may serve as crutches, preventing learning from errors (natural feedback) which may be a superior learning mode' (1996: 265). One has only to watch skateboarders practising techniques (no manuals, no adults to offer feedback) to see the point of this claim.

Feedback has been a key element in this discussion of validity because of its critical role in leading to further learning, the concept at the heart of consequential validity in formative assessment. What has to be recognized is the complexity of feedback processes, and how activities that pass for feedback may not be valid. The challenge is whether the consequence of the feedback is further learning, rather than improved motivation or changes to self-esteem. These may have a place, but are not themselves formative assessment. A further thought is that some forms of feedback may sometimes undermine the deep learning we claim to encourage.

What has not been considered so far is the role of reliability in these formative assessment processes. Does it pose a threat to validity in the same way as it does in summative assessment?

Reliability and formative assessment

Unlike summative assessments, conventional concepts of reliability such as marker consistency do not play a part in this particular validity argument. For

145

formative purposes judgements are essentially student-referenced rather than needing to be consistently applied, since a variety of students with similar outcomes may need different feedback to 'close the gap' in their learning. This is a strength rather than a problem.

How is reliability to be interpreted in relation to formative assessment? Reconceptualizing reliability in terms of the trustworthiness of the teacher's assessment has potential in relation to formative assessment. Wiliam (1992: 13) has proposed the useful concepts of disclosure ('the extent to which an assessment produces evidence of attainment from an individual in the area being assessed') and fidelity ('the extent to which evidence of attainment that has been disclosed is recorded faithfully') as alternative ways of thinking about reliability. The concept of disclosure is useful in thinking about the reliability of formative assessment. Has the formative assessment gathered the quality of evidence needed to understand where the learner is? Would a different task have led to a different understanding? While, ideally, feedback is repeated and informal and errors in interpretation will be self-correcting, the intention is to provide relevant feedback. 'Unreliable', in the sense of the limited dependability of the quality of interpretation and feedback, may have some salience. This is particularly relevant when feedback is being given in relation to any form of criterion-related standards, since any misinterpretation of these by the teacher could lead to feedback that misdirects learning.

Conclusion

Validity is central to any assessment. It is directly related to the purpose, form and context of an assessment; as these vary, so do the key threats to the validity of an assessment. The validation process involves judgements about the inferences and consequences of an assessment and what may undermine confidence in these. Reliability issues are part of this process in relation to summative assessment, but less so to formative assessment since unreliable results will undermine the dependability of the inferences that are made. So too will a failure to sample effectively the construct being assessed, even if the assessment is reliable.

In formative assessment validity is about consequences. Did further learning take place as a result of formative assessment? The threats to validity are those things that get in the way of this learning. These may be related to the classroom context, itself affected by the larger socio-cultural context, and the conditions for learning. This is exemplified in how feedback, a key concept in formative assessment, is used in classroom interactions. Many current feedback practices may not lead to further learning, and therefore may not be valid formative assessment.

Part IV Policy

Chapter 9

Constructing Assessment for Learning in the UK Policy Environment

Richard Daugherty and Kathryn Ecclestone

The rise of interest in assessment for learning in the UK has, as earlier chapters show, produced a parallel increase in theoretical and technical activity in relation to teachers' assessments of their own students and in mechanisms to promote the validity and reliability of such assessments. All of these dimensions have important policy implications for national assessment systems. The chapters on teachers' practice show that there was also, over the same period, a growing professional interest in assessment for learning. However, despite attempts in the late 1980s to include notions of assessment for learning within national curriculum assessment in England and Wales, UK policy makers have only recently taken an interest in this crucial aspect of the assessment of students' attainments. For example in England, where the policy environment had appeared to be unfavourable, policy makers have at the time of writing linked assessment's role in support of learning to the 'personalization' of learning, which is a central plank in the current Labour government's approach to 'personalized public services' (see Leadbetter, 2004).

This chapter explores the rise of assessment for learning as a feature of education policy in the four countries of the UK and shows how assessment policies are a pivotal element in the distinct, and increasingly divergent, policy environments in England, Scotland, Wales and Northern Ireland. Each of the four countries of the UK is evolving its own education system and this process has accelerated since 1999 when structural changes in the constitution of the UK resulted in increased policy-making powers for the Scottish parliament and for assemblies in Wales and in Northern Ireland. The chapter considers the rising prominence of assessment for learning within the broader education policy scene as one of the major ways in which governments aim to alter professional and public expectations of assessment systems.

We take as our starting point Broadfoot's (1996) reminder that assessment practices and discourses are embedded in and emanate from cultural, social and political traditions and assumptions. These affect policies and teachers' practices in subtle, complex and often contradictory ways. In relation to assessment, the past thirty years have seen fundamental changes in expectations about the social, political and educational purposes that assessment systems must serve. Growing political interest in assessment for learning has occurred partly in response to a shift from norm-referenced systems engineered to select the highest achieving students, towards various forms of criterion-based systems that aim to be both meritocratic and inclusive. At the same time, attempts to introduce more holistic approaches to assessment in post-14 and post-compulsory education and training, such as records of achievement and portfolio assessment, aim to expand the range of outcomes that can be certificated and recognized formally (see Broadfoot, 1986; Hargreaves, 1995; Jessup, 1991).

The broader background of changing ideas about what counts as legitimate, educational and useful assessment forms the context for considering debates and policy shifts around assessment for learning. This chapter will explore debates inside policy processes and among academic and professional constituencies about assessment for learning in the compulsory school system. In the first part we will outline some theoretical tools that are useful for analysing these debates and processes. In the second part we will show how in England ideas about assessment for learning were debated and contested amongst policy makers, academics and professional constituencies as national curriculum assessment was developed and implemented. In the third part we will explain how policies and politics in Scotland set up a quite different context for debate and practice in relation to assessment for learning. In the fourth part we will refer to policy developments in Wales and Northern Ireland and also review a range of recent policy initiatives across all four countries. Finally, we shall summarize the main shifts in conceptions and enactments of assessment for learning in order to show how its educational potential for making learning deeper and more motivating can be subverted.

Analysing assessment policy

It is important to define 'policy' and while Ball acknowledges that this is fraught with conceptual confusion, he offers a useful working definition:

> [policies] are pre-eminently, statements about practice – the way things could or should be – which rest upon, derive from, statements about the world – about the way things are. They are intended to bring about individual solutions to diagnosed problems. (1990: 22)

Further clarification about what we mean here by 'policy' is offered by Dale who differentiates between the 'politics of education' as the broader agenda for education, created through particular processes and structures, and 'education politics' as processes that operate inside official government departments and agencies and through engagement with other interested groups. These processes are convoluted, often contentious and opaque to those outside them, but they work to translate a political agenda into proposals to which institutions and practitioners respond (Dale, 1994). He argues that a focus on education politics makes little sense unless there is 'A more or less explicit reference to, and appreciation of, the politics of education' (1994: 35).

Following these broad notions of policy and politics, one approach to analysis in this chapter would be to locate debates about assessment for learning in a broader structural analysis of the ways in which the economy, education and culture interact. Or, we could analyse how various groups, individuals and interested constituencies interact both within formal policy processes and broader advocacy and the 'epistemic communities' that contribute ideas and information to policy makers. We could also undertake a discursive analysis of how a particular notion, in this case assessment for learning, is symbolized and then enacted through political conceptualization, formation and transmission. Combining all three approaches enables an analysis of assessment for learning as a prominent theme in education policy and the politics of education to be traced to previous problems and debates (see for example, Ecclestone, 2002).

We recognize here the need to remember broader structural and cultural influences on debates about assessment for learning. We also acknowledge the need to know more about the effects of debates about assessment for learning at macro-, meso- and micro- levels of policy and practice and how these connect national policy, institutional responses to policy, and the shaping of individual identity and social actions in classrooms. However, for reasons of space and clarity, we will confine our analysis of assessment for learning in recent assessment policy to two notions offered by Ball and other colleagues, namely 'policy as text' and 'policy as discourse' (Ball, 1990,1994; Bowe et al., 1992).

Policy as text

Key texts, such as acts of parliament are translated at various levels of the policy process into other official texts, such as national curriculum policy statements and regulations, and then into what Bowe et al. call 'secondary texts', such as non-statutory guidelines and advice on practice. At all stages of the policy process official positions about assessment emerge in subtle and often contradictory ways through various texts and discussions. Texts, therefore, represent policy and encode it in complex ways through the struggles, compromises and public interpretation of political intentions. Texts are then decoded through implementations and new interpretations, by individuals and constituencies, moving in and out of policy processes. As Ball points out, attempts to present policy may spread confusion as various mediators of policy try to relate their understandings of policy to particular contexts. It is therefore crucial to recognize that texts are not

> *clear or closed or complete [but] the products of compromises at various stages (at points of initial influence, in the micropolitics of legislative formation, in the parliamentary process and in the politics and micropolitics of interest group articulation). (1994: 16)*

Interest in assessment for learning at all levels of the UK's education system has generated a deluge of texts that follow on from the official key texts: draft and final assessment specifications; guidance to specification writers; advice to teachers; guidelines to awarding body officers; decisions and debates recorded in minutes of policy meetings and public documents such as policy papers and text books. In addition, interest groups and professional bodies offer their own interpretations of assessment for learning while the speeches of policy makers, official videos and websites add further layers of meaning. These texts can all be seen as ' ... cannibalized products of multiple (but circumscribed) influences and agendas. There is ad hocery, negotiation and serendipity within the state, within policy formation' (Ball, 1994: 16).

In addition, as Bowe et. al argue, texts vary in the extent to which they are 'readerly' and offer minimum opportunities for interpretation by readers, or 'writerly', where they invite the reader to join in, to co-operate and feel some ownership of the ideas. Making sense of new texts leads people into a ' ... process of trying to translate and make familiar the language and attendant embedded logics' (1992: 11).

For teachers, parents, professional bodies, policy makers and implementers of policy, such as inspectors, a plurality of texts produces a plurality of readings. Such complexity means that we need to bear in mind constantly, as we review policy debates about assessment for learning, that ' ... the expression of policy is fraught with the possibility of misunderstandings, texts are generalized, written in relation to idealizations of the "real world" and can never be exhaustive' (1992: 21).

Assessment for learning may therefore be robustly and overtly defined, or it may emerge in subtle and more implicit ways. Its various representations reflect, again in overt and implicit ways, beliefs about desirable educational goals and practices. In addition, further negotiation and understanding come from a very diverse range of bodies and individuals who make use of policy texts. These include awarding body officers, inspectors, staff development organizers, unions and professional organizations, local education authority advisers, teachers, students, parents and employers. All create and amend the official texts and offer competing interpretations of policy aims. Exploration of different texts can therefore reveal the influences and agendas viewed as legitimate both inside policy processes and within institutions. It also reveals how these change over time as key actors move on or are removed from processes and debates. Charting how policy texts have evolved enables us to understand more about how teachers and students interpret their intentions and turn them into 'interactive and sustainable practice' within particular social, institutional and cultural contexts (Ball, 1994: 19).

Policy as discourse

Despite the importance of texts for understanding policy debates and processes, focusing analysis too heavily on them can produce an over-rational and linear account of debates about assessment for learning. The notion of 'policy as discourse' is therefore a crucial parallel notion because it enables researchers, practitioners and implementers of policy to see how discourses in policy construct and legitimize certain possibilities for thinking and acting while tacitly excluding others. Through language, symbols and codes and their presentation by different authors, discourses embody subtle fusions of particular meanings of truth and knowledge through the playing out of power struggles inside and outside policy. They construct our responses to policy through the language, concepts and vocabulary that they make available to us, and legitimize some voices and constituencies as legitimate definers of problems and solutions whilst silencing others (Ball, 1994). Focusing on discourse encourages analysts of texts to pay close attention to the language and to its adequacy as a way of thinking about and organizing how students learn. It also reminds us how texts reflect shifts in the locus of power between different groups and individuals in the struggle to maintain or change views of schooling.

However, analysis of the ways in which particular discourses legitimize voices, problems and solutions must also take account of the 'silences' in the text, namely the voices and notions that it leaves out. Silences operate within a text to affect how we view educational problems and policies, but they also come from other discourses and the policy processes that produce them. For example, a discourse about assessment for learning needs to be interpreted in the light of discourses in other texts about accountability or the need for nationally reliable assessment.

In this chapter we will focus on selected texts in order to identify the interactions and goals of different bodies in the production of texts and the discourses of assessment for learning that permeate them, either overtly or more subtly.

Assessment for learning in England

The introduction of national curriculum assessment

The transformation of education policy brought about by the Education Reform Act of 1988 included within it, for the first time in the modern era, provision for a statutory national curriculum and associated 'assessment arrangements' covering the years of compulsory schooling (ages 5 to 16). With relatively little prior thought seemingly having been given to what form such arrangements might take, the Minister for Education remitted an expert group chaired by an academic, Professor Paul Black, to draw up proposals.

The Task Group on Assessment and Testing (TGAT), working to an open-ended all-purpose remit from government, chose to place assessment of students by their teachers at the centre of its framework for assessment. The group's recommendations (DES/WO, 1988a) drew on experience in the 1970s and 1980s, in particular in relation to graded tests, of teachers' assessments contributing both to students' learning and to periodic summative judgments about their attainments. In the earliest paragraphs of the report – 'our starting point' – the formative purpose of assessment is identified as a central feature of the work that teachers undertake:

Promoting children's learning is a principal aim of schooling. Assessment lies at the heart of this process. (para. 3)

... the results [of national assessments] should provide a basis for decisions about pupils' further learning needs: they should be formative. (para. 5)

The initial formal response of ministers to the TGAT recommendations was to signal acceptance of what would clearly be an innovative system for assessing students' attainments and their progress. The minister responsible, Kenneth Baker, echoed TGAT's focus on the individual student in his statement to parliament accepting the group's main and supplementary reports and most of its recommendations:

The results of tests and other assessments should be used both formatively to help better teaching and to inform next steps for a pupil, and summatively at ages 7, 11, 14 and 16 to inform parents about their child's progress. (quoted by Black, 1997: 31)

Yet it is clear, from the memoirs of the politicians in key roles at the time (Baker, 1993; Thatcher, 1993) as well as from the work of academics (Ball, 1990; Callaghan, 1995; Taylor, 1995), that formal government acceptance of most of the TGAT recommendations did not mean acceptance either of a discourse of formative assessment or of its translation into ideas for practice. From a very early stage of policy development, though only the proposals for the consistency of teachers' assessments to be enhanced by group moderation (DES/WO, 1988b) had actually been formally rejected by the minister, the discourse amongst policy makers concerned test development at each of the first three 'key stages'. The ideas that had shaped the TGAT blueprint for national curriculum assessment quickly came to be 'silences' in the policy discourse and in the texts about assessment that emanated from government and its agencies.

As Black's own account of *Whatever happened to TGAT* makes clear, several factors including the growing influence of the 'New Right' had the effect of undermining TGAT and transforming national curriculum assessment into a very differently oriented set of assessment policies (Black, 1997). The need for national assessments to supply indices of school performance for accountability purposes, an aspect of the policy that had been downplayed when the government was enlisting support for the Education Act's passage through parliament, came to the fore once the legislation was in place. The ideological nature of the debates about TGAT within the governing party is evident from the characteristically blunt comments of the then Prime Minister in her memoirs:

The fact that it [the TGAT Report] was welcomed by the Labour Party, the National Union of Teachers and the Times Educational Supplement was enough to confirm for me that its approach was suspect. It proposed an elaborate and complex system of assessment – teacher dominated and uncosted. (Thatcher, 1993: 594)

In short, TGAT was perceived as the work of an insidious left-leaning 'education establishment' intent upon subverting the government's best intentions to raise educational standards. This neo-conservative discourse, epitomized by the language used in Marsland and Seaton's *The Empire Strikes Back* (1993), was in the ascendancy amongst education policy makers in England in the early 1990s (see Black, 1995, for a fuller discussion of this). Even though its influence was beginning to wane by the time of the Dearing Review of the national curriculum and its assessment in the middle of the decade, the voice of the Centre for Policy Studies (Lawlor, 1993) was still a prominent feature of the policy discourse at national level.

As detailed policies for each element in the new assessment system were developed, the national curriculum assessment arrangements emerged as a system of time-limited and end-of-stage tests in the 'core' subjects only, the main purpose of which was to supply data that would place each student on a 10 (later 8+) level scale (Daugherty, 1995). It also became increasingly obvious that such data would be aggregated and published as indicators of the performance of teachers, schools, local education authorities and the system as a whole. Although TGAT had envisaged arrangements that would focus on the formative use of data on individual students, the evaluative use of aggregate data coloured the multifarious texts spawned by national curriculum assessment. In parallel, policy discourses associated with those texts reinforced this performance indicator and target-driven view of assessment. Without ever being superseded by a revised policy, the TGAT recommendations were distorted and then abandoned, thereby illustrating how policy texts are reworked at the whole system level as policies move from an initial blueprint through development and implementation. In this respect the discourse of assessment for learning carried the ominous silence, of accountability and concerns about the reliability of teacher assessment, from other parallel discourses.

Over the same period, agencies and individuals responsible for implementation were interpreting and mediating those policies. There is substantial research evidence about the ways in which national curriculum assessment came to be understood and operationalized, both by officials in departments and agencies of government and by the headteachers and teachers in schools on whose practices the system depended. This was happening in spite of government antipathy to teachers' practices as biased and too student-centred and the low profile of 'teacher assessment' in the policy texts of the time. Evidence of the impact of those policies can be found in findings both from large-scale longitudinal studies in the primary curriculum (Osborn et al., 2000; Pollard et al., 2000 – see also Chapter 4) and from many other empirical studies reporting on assessment practices in schools (for example, Tunstall and Gipps, 1996; Torrance and Pryor, 1998; Reay and Wiliam, 1999). Taken together, these studies show the effects of a target-led approach to assessment and the subtle changes to teachers' and students' roles and perceptions of the purposes and outcomes of assessment.

The potential for local education authorities to have a significant role in implementing, moderating and monitoring national curriculum assessment was never fully developed because policy makers at the national level, more often implicitly than explicitly, acted as if what was decreed in London would be accepted and acted upon in every classroom in every school in every LEA in the country. Local education authorities were also perceived by some policy activists on the political right as being prime movers in a malign influence of the 'education establishment' on the education system. However, as agencies that provided training for teachers and therefore mediated the texts published at the centre, their influence on schools and teachers would be considerable. As Conner and James have shown, some local authorities went beyond the 'attempt to accommodate state policy within a broad framework of local values and practice' (1996: 164), developing local initiatives such as procedures for moderating teachers' assessments of their students. Local moderation as a necessary component in any national system that makes use of teachers' judgments had, once TGAT's proposals in this respect had been rejected, been neglected by policy makers at the national level.

Education policies in general, including assessment policies, were being shaped by what Broadfoot (2000) and Ball (2000), using Lyotard's term, have characterized as a culture of 'performativity'. Performativity came to dominate the thinking of policy makers in government during that period to such an extent that

> the clear policy emphasis [of the 1990s was] on assessment as a measurement device, the results of which are used to goad students, teachers and institutions as a whole to try harder. It is not surprising that, faced with these pressures, schools have typically succumbed to them. (Broadfoot, 2000: 143)

As both Broadfoot (2000) and Ball (2000) have argued, the setting and regulation of political targets influence teachers in subtle and profound ways. Summative assessment by teachers of their own students, a residual feature from the original TGAT framework, was still given a notional status in the overall framework, for example in the Dearing Review of curriculum and assessment in 1993/4. But the policy texts and associated discourses of that period showed that recognition of the teacher's role in using assessment to guide and support learning disappeared from sight. Black and Wiliam conclude that

> ... by 1995 nothing was left of the advances made in the previous decades. Government was lukewarm or uninterested in formative assessment: the systems to integrate it with the summative had gone, and the further development of tools was only weakly supported. (2003: 626)

The strengthening of academic and professional discourses

In contrast, academic and professional assessment discourses retained formative assessment as a crucial aspect of assessment practice in educational institutions. In addition, such discourses presented formative assessment as a necessary component of any assessment policy that sought to meet several purposes, which might be served by student data. For example, Torrance (1993) was writing about the 'theoretical problems' and 'empirical questions' associated with formative assessment. Contributions by academics to wider theoretical debates about assessment such as by Gipps (1994), and texts written by academics for practitioners such as by Stobart and Gipps (1990 and subsequent editions), also recognized and promoted the importance of formative assessment. Crooks's (1988) review of the impact of assessment practices on students and Sadler's (1989) seminal paper on formative assessment helped fuel continuing debates in academic circles that were in contrast to the preoccupation amongst policy makers in England with the summative and evaluative uses of assessment data.

In this context, and with the explicit aim of influencing assessment policy discourses and texts, a small group of academics was established in 1989 as one of several British Educational Research Association policy task groups and continued as an unaffiliated Assessment Reform Group after 1997. Among its early publications was a critical commentary on the development of national curriculum assessment which reiterated the role of assessment in 'the improvement of education' (Harlen et al., 1992). The group then obtained funding for a survey of the research literature on formative assessment, undertaken by Paul Black and Dylan Wiliam. The outcomes of that review, published both in the form of a full report in an academic journal (Black and Wiliam, 1998a) and in a pamphlet for wider circulation to practitioners and policy makers (Black and Wiliam, 1998b), would in time be acknowledged as a major contribution to reorienting the discourse associated with assessment policies in the UK (see also Chapter 1).

This initial optimistic foray by a group of academics hoping to influence policy was supplemented by later publications from the team working with Black and Wiliam at King's College, London and from the Assessment Reform Group. As part of a strategy for communicating more effectively with policy makers, making use of pamphlets and policy seminars, the Assessment Reform Group chose the more accessible term 'assessment for learning' rather than using the technical terminology of 'formative assessment'. Assessment for learning also became increasingly prominent in the professional discourse about assessment, supported by organizations such as the AIAA, with its membership mainly drawn from assessment inspectors and advisers in local government, and by other advocates of formative assessment operating from a base in higher education such as Clarke (2001).

New government, continuing discourse

Government policy on curriculum and assessment in England during the late 1990s remained strongly wedded to the notion that the 'raising of standards' of attainment in schools should be equated with improvement in the aggregate scores of successive cohorts of students as they passed through the 'key stages' of the national curriculum. This applies at least as much to the 'Blairite' education policies of the Labour administrations since 1997 as to the policies of the Conservative governments of the 1980s and the early to mid 1990s. In some respects, the education policies of the incoming government in 1997 gave a fresh impetus to the culture that had dominated policy texts and discourses earlier in the decade, endorsing rather than seeking to change the ideological stance that had underpinned education policies:

... many of New Labour's changes to the Conservative agenda were largely cosmetic. In some of its manifestations New Labour's so-called Third Way looked remarkably similar to quasi-markets. (Whitty, 2002: 127)

Reinforcing a general perception that the most important role for data from national curriculum assessments was to fuel performance indicators, the new government's first major policy paper *Excellence in Schools* (DfEE, 1997) signalled that schools and local authorities would be expected to set and meet 'benchmarking' targets. The then Secretary of State for Education, David Blunkett, raised the public profile of benchmarking by stating that he would resign if the government's national targets, based on national curriculum test data, were not met. At the school and local authority level these policies were policed by an inspection agency, OFSTED, whose head revelled in his public image as the scourge of 'low standards' in classrooms and in schools. This discourse was dominated by the role of assessment in relation to accountability and alongside this centrally-driven national strategies emerged, first in literacy (from 1998) and then in numeracy (from 1999). Both were underpinned by the publication of pedagogical prescriptions in which the formative functions of classroom assessment had no official role.

The performativity culture was thus retaining its hold on policy makers and also on practitioners whose performance, individually and collectively, was being judged in those terms. Looking back on the first five years of Labour education policies in England, Reynolds sums up in these terms:

[The Labour government] kept in its virtual entirety the 'market-based' educational policies introduced by the Conservative government from 1988 to 1997, involving the systematic tightening of central control on the nature of the curriculum and on assessment outcomes, combined with devolution to schools of the determination of the 'means', at school and classroom level, to determine outcomes. (2002: 97)

In such circumstances, there was no place in the official policy discourse in England for assessment's role as an informal and personal source of support for the learner or as a key element in learners' genuine engagement with learning. Instead, the silences in both texts and discourses in relation to formative assessment as integral to meaningful learning led to an implicit presentation of it as an instrumental adjunct to the goal of raising formal levels of achievement. In policy discourse and text, 'achievement' and 'learning' became synonymous. This image of assessment prevailed amongst English policy makers into the middle years of the next decade, with no acknowledgment that an assessment culture which geared every aspect of the classroom experience to test performance – 'a SATurated model of pupildom' (Hall et al., 2004) – was not conducive to fostering effective assessment for learning. And the research into primary and secondary school students' attitudes to assessment and learning, cited above, showed just how strong an influence a summative image of assessment was.

Scotland – distinct politics, distinctive policies

From guidelines to national survey

Scotland did not experience the kind of major transformation of its schools that the Education Reform Act brought about in England and Wales, relying instead on a series of directive but not statutory national 'guidelines'. In relation to assessment policy, it retained a national system of periodic sampling of student attainments introduced in 1983 – the Assessment of Achievement Programme (AAP) – and did not follow England in introducing a statutory curriculum backed up by a system of external tests. Assessment for learning as a major official policy priority emerged in the early years of the twenty-first century as a product of a different political environment and distinctive policy processes in Scotland (Humes, 1997, 1999) that predated the establishment of a Scottish Parliament in 1999 (Bryce, 1999; Bryce and Humes, 1999; Paterson, 2003; Finlay, 2004).

Concurrently with the passage of the Education Reform Act through the UK parliament, the Scottish Office published in November 1987 a policy text, *Curriculum and Assessment in Scotland: A Policy for the 1990s*, which set out aims for education of the 5 to 14 age group. In terms of policy process some Scottish Office ministers favoured statutory regulation. However, after strong opposition from parents and teachers to proposals for statutory testing, the guidelines published in the early 1990s were to be the Scottish response to the broader trend, within the UK and internationally, towards greater central government control of the curriculum and assessment. Although this was a seemingly softer approach to regulation of the curriculum and assessment in schools than was found elsewhere in the UK, Finlay has argued that too much should not be made of the use of the word 'guidelines'.

> Her Majesty's Inspectors of Education ... use the guidelines as the basis of inspections of primary schools and lower secondaries and the expectation is that they will find a close correspondence between the guidelines and practice. (Finlay, 2004: 6)

According to Hayward et al. (2004: 398) the guidelines on assessment, *Assessment 5–14* (SOED, 1991), ensured that there were 'clear principles, advocating the centrality of formative assessment'. And yet, in spite of a supportive policy discourse, it became apparent from both academic studies (Swann and Brown, 1997) and from a report by the schools inspectorate (HMI, 1999) that the impact of Assessment 5–14 on the ground in schools was patchy. A national consultation on future assessment policies for Scottish schools, prompted by the findings of the 1999 HMI survey, was undertaken by the Scottish Executive Education Department (SEED) (Hayward et al., 2004). The consultation revealed 'clear, almost unanimous support for the principles of Assessment 5–14' (Hayward et al., 2004). However, by the late 1990s it was clear that the overall assessment system was fragmented and fulfilling none of its purposes particularly effectively.

Among the issues to emerge from the consultation report was the difficulties teachers faced in establishing 'assessment for learning' practices in their classrooms and the tensions within an education culture where teachers were expected to be able to reconcile expectations that assessment practices should serve both formative and accountability purposes. Interestingly, the seeds of subsequent developments were already in evidence in that report with overtly supportive reference being made to Black and Wiliam's review of research. The academic discourse developing from that review came to have a more direct influence on government policy over the next few years in Scotland than was the case in England.

There were other assessment policy initiatives during the 1990s from the Scottish Executive which was still answerable at that time, via the Secretary of State for Scotland, to the UK parliament. These had their roots in the priorities of the UK government but took a different form from parallel developments in the three other UK countries. 'Neither the National Test system nor the AAP survey had been designed to meet the new data requirements; the 'test when ready' system did not provide conventional test scores that could readily be used for monitoring and accountability purposes' (Hutchinson, 2005). The perceived need to make available evidence about students' attainments in key curriculum areas, the driver behind publication of school performance tables in England, led to the introduction of the National 5–14 Survey of Achievement in 1998. Up until that point, the national tests in Scotland had been offered to schools as test units in reading, writing and maths, devised by what was to become the Scottish Qualifications Authority, to be used by teachers to confirm their judgments as to the attainment levels (A to F) which students had reached. After 1998, SEED collected aggregate attainment information from every school in those curriculum areas and there was an associated expectation that the reported levels would have been confirmed by national tests. Taken together, these moves represented a considerable raising of the stakes because test data became an overt part of the accountability policy discourse.

The 'Assessment is for Learning' Project

Despite these influences, politics and policy making in Scotland had given rise to a distinctive set of assessment policies during the 1990s, and the establishment of a Scottish Parliament in 1999 gave fresh impetus to a wide range of policies on education. A flurry of activity in education – a major responsibility of the new devolved legislature – led to the passing by parliament of the Standards in Scotland's Schools Act with its five 'National Priorities'. The Minister for Education and Young People initiated a 'National Debate on Education' in 2001 and published *Educating for Excellence* in 2003, setting out the Executive's response to views expressed in the National Debate. Assessment policy for Scottish schools was the subject of a major parliamentary debate in 2003. Political power was in the hands of a Labour/Liberal Democrat coalition, with influential individuals such as Jack McConnell, initially the minister responsible for schools policy and subsequently First Minister, to the fore. National agencies, such as Learning and Teaching Scotland (LTS) and Her Majesty's Inspectorate of Education (HMIE), were drawn into policy development but the shaping of education policy in the early years of the new century was driven from within the Executive and strongly supported by key politicians.

The establishment of an Assessment Action Group was the next stage in assessment policy development, drawing in a range of interest groups including national agencies, representatives of teachers, parents and researchers. Its role was to oversee a programme that developed assessment for students from 3 to 14. This programme was subsequently, and significantly, entitled 'Assessment is for Learning' (AifL). The AifL programme had considerable resources invested in it, mainly to allow teachers time away from the classroom to engage in developing their practice. And yet, though strongly led and guided from the centre, the developmental model adopted was for teachers at school level across Scotland being recruited to a series of parallel projects and given opportunities to shape and to share their practice.

One of those projects focused on 'Support for Professional Practice in Formative Assessment' and was explicitly based on the work of Black and Wiliam, involving a team from King's College London led by them as consultants. The report of its external evaluation (Hallam et al., 2004) is positive in tone: 'relatively few difficulties in implementation', 'dramatic improvement in pupils' learning skills', 'a shift from teacher-centred pedagogy'. And yet, whilst recognizing that progress had been made in the pilot schools, the evaluators also highlighted the challenges ahead if the project's gains in terms of improving learning through formative assessment were to be sustained and disseminated more widely. Perceived obstacles to further successful development included the tensions between formative assessment strategies and what was required of teachers in relation to summative assessment. Some teachers reported that time pressures militated against being able to cover required curriculum content. Evaluators of the programme also argued that it was crucial to continue teacher 'ownership' of the policy development process:

> The project has had a promising start ... [but] successful dissemination requires continued funding to enable new participants to have sufficient time to develop and implement their ideas and reflect upon and evaluate their progress. (Hallam et al., 2004: 13)

The evaluators' conclusions, together with insights from other studies of the programme such as Hayward et al's (2004), offer helpful pointers to the issues that need to be addressed in any policy context which aspires to the major pedagogical innovation that the widespread adoption of assessment for learning classroom practices entails.

In November 2004, Scotland's policy journey from the generalities of the 1991 guidelines through reformulation and reinvigoration of policy priorities reached the point where, in *Assessment, Testing and Reporting 3–14: Our Response* (SEED, 2004a), ministers adopted most of the main policy recommendations of the consultation earlier that year on the AifL programme. By early 2005, officials in the SEED were embarking on plans for implementing this latest policy text on assessment in Scotland in parallel with the equivalent official published text, *A Curriculum for Excellence: Ministerial Response* (SEED, 2004b), setting priorities and targets for the curriculum.

How had Scotland come to take this particular route to rethinking assessment policy? In his review of Scottish education policies Finlay (2004) argues that almost all of the major policy developments in education would have been possible in the pre-1999 era of 'administrative devolution'; indeed many of those developments were initiated and had progressed prior to 1999:

> *The contribution of political devolution in Scotland has been the realized opportunity to engage the* demos *much more widely in democratic processes. Inviting people to contribute at early stages to identifying long term political priorities is quite different from giving them the freedom to choose much more widely in democratic processes. (2004: 8, emphasis in original)*

With Scotland being the first of the four UK countries to identify assessment for learning as a policy priority and to move, from 2005, into whole system implementation it will be interesting to see the extent to which that distinctive political ideology continues to colour the realization of assessment for learning in the day-to-day practices of schools and classrooms.

Multiplying policies – proliferating discourses

Whilst assessment policies in Scotland and England diverged during the 1990s Wales, operating within the same legislative framework as England, used the limited scope allowed by 'administrative devolution' to be more positive about the value of teachers' assessments and to adopt a less aggressive accountability regime (Daugherty, 2000). The absence of primary school performance tables, a different approach to the inspection of schools (Thomas and Egan, 2000) and an insignificant Wales-based daily press all meant that the media frenzy about 'failing' teachers and schools was not a feature of the Welsh public discourse.

There is evidence (see for example, Daugherty and Elfed-Owens, 2003) from the pre-1999 era of administrative devolution that a distinctive policy environment in Wales resulted in the recontextualizing of London-based policies. However, after 1999 political devolution undoubtedly speeded up the pace of change as Wales became an arena for policy formulation as well as policy implementation. The rhetoric of *The Learning Country* published by the Welsh Assembly government in 2001, was followed up by, amongst other policy decisions, the abolition of national testing for 7-year-olds from 2002. Assessment for learning did not become a feature of the policy agenda in Wales until the Daugherty Assessment Review Group, established by the Assembly Minister for Education in 2003, published its recommendations (Daugherty, 2004). Encouraged by the minister's espousal of 'evidence-informed policy-making', the group was influenced by research evidence from the Black and Wiliam review, from the Assessment Reform Group and from other assessment specialists. One of its main recommendations was that 'The development of assessment for learning practices should be a central feature of a programme for development in Wales of curriculum and assessment' (2004: 31).

The discourse of assessment policy in Wales, without the steady evolution since 1991 that had led to the Scottish Executive's endorsement of assessment for learning, had thus changed markedly after 1999. By 2004 assessment for learning was an uncontested aspect of official policy in Wales. As part of its more broadly based recommendations the agency with statutory responsibility for advising the Welsh Assembly government also quoted the Assessment Reform Group's definition of assessment for learning in its advocacy of policy change: 'ACCAC recommends that it should be remitted to establish a programme to develop assessment for learning' (ACCAC, 2004: 41).

The minister in Wales, Jane Davidson, announced in July 2004 that she would be implementing these recommendations from the Review Group and from ACCAC and her support for a new assessment policy framework was unequivocal:

There is clear evidence ... that change is needed if we are to get the best from our pupils, the curriculum and our teachers. I propose, therefore, to move away over the next four years from the current testing regime to a system which is more geared to the pupil, focuses more on skills and puts teacher assessment at its heart. (Davidson, 2004: 2)

In Wales, as in Scotland, political devolution had given a fresh impetus to the rethinking of education policies in general (Rees, 2005).

Northern Ireland, since its establishment as a state in 1922, had developed what McKeown refers to as a tradition of

adoption (sometimes with minor adaptation) of policy from GB so as to obtain parity of provision, the non-implementation of GB policy when deemed inappropriate, and the development of policy initiatives, where feasible, which are relevant specifically to Northern Ireland.(2004: 3)

Any review of assessment policies in that part of the UK can be framed in those terms although England, rather than Wales or Scotland, was usually the source for policy borrowing rather than 'GB'. Thus the Northern Ireland framework is recognizably a first cousin of that to be found in England (and in Wales), but the system of mainly faith-based schooling and the continued existence of academic selection for secondary schooling at age 11 are the product of the country's distinctive social context.

A culture in which 'assessment' is closely associated with the testing of 11-year-olds would not appear to be favourable to the development, politically or professionally, of assessment for learning. And yet, even in a policy environment where deep and longstanding political conflicts stalled the establishment of a devolved legislative assembly, initiatives taken by the agency responsible for advising on curriculum and assessment brought assessment for learning into the policy discourse (CCEA, 2003; Montgomery, 2004). As White's commentary on the CCEA 'Pathways' proposals notes:

> *The major priority is that assessment should help pupils to learn, teachers to teach, and parents – as co-educators – to support and supplement what goes on in schools. This is why the emphasis ... is on assessment for learning rather than assessment of learning. (White, 2004: 14)*

The emphasis in the policy discourses in Northern Ireland has now been consolidated with the key assessment for learning approaches established within the Key Stage 1 and 2 curriculum as 'Ongoing Integrated Assessment' (CCEA, 2004: 10). At Key Stage 3 CCEA's Pathways consultation document proposed that the '... research carried out by the Assessment Reform Group and others has produced substantial evidence to show that by adopting these approaches [assessment for learning], the progress and achievement of pupils in all ability ranges and the professional competences of teachers can be significantly enhanced' (2003: 103). The then minister for education, Barry Gardiner, gave the final go ahead for all of the curriculum proposals in June 2004.

In England there were, during the second term of the Blair government (from 2001), two notable patterns of development relating to assessment for learning. The first was the increasing attention to it in publications by England-based organizations representing teachers (SHA, 2002; Swaffield and Dudley, 2002; NUT, 2004; GTC(E), 2004). A joint publication from three of the teacher associations, directed at ministers in England, made the case for assessment for learning to become a significant part of the government's policy agenda for 'raising standards' whilst also airing doubts about the way in which that term had become part of the official policy discourse:

> *The model of assessment for learning now being proposed by government relies mainly on teachers' analysis and management of data to diagnose and target pupils' learning needs. This is in direct contradiction to, for example, the effectiveness of the highly successful approach to assessment for learning adopted by King's College, London and by the national Assessment Reform Group. (ATL, NUT and PAT, 2004: 4)*

Within these texts not only are the well-established differences on policy between teacher representatives and government apparent but there are also substantial variations in the ways in which the teacher organizations define assessment for learning and how its potential might be realized.

The second significant series of developments during Blair's second term brought 'assessment for learning' for the first time into the official discourses associated with education policy in England. The second term of a Blair-led government was as wedded as the first had been to 'strategies', accompanied by weighty documentation and an infrastructure of agencies implementing national directives. The language of target-setting and the discourse of performativity remained, but attempts were also made in some policy texts to leaven the discourse with a 'softer' message in which the individual student's needs were acknowledged. The 2004 Primary Strategy (for students aged 5 to 11) included guidance materials for schools and teachers in which assessment for learning figured prominently. And yet, as a critique of the materials by an organization representing assessment professionals points out, the materials are 'problematic' and based on a model of assessment that is one of 'frequent summative assessment not formative assessment' (AAIA, 2005a: para 4.3) The Key Stage 3 Strategy (for students aged 11 to 14), whilst drawing more directly on the work of Black and Wiliam and the Assessment Reform Group, also appeared trapped in a mindset that sees target-setting by teachers and schools as the only route to higher achievement. That same uneasy mix of disparate discourses was apparent in a ministerial speech early in 2004 which placed 'personalized learning' at the centre of the government's new policy agenda for schools. Assessment for learning would be one of five 'key processes' in realizing this ambition to 'personalize' learning: 'Assessment for Learning that feeds into lesson planning and teaching strategies, sets clear targets, and clearly identifies what pupils need to do to get there' (Miliband, 2004: 4).

Developing student autonomy through self- and peer assessment, which is central to the view of assessment for learning that its academic advocates had been promoting, is nowhere to be seen in this teacher-led and target-dominated usage of the term.

The report in 2005 of a 'Learning Working Group', commissioned by the Minister for Schools in England but without any official status in the policy process, refers both to the growing awareness of assessment for learning and to the proliferation of discourses when it comments that

> Assessment for learning is spreading rapidly, in part because it, or more accurately a version of it (some would argue a perversion), contributes to the Key Stage 3 Strategy in England, and in part because teachers find that it works – the scientific evidence and the practice evidence are aligned and mutually supportive. (Hargreaves, 2005: 9)

Assessment for learning had, by 2005, been incorporated into the official policy discourses in the other three UK countries and the term was increasingly featured in policy-related texts and associated discourses in England. But doubts remained about the commitment to it of policy makers and ministers:

> … 'assessment for learning' is becoming a catch-all phrase, used to refer to a range of practices. In some versions it has been turned into a series of ritualized procedures. In others it is taken to be more concerned with monitoring and record-keeping than with using information to help learning. (James, 2004: 2)

Conclusion

Within less than a decade assessment for learning became established as an element in the official policy discourses in each of the four countries of the UK. It did so in ways that reflected the distinctive cultures, policy environments and policy processes of each country. Whilst there are some common roots discernible in discourses across the UK there are also aspects of the process of policy development that are fundamentally different and can be expected to give rise to differences in the impact of policy on practice.

The academic discourse within the UK as a whole, though mainly based on the English experience, evolved during the 1990s. By the end of the century there was an enriched literature, drawing on a growing body of empirical evidence. The work of the PACE project is significant in this respect (Osborn et al., 2000; Pollard et al., 2000) as is that of Torrance and Pryor (1998) with its theorizing in terms of 'convergent' and 'divergent' modes of assessment. But it was the review by Black and Wiliam (1998a), supported by the ways in which its authors and the Assessment Reform Group targeted policy-makers in advocating formative assessment, which was increasingly recognized and reinterpreted in the professional and policy discourses. The new post-devolution administrations in Scotland and Wales made overt commitments to 'evidence-informed policy'. This contributed to the evidence and argument from Black and Wiliam's review of research, mediated by the review's authors in Scotland and by Daugherty in Wales, and becoming an explicit influence on the assessment policy decisions announced during 2004.

In contrast, the dominant policy discourses and the main official policy texts in England seemed at first to be largely unaffected by the evidence from research or the advocacy of academics. Instead, it was developments in certain localities, such as the KMOFAP and Learning How to Learn Project (see Chapters 1 and 2) plus the work with groups of teachers by others such as Shirley Clarke that fuelled a groundswell of interest in schools. Only when that growth in interest amongst teachers found echoes in some of the continuing centrally-driven policy initiatives of the DfES from 2003 onwards did the language of assessment for learning enter the policy discourses at national level in England.

Yet, as is evident from the examples quoted above, this infiltration into the official discourses brought with it sometimes worryingly disparate versions of both the 'why' and the 'how' of assessment for learning. 'Personalized learning', with assessment for learning as one of five key components, was highlighted in England in the run-up to elections in 2005 as the educational dimension of the government's new drive to 'personalize' public services. Pollard and James welcome its potential to re-orientate policies for schools towards the needs of learners whilst also warning of the dangers of 'slipping back into over-simplified consideration of teaching provision and associated systems' (2005: 5). But an accountability culture so strongly coloured by performativity has meant that, for many English professionals working at the local level, discourses associated with student assessments are linked to parental choice of schools and public measures of school performance.

It is here that the concept of 'policy as discourse' is powerful. The 'silences' of an enthusiastic policy rhetoric about assessment for learning come from another, seemingly separate discourse – that of performativity. Other silences lie within the new discourse of personalized learning which is suggesting an individualized approach to assessment that is far from the constructivist and social learning notions that underpin assessment for learning (see Chapter 3). Such silences speak louder to many than do the official policy texts in England which now refer routinely to 'learning', displacing the discourse of 'what must be taught' that had been dominant in the 1990s.

The distinctive social and political cultures of these four countries are thus increasingly apparent. For example, the assessment policy texts and discourses at national level in Scotland and Wales acknowledge the reality of the tensions created by trying to use evidence from assessment directly in support of learning whilst also using data, both about individuals and on cohorts of students, for summative and evaluative purposes. The Scottish Executive's approach to accountability was through the active involvement by representatives of all stakeholder interests in developing policy. This is in marked contrast to the English approach which seeks to empower people by offering them choice in a supposed market for schools, with aggregate data from student assessments as the main indicator of school performance. The emphasis on school self-evaluation in the Scottish policy framework is another contribution to changing how assessment data are used, thereby changing the perceived role of assessment in the school system. Wales has been distancing itself from the inheritance of an 'England and Wales' assessment policy. But it is not yet clear whether those responsible for policy in Wales, whether at national level or in schools and local education authorities, realize how much of a culture shift is needed for teachers to be able to develop their assessment practices in ways that ensure assessment for learning is a major priority.

Understanding the social and political context is therefore crucial for an understanding of the current status of assessment for learning in each of the four countries. Understanding the interplay of discourse and text within each country is also crucial for any judgement about the prospects for assessment that supports learning and fosters student autonomy becoming embedded in the routine practices of thousands of schools and tens of thousands of teachers.

It will be evident from this chapter that there are four 'policy trajectories' to be found within the UK. At one level those who have long argued that formative assessment has been neglected as a policy priority can be encouraged by the fact that assessment for learning has moved up the official policy agenda in all four countries over the past decade. But it must also be remembered that the policy developments reviewed here have all been located at the early stages of the policy cycle, namely those concerned with initiating policy at the national level and articulating broad policy intentions for the system as a whole.

For a short time in the late 1980s, the TGAT Report put formative assessment at the centre of a framework for national curriculum assessment for England and Wales; the stages of policy development and implementation which followed that Report ensured that, in 'policy as practice', it disappeared without trace during the 1990s. A markedly more favourable social and political context, at least in Scotland and Wales, now offers better prospects for the ambitions of recent policy texts in those countries being implemented in ways that, while inevitably mediated by practitioners, do not lose sight of the original policy aims. In all four countries the policy cycle is only now beginning to unfold.

Chapter 10

Assessment for Learning: Why no Profile in US Policy?

Dylan Wiliam

The aim of this chapter is not to provide an overview of assessment for learning in US schools' policy – given the lack of good evidence on this point, such a chapter would either be very short, or highly speculative. Instead, it is to attempt to account for the current position with regard to assessment for learning in the USA in the light of the history of assessment more generally. In the broadest terms, the expectation of high reliability and objectivity in the assessment of students' learning within a culture of accountability and litigation when things go wrong, has tended to deflect policy developments from any consideration of improving learning through assessment.

The main story of this chapter, therefore, is how one highly specialized role for assessment, the selection of students for higher education, and a very specialized solution to the problem, the use of an aptitude test, gained wide acceptance and usage. By eventually dominating other methods of selecting students for university and ultimately influencing the methods of assessment used for other purposes, such approaches to assessment have eclipsed the use of and to some extent discourse on formative assessment; that is, assessment designed to support learning.

The chapter begins with a brief account of the creation of the College Entrance Examinations Board and its attempts to bring some coherence to the use of written examinations in university admissions. The criticisms that were made of the use of such examinations led to explorations of the use of intelligence tests, which had originally been used to diagnose learning difficulties among Parisian school students but which had been modified in the USA to enable blanket testing of army recruits in the closing stages of the First World War. Subsequent sections detail how the army intelligence test was developed into the Scholastic Aptitude Test and how this test came to dominate university admissions in the USA. The final sections discuss how assessment in schools developed over the latter part of the twentieth century, including some of the alternative methods of assessment such as portfolios which were explored in the 1980s and 1990s. These methods, with clear links to assessment for learning, were ultimately eradicated by the press for cheap scalable methods of testing for accountability – a role that the technology of aptitude testing was well-placed to fill.

Assessment in US schools

For at least the last hundred years, the experience of US school students has been that assessment means grading. From the third or fourth grade (age 8 to 9), and continuing into graduate studies, almost all work that is assessed is evaluated on the same literal grade scale: A, B, C, D or F (fail). Scores on tests or other work that is expressed on a percentage scale are routinely converted to a letter grade, with cut-offs for A typically ranging from 90 to 93, B from 80 to 83, C from 70 to 73 and D from 60 to 63. Scores below 60 are generally graded as F. In high schools (and sometimes earlier) these grades are then cumulated by assigning 'grade-points' of 4, 3, 2, 1 and 0 to grades of A, B, C, D and F respectively, and then averaged to produce the grade-point average (GPA). Where students take especially demanding courses, such as Advanced Placement courses that confer college credit, the grade-point equivalences may be scaled up, so that an A might get 5. However, despite the extraordinary consistency in this practice across the USA, exactly what the grade represents and what factors teachers take into account in assigning grades and assessing students in general are far from clear (Madaus and Kellaghan, 1992; Stiggins et al., 1986), and there are few empirical studies on what really goes on in classrooms.

Several studies conducted in the 1980s found that while teachers were required to administer many tests, they had relied on their own observations or tests they had constructed themselves in making decisions about students (Stiggins and Bridgeford, 1985; Herman and Dorr-Bremme, 1983; Dorr-Bremme et al., 1983; Dorr-Bremme and Herman, 1986). Crooks (1988) found that such teacher-produced tests tended to emphasize low-order skills such as factual recall rather than complex thinking. Stiggins et al. (1989) showed that the use of grades both to communicate to students and parents about student learning on the one hand, and to motivate students on the other, was in fundamental conflict.

Perhaps because of this internal conflict, it is clear that the grade is rarely a pure measure of attainment and will frequently include how much effort the student put into the assignment, attendance and sometimes even behaviour in class. The lack of clarity led Dressel to define a grade as 'an inadequate report of an inaccurate judgment by a biased and variable judge of the extent to which a student has attained an undefined level of mastery of an unknown proportion of an indefinite material' (Chickering, 1983).

Inconsistency in the meanings of grades from state to state and even district to district may not have presented too many problems when the grades were to be used locally, but at the beginning of the twentieth century as students applied to higher education institutions increasingly further afield, and as universities switched from merely recruiting to selecting students, methods for comparing grades and other records from different schools became increasingly necessary.

Written examinations

Written examinations were introduced into the Boston public school system in 1845 when the superintendent of instruction, Mann, decided that the 500 most able 14-year-olds should take an examination on the same day (Travers, 1983). The idea was quickly taken up elsewhere and the results were frequently used to make 'high-stakes' decisions about students such as promotion and retention. The stultifying effects of the examinations were noted by the superintendent of schools for Cincinatti:

> ... they have occasioned and made well nigh imperative the use of mechanical and rote methods of teaching; they have occasioned cramming and the most vicious habits of study; they have caused much of the overpressure charged upon schools, some of which is real; they have tempted both teachers and pupils to dishonesty; and last but not least, they have permitted a mechanical method of school supervision. (White, 1888: 519)

Admission to higher education institutions in the USA at the time was a rather informal process. Most universities were recruiting rather than selecting students; quite simply there were more places than applicants, and at times, admission decisions appear to have been based on financial as much as academic criteria (Levine, 1986).

In the period after the civil war, universities had begun to formalize their admissions procedures. In 1865 the New York Board of Regents, which was responsible for the supervision of higher education institutions, put in place a series of examinations for entry to high school. In 1878, they added to these examinations for graduation from high schools which were used by universities in the state to decide whether students were ready for higher education. Students who did not pass the Regents examinations were able to obtain 'local' high school diplomas if they met the requirements laid down by the district.

Another approach, pioneered by the University of Michigan, was to accredit high schools so that they were able to certify students as being ready for higher education (Broome, 1903) and several other universities adopted similar mechanisms. Towards the end of the century, however, the number of higher education institutions to which a school might send students and the number of schools from which a university might draw its students both grew. In order to simplify the accreditation process, a large number of reciprocal arrangements were established. Although attempts to co-ordinate these were made (see Krug, 1969), particularly in the elite institutions, it appears that university staff resisted that loss of control over admissions decisions. The validity of the Michigan approach was also weakened by accumulating evidence that teachers' grading of student work was not particularly reliable. Not only did different teachers give the same piece of work different grades, but even the grades awarded by a particular teacher were inconsistent over time (Starch and Elliott, 1912, 1913).

As an alternative, the Ivy League universities (Brown, Columbia, Cornell, Dartmouth, Harvard, Pennsylvania, Princeton and Yale) proposed the use of common written entrance examinations. Many universities were already using written entrance examinations, for example Harvard and Yale since 1851 (Broome, 1903), but each university had its own system with its own distinctive focus. The purpose behind the creation of the College Entrance Examination Board in 1899 was to establish a set of common examinations scored uniformly that would bring some coherence to the high school curriculum, while at the same time allowing individual institutions to make their own admission decisions. Although the idea of a common high school curriculum and associated examinations was resisted by many institutions, the College Boards as the examinations came to be known gained increasing acceptance after their introduction in 1901.

The original College Boards were highly predictable tests – even the specific passage of Homer or Virgil that would be tested was made public – and so there was concern that the tests assessed the quality of coaching rather than the talent of the student. For this reason the College Board introduced its New Plan examinations in 1916, focusing on just four subjects and placing greater emphasis on higher-order skills. Originally the New Plan examinations were taken almost exclusively by students applying for Harvard, Princeton or Yale. However, other universities quickly began to see the benefits of the 'New Plan' examinations and for two reasons. Firstly, they provided information about the capability of applicants to reason critically as opposed to regurgitating memorized answers, and secondly, they freed schools from having to train students on a narrow range of content. Although there was also some renewed interest in models of school accreditation (for example in New England), the New Plan examinations became increasingly popular and were quickly established as the dominant assessment for university admission.

However, these examinations were still a compromise between a test of school learning and a test of 'mental power'; more focused on the latter than the original College Boards, but still an assessment that depended strongly on the quality of preparation received by the student. It is hardly surprising, therefore, that the predominance of the 'College Boards' was soon to be challenged by the developing technology of intelligence testing.

The origins of intelligence testing

The philosophical tradition known as British empiricism held that all knowledge comes from experience (in contrast to the continental rationalist tradition which emphasized the role of reason and innate ideas). Therefore, when Galton sought to define measures of intellectual functioning as part of his arguments on 'hereditary genius' it is not surprising that he focused on measures of sensory acuity rather than knowledge (Galton, 1869). Building on this work, in 1890 Cattell published a list of ten mental tests that he proposed might be used to measure individual differences in mental processes. To a modern eye, Cattell's tests look rather odd. They measured grip strength, speed of movement of the arm, sensitivity to touch and pain, the ability to judge weights, time taken to react to sound and to name colours, accuracy of judging length and time and memory for random strings of letters.

In contrast, Binet had argued throughout the 1890s that intellectual functioning could not be reduced to sensory acuity. In collaboration with Simon he produced a series of 30 graduated tests that focused on attention, communication, memory, comprehension, reasoning and abstraction. Through extensive field trials, the tests were adjusted so as to be appropriate for students of a particular age. If a child could answer correctly those items in the Year 4 tests, but not the Year 5 tests, then the child could be said to have a mental age of four. However, the results were interpreted as classifications of children's abilities, rather than measurements, and were used in particular to identify those students who would require additional teaching to make adequate progress. In fact, Binet stated explicitly

> I do not believe that one may measure one of the intellectual aptitudes in the sense that one measures a length or a capacity. Thus, when a person studied can retain seven figures after a single audition, one can class him, from the point of his memory for figures, after the individual who retains eight figures under the same conditions, and before those who retain six. It is a classification, not a measurement. (cited in Varon, 1936: 41)

Binet's work was brought to the USA by Goddard who translated the tests into English and administered them to the children at the New Jersey Training School in Vineland. He was somewhat surprised to discover that the classification of children on the basis of the tests agreed with the informal assessments made by Vineland teachers; 'It met our needs. A classification of our children based on the Scale agreed with the Institution experience' (1916: 5).

In the same year, Terman (1916) adopted the structure of the Binet-Simon tests, but discarded items he felt were inappropriate for US contexts. He added 40 new items, which enabled him to increase the number of items per test to six.

The resulting tests, known as the Stanford-Binet tests, were then developed in multiple-choice versions for use with army recruits. Known as Army Alpha and Army Beta tests, the US Army trials proved successful, providing scores that correlated highly with officers' judgments about the capabilities of their men. This resulted in their full adoption and by the end of January 1919, the tests had been administered to 1,726,966 men (Zenderland, 2000).

Intelligence tests in university admissions

The Army Alpha test results demonstrated the feasibility of large-scale, group-administered intelligence tests and shortly after the end of the First World War, many universities began to explore the utility of intelligence tests for a range of purposes.

In 1919, both Purdue University and Ohio University administered the Army Alpha to all their students and, by 1924, the use of intelligence tests was widespread in US universities. In some, the intelligence tests were used to identify students who appeared to have greater ability than their work at university indicated; in others, the results were used to inform placement decisions both between programmes and within programmes (that is, to 'section' classes to create homogeneous ability groups). Perhaps inevitably, the tests were also used as performance indicators: to compare the ability of students in different departments within the same university and to compare students attending different universities. In an early example of an attempt to manipulate 'league table' standings, Terman, still at Stanford which was at the time regarded as a 'provincial' university, suggested selecting students on the basis of intelligence test scores in order to improve the university's position in the reports of university merit then being produced (Terman, 1921).

Around this time, many universities began to experience difficulties in meeting demand. The number of high school graduates had more than doubled from 1915 to 1925 and although many universities had tried to expand their intake to meet demand, some were experiencing substantial pressure on places. As Levine noted '… a small but critical number of liberal arts colleges enjoyed the luxury of selecting their student bodies for the first time' (1986: 136). In order to address this issue, in 1920 the College Board established a commission '… to investigate and report on general intelligence examinations and other new types of examinations offered in several secondary school subjects'. The task of developing 'new types of examinations' of content was given to Thorndike and Wood of Columbia Teachers' College, who presented the first 'objective examinations' (in algebra and history) to the College Board in 1922.

Four years earlier, some of the leading public universities had founded the American Council on Education (ACE) to represent their interests. In 1924 ACE asked Thurstone, a psychologist at the Carnegie Institute of Technology, to develop a series of intelligence tests. Thurstone had hoped that his work would be embraced by the College Board but they in turn set up their own Committee of Experts to investigate the use of 'psychological tests'. Although the committee included notable psychologists, no-one from Teachers' College was invited, despite the foundational work of Thorndike and Wood in both intelligence testing and the development of 'objective' tests of subject knowledge. This was to have severe and far-reaching implications for the development of the test that came to be known as the Scholastic Aptitude Test. As Hubin notes '… from its inception, the Scholastic Aptitude Test was isolated from advances in education and learning theory and ultimately isolated from the advances in a field that decades later would be called cognitive psychology' (1988: 198).

The Scholastic Aptitude Test

The first version of the Scholastic Aptitude Test was produced in 1926 and administered to 8026 students. As Brigham wrote in the introduction to the manual that accompanied the tests:

The term 'scholastic aptitude test' has reference to the type of examination now in current use and variously called 'psychological tests', 'intelligence tests', 'mental ability tests', 'mental alertness tests' et cetera. The committee uses the term 'aptitude' to distinguish such tests from tests of training in school subjects. Any claims that aptitude tests now in use really measure 'general intelligence' or 'general ability' may or may not be substantiated. It has, however, been very generally established that high scores in such tests usually indicate ability to do a high order of scholastic work. The term 'scholastic aptitude' makes no stronger claim for such tests than that there is a tendency for individual differences in scores in these tests to be associated positively with individual differences in subsequent academic attainment. (1926: 1)

Initially, the acceptance of the SAT was slow. Over the first eleven years, the number of test takers grew only 1.5 per cent per year. Most members of the College Board (including Columbia, Princeton and Yale) required students to take the examination but two (Harvard and Bryn Mawr) did not, although since most students applied to more than one institution both Harvard and Bryn Mawr did have SAT scores on many of its students which provided evidence that could be used in support of the SAT's validity, and this evidence was crucial when Conant, appointed as president of Harvard in 1933, began his attempts to make Harvard more meritocratic.

One of Conant's first acts was to establish a new scholarship programme and he determined that the SAT, together with school transcripts and recommendations, should form the basis of the Harvard National Scholarships administered in 1934–6. The SAT proved to be an immediate success. Students awarded scholarships on the basis of SAT scores did well at Harvard; indeed the 1981 Nobel Prize winner (Economic Science), James Tobin, was one of the early recipients of a Harvard scholarship. Emboldened by the success of the SAT, Conant persuaded 14 of the College Board universities to base all scholarship decisions on objectively scored multiple-choice tests from 1937 onwards.

From its first use in 1926, the outcomes on the SAT had been reported on the familiar 200 to 800 scale, by scaling the raw scores to have a mean of 500 and a standard deviation of 100. From 1926–40, this norming was based on the students who took the SAT each year, so that the meaning of a score might change from year to year according to the scores of the students who took the test. Since the early period of the SAT was one of experimentation with different sorts of items and formats, the difference in meaning from year to year may have been quite large even if the population of test-takers did not change much. Responding to complaints from administrators, in 1941 the College Board introduced a system of equating tests so that each form of the verbal test was equated to the version administered in April 1941 (Angoff, 1971) and the mathematics test to that administered in April 1942. At the same time, the traditional College Board written examinations were withdrawn.

At the time of these changes, the test was taken by less than 20,000 students but by 1951, three years after the Educational Testing Agency began to administer them, the number of SAT takers had grown to 81,000 and by 1961 to 805,000. In 2004, the SAT was taken by 1,419,007 students (College Board, 2004). While the SAT remained substantially unchanged for over sixty years, its name has not. In 1990, the College Board changed its name to the Scholastic Assessment Test, and in 1996, it decided that the letters did not stand for anything. It was just the SAT.

The most serious and enduring challenge to the predominance of the SAT came in 1959, when Linquist and McCarrell of Iowa University established American College Testing (now called simply ACT). Lindquist was an acknowledged leader in the field of psychometrics and had edited the first edition of the field's 'bible', *Educational Measurement* (Lindquist, 1951). ACT was strong where the College Board was weak. They had very strong links with public universities, especially in the mid-west, and had a strong track-record in measuring school achievement. And where the College Board was interested in helping the elite universities in selecting students, ACT was much more interested in placement – helping universities decide which programmes would suit an individual. In reality, however, the differences between the ACT and the SAT are not that clear cut. Despite its origins in the idea of assessing intelligence, the SAT has always been a test of skills that are developed at school; students with higher levels of reasoning skills find mastering the material for the ACT easier. In fact, the correlation between the scores on the SAT and the ACT is 0.92 (Dorans et al., 1997; Dorans, 1999). To all intents and purposes, the two are measuring the same thing. Nevertheless, many students take both tests in order to maximize their chances of getting into their chosen university, and almost as many students take the ACT each year (1,171,460 in 2004) as take the SAT (ACT, 2004).

Ever since its introduction, the SAT has been subjected to much critical scrutiny (again, see Lemann, 1999 for a summary), but things came to a head in 2001 when Richard Atkinson, president of the University of California, announced that he had asked the senate of the university not to require SAT reasoning test scores in considering applicants. In doing so, he said:

> *All too often, universities use SAT scores to rank order applicants in determining who should be admitted. This use of the SAT is not compatible with the US view on how merit should be defined and opportunities distributed. The strength of US society has been its belief that actual achievement should be what matters most. Students should be judged on the basis of what they have made of the opportunities available to them. In other words, in America, students should be judged on what they have accomplished during four years of high school, taking into account their opportunities. (Atkinson, 2001)*

Because the SAT and the ACT are, as noted above, essentially measuring the same thing, these criticisms are not well-founded in terms of the quality of decisions made on the basis of test scores. The criticism is really one about the message that is sent by calling something 'general reasoning' rather than 'school achievement' – essentially an issue of value implications (Messick, 1980). Nevertheless, the threatened loss of income was enough to make the College Board change the SAT to focus more on achievement and to include a writing test. The new test was administered for the first time in March 2005.

The SAT therefore appears set to dominate the arena of admissions to US universities for years to come. No-one really understands what the SAT is measuring, nor how a three-hour test is able to predict college grades almost as well as the high-school grade point average (GPA) which is built up from hundreds of hours of assessed work. Nevertheless, the SAT works. It works partly because it is uniquely attuned to the US higher education system. In most European universities, selection to university is combined with placement into a specific pro-gramme, so information is needed on the applicant's aptitude for a particular programme of study. In US universities, students do not select their 'major' until the second or third year, so at admission information on specific aptitudes is not needed. The SAT works also because it is well-suited to a society with a propensity to litigate. The reliability of the SAT is extremely high (over 0.9) and there is little evidence of bias (minority students get lower scores on the test, but also do less well at college).

In terms of what it sets out to do, therefore, the SAT is a very effective assess-ment. The problem is that it set the agenda for what kinds of assessment are acceptable or possible. As the demand to hold schools accountable grew during the final part of the twentieth century, the technology of multiple-choice testing that had been developed for the SAT was easily pressed into service for the assessment of younger children.

The rise and rise in assessment for accountability

One of the key principles of the constitution of the USA is that anything that is not specified as a federal function is 'reserved to the states', and this notion (that has within the European Union been given the inelegant name of 'subsidiarity') is also practised within most states. Education in particular has always been a local issue in the US, so that for example decisions about curricula, teachers' pay and conditions of service and organizational structures are not made at the state level but in the 17,000 school districts. Most of the funding for schools is raised in the form of taxes on local residential and commercial property. Since the school budget is generally determined by locally elected Boards of Education there is a very high degree of accountability, and the annual surveys produced by the Phi Delta Kappan organization indicate that most communities are happy with their local schools.

From the 1960s, however, state and federal sources had become greater and greater net contributors (Corbett and Wilson, 1991: 25), which led to demands that school districts become accountable beyond the local community and the state has thus played a greater and greater role in education policy and funding. For example, in 1961 California introduced a programme of achievement testing in all its schools although the nature of the tests was left to the districts. In 1972, the California Assessment Program was introduced which mandated multiple choice tests in language, arts and mathematics in grades 2, 3, 6 and 12 (tests for grade 8 were added in 1983). Subsequent legislation in 1991, 1994 and 1995 enacted new state-wide testing initiatives that were only partly imple-mented. However, in 1997 new legal requirements for curriculum standards were passed which in 1998 led to the Standardized Testing and Reporting (STAR) Program. Under this programme, all students in grades 2 to 11 take the Stanford Achievement Test – a battery of norm-referenced tests – every year. Those in grades 2 to 8 are tested in reading, writing, spelling and mathematics, and those in grades 9, 10 and 11 are tested in reading, writing, mathematics, science and social studies. In 1999 further legislation introduced the Academic Performance Index (API), a weighted index of scores on the Stanford Achievement Tests, with awards for high-performing schools and a combination of sanctions and additional resources for schools with poor performance. The same legislation also introduced requirements for passing scores on the tests for entry into high school, and for the award of a high-school diploma.

Portfolios

Many states have experimented with alternatives to standardized tests for monitoring the quality of education and for attesting to the achievements of individual students. In 1974, the National Writing Project (NWP) had been established at the University of California, Berkeley. Drawing inspiration from the practices of professional writers, the National Writing Project emphasized the importance of repeated redrafting in the writing process and so, to assess the writing process properly, one needed to see the development of the final piece through several drafts. In judging the quality of the work, the degree of improvement across the drafts was as important as the quality of the final draft.

The emphasis on the process by which a piece of work was created, rather than the resulting product, was also a key feature of the Arts-PROPEL project – a collaboration between the Project Zero research group at Harvard University and the Educational Testing Service. The idea was that students would '... write poems, compose their own songs, paint portraits and tackle other "real-life" projects as the starting point for exploring the works of practising artists' (Project Zero, 2005). Originally, it appears that the interest in portfolios was intended to be primarily formative but many writers also called for performance or authentic assessments to be used instead of standardized tests (Berlak et al., 1992; Gardner, 1992)

Two states in particular, Vermont and Kentucky, did explore whether portfolios could be used in place of standardized tests to provide evidence for accountability purposes, and some districts also developed systems in which portfolios were used for summative assessments of individual students. However, the use of portfolios was attacked on several grounds such as being '... costly indeed, and slow and cumbersome' and '... its biggest flaw as an external assessment is its subjectivity and unreliability' (Finn, cited in Mathews, 2004).

In 1994, the RAND Corporation released a report on the use of portfolios in Vermont (Koretz et al., 1994), which is regarded by many as a turning point in the use of portfolios (see for example, Mathews, 2004). Koretz and his team found that the meanings of grades or scores on portfolios were rarely comparable from school to school because there was little agreement about what sorts of elements should be included. The standards for reliability that had been set by the SAT simply could not be matched with portfolios. While advocates might claim that the latter were more valid measures of learning, the fact that the same portfolio would get different scores according to who did the scoring made their use for summative purposes impossible in the US context.

In fact, even if portfolios had been able to attain high levels of reliability, it is doubtful that they would have gained acceptance. Teachers did feel that the use of portfolios was valuable, although the time needed to produce worthwhile portfolios detracted from other priorities. Mathematics teachers in particular complained that portfolio activities took time away from basic skills and computation. Furthermore, even before the RAND report, the portfolio movement was being eclipsed by the push for 'standards-based' education and assessment (Mathews, 2004).

Standards

In 1989, President Bush convened the first National Education Summit in Charlottesville, Virginia, led by (the then) Governor Clinton of Arkansas. Those attending the summit, mostly state governors, were perhaps not surprisingly able to agree on the importance of involving all stakeholders in the education process, of providing schools with the resources necessary to do the job, and to hold schools accountable for their performance. What was not so obvious was the agreement that all states should establish standards for education and they should aspire to having all students meet those standards. In many ways this harked back to the belief that all students would learn if taught properly, a belief that underpinned the 'payment by results' culture of the first half of the nineteenth century (Madaus and Kellaghan, 1992).

The importance attached to 'standards' may appear odd to Europeans but the idea of national or regional standards has been long established in Europe. Even in England, which lacked a national curriculum until 1989, there was substantial agreement about what should be in, say, a mathematics curriculum since all teachers were preparing students for similar sets of public examinations.

Prominent in the development of national standards was the National Council of Teachers of Mathematics (NCTM), which published its *Curriculum and Evaluation Standards for Mathematics* in 1989 and *Professional Standards for Teaching Mathematics* two years later (NCTM, 1989, 1991). Because of the huge amount of consultation which the NCTM had undertaken in constructing the standards they quickly became a model for states to follow, and over the next few years every state in the USA except Iowa adopted state-wide standards for the major school subjects. States gradually aligned their high-stakes accountability tests with the state standards, although the extent to which written tests could legitimately assess the high-order goals contained in most state standards is questionable (Webb, 1999).

Texas had introduced a state-wide high-school graduation test in 1984. In 1990, the graduation tests were subsumed within the Texas Assessment of Academic Skills (TAAS), a series of untimed standards-based achievement tests for grades 3 to 10 in reading, writing, mathematics and social studies. Apart from writing, these tests are in multiple-choice format. Massachusetts introduced state-wide testing in 1986. The original aim of the assessment was to provide information about the quality of schools across the state, much in the same way as the National Assessment of Educational Progress (NAEP) had done for the country as a whole (Jones and Olkin, 2004). Students were tested in reading, mathematics and science at grade 4 and grade 8 in alternate years until 1996, and only scores for the state as whole were published. In 1998, however, the state introduced the Massachusetts Comprehensive Assessment System (MCAS), which tests students at grades 4, 8 and 10 in English, mathematics, science and technology, social studies and history (the last two in grade 8 only). The tests use a variety of formats including multiple-choice and constructed response items.

In reviewing the development of state-wide testing programmes, Bolon suggests that many states appeared to be involved in a competition which might be called 'Our standards are stiffer than yours' (2000: 11). Given that political timescales tend to be very short, it is perhaps not surprising that politicians have been anxious to produce highly visible responses to the challenge of raising student achievement. However, the wisdom of setting such challenging standards was called into question when, in January 2002, President Bush signed into law the No Child Left Behind (NCLB) Act of 2001.

No Child Left Behind

Technically, NCLB is a reauthorization of the Elementary and Secondary Education Act originally passed in 1965 (in the USA much legislation expires unless reauthorized) and is a complex piece of legislation, even by US standards. The main requirement of the act is that, in order to receive federal funds, each state must propose a series of staged targets for achieving the overall goal of all students in grades 3–8 to be proficient in reading and mathematics by 2014 (although the definition of 'proficient' is left to each state). Each school is judged to be making 'adequate yearly progress' (AYP) towards this goal if the proportion of students being judged as 'proficient' on annual state-produced standards-based tests exceeds the target percentage for the state for that year. Furthermore, the AYP requirements apply not only to the totality of students in a grade but also to specific sub-groups of students (for example ethnic minority groups), so that it is not possible for good performance by some student subgroups to offset poor performance in others. Among the many sanctions that the NCLB mandates, if schools fail to make AYP then parents have the right to have their child moved to another school at the district's expense.

It has been claimed by some (see for example, Robson, 2004) that NCLB was designed by Republicans to pave the way for mass school privatization by showing the vast majority of public schools to be failing. In fact, the act had strong bipartisan support. Indeed some of the most draconian elements of the legislation, such as the definition of 'adequate yearly progress', were insisted on by Democrats because they did not want schools to be regarded as successful if low performance by some students (for example those from minority ethnic communities) were offset by high performance by others. However, it is clear that the way that the legislation was actually put into practice appears to be very different from what was imagined by some of its original supporters, and an increasing number of both Republican and Democratic politicians are calling for substantial changes in the operation of the Act.

Failure to make AYP has severe consequences for schools, and as a result many schools and districts have invested both time and money in setting up systems for monitoring what teachers are teaching and what students are learning. In order to ensure that teachers cover the curriculum, most districts have devised 'curriculum pacing guides' that specify which pages of the set texts are to be covered every week (and sometimes each day). With such rigid pacing, there are few opportunities for teachers to use information on student performance to address learning needs.

Very recently, there has also been a huge upsurge of interest in systems that monitor student progress through the use of regular formal tests that are designed to predict performance on the annual state tests – some reports suggest that this may be the fastest growing sector of the education market. The idea of such regular testing is that students who are likely to fail the state test, and may therefore prevent a school from reaching its AYP target, can be identified early and given additional support. For this reason these systems are routinely described in the USA as 'formative assessment', even though the results of the assessments rarely impact on learning and as such might be better described as 'early-warning summative'. In many districts such tests are given once a week on a Friday. Thursdays are consumed with preparation for the test, and Mondays with reviews of the incorrect answers, leaving only 40 per cent of the available subject time for teaching. While the pressure on schools to improve the performance of all students means that schools in the USA are now more than ever in need of effective formative assessment, the conditions for its development seem even less promising than ever.

Conclusion

In Europe, for most of the twentieth century, education beyond the age of 15 or 16 was intended only for those intending to go to university. The consequence of this has been that the alignment between school and university curricula is very high – indeed it can be argued that the academic curriculum for 16 to 19-year-olds in Europe has been determined by the universities, with consequent implications for the curriculum during the period of compulsory schooling. In the USA, however, despite the fact that for most of the twentieth century a greater proportion of school leavers went on to higher education, the high-school curriculum has always been an end in itself and determined locally. The advantage of this approach is that schools are able to serve their local communities well. The disadvantage is that high school curricula are often poorly aligned with the demands of higher education and this has persisted even with the introduction of state standards (Standards for Success, 2003).

When higher education was an essentially local undertaking the problems caused by lack of alignment could be addressed reasonably easily, but the growth of national elite universities rendered such local solutions unworkable. At the time of its 'ossification' in 1941, the SAT was being taken by less than 20,000 students each year (Hubin, 1988), and it is entirely possible that it would have remained a test required only of those students applying for the most selective universities, with a range of alternatives including achievement tests also in use. It would be unfair to blame the SAT for the present condition of assessment in US schools, but it does seem likely that the dominance of the SAT and the prevalence of multiple-choice testing in schools are both indications of the same convictions, deeply and widely held in the USA, about the importance of objectivity in assessment.

Once multiple-choice tests were established (and not long afterwards, the machine marking of tests – see Hubin, 1988), it was probably also inevitable that any form of 'authentic' assessment such as examinations that required extended responses let alone portfolios would have been found wanting in comparison. This is partly due to such assessments tending to have lower reliability than multiple-choice items because of the differences between raters, although this can be addressed by having multiple raters. A more important limitation, within the US context, is the effect of student-task interaction – the fact that with a smaller number of items, the particular set of items included may suit some students better than others. In Europe, such variability is typically not regarded as an aspect of reliability – it's just 'the luck of the draw'. However, in the USA, the fact that a different set of items might yield a different result for a particular student would open the possibility of expensive and inconvenient litigation.

Once the standards-based accountability movement began to gather momentum, in the 1980s, the incorporation of the existing technology of machine-scored multiple-choice tests was also probably inevitable. Americans had got used to testing students for less than $10 per test and to spend $30 or more for a less reliable test as is commonplace in Europe, whatever the advantages in terms of validity, would be politically very difficult.

However, even with annual state-mandated multiple-choice testing it could be argued that there was still space for the development of effective formative assessment. After all, one of the key findings of the research literature in the field was that attention to formative assessment raises scores even on state-mandated tests (Crooks, 1988; Black and Wiliam, 1998a), Nevertheless, the prospects for the development of effective formative assessment within US education seem more remote than ever. The reasons for this are of course complex, but two factors appear to be especially important.

The first is the extraordinary belief in the value of grades, both as a device for communication between teachers on the one hand and students and parents on the other, and also as a way of motivating students despite the large and mounting body of evidence to the contrary (see Chapter 4).

The second is the effect of an extraordinary degree of local accountability in the USA. Most of the 17,000 district superintendents in the USA are appointed by directly-elected boards of education, which are anxious to ensure that the money raised in local property taxes is spent efficiently. Under NCLB, the superintendents are required to ensure that their schools make 'adequate yearly progress'. The adoption of 'early-warning summative' testing systems therefore represents a highly visible response to the task of ensuring that the district's schools will meet their AYP targets.

There are districts where imaginative leaders can see that the challenge of raising achievement, and reducing the very large gaps in achievement between white and minority students that exist in the USA, requires more than just 'business as usual, but with greater intensity'. But political timescales are short and educational change is slow. A superintendent who is not re-elected will not change anything. Satisfying the political press for quick results with the long-term vision needed to produce effective long-term improvement is an extraordinarily difficult and perhaps impossible task. There has never been a time when the USA needed effective formative assessment more but, perversely, never have the prospects for its successful development looked so bleak.

Chapter 11

Policy and Practice in Assessment for Learning: the Experience of Selected OECD Countries

Judy Sebba

Studies of assessment for learning in countries other than the USA or those in the UK potentially provide a rich and stimulating source of evidence for understanding practices in assessment for learning. In Chapter 9, Daugherty and Ecclestone provide an analysis of policy developments in the four countries of the UK and in Chapter 10, Wiliam outlines reasons for assessment for learning not featuring in policy in the USA. This chapter draws on illustrative examples of practice from selected countries that participated in an OECD study of formative assessment. Daugherty and Ecclestone quoted Ball (1990) as suggesting that policies are pre-eminently statements about practice, intended to bring about solutions to problems identified by individual teachers and schools. Classroom practice can thus be seen as a key measure of policy implementation and it is examples of classroom practice from different countries that are presented and analysed in this chapter. Some brief comments are made about policies in these countries but a comprehensive analysis of educational policies in these countries is beyond the scope of this chapter.

In 2005, the Centre for Educational Research and Innovation (CERI) at OECD published research (OECD, 2005[1]) on 'formative assessment' in lower secondary education, drawing on case studies involving eight countries: Canada, Denmark, England, Finland, Italy, New Zealand, Australia and Scotland. I undertook the case study of Queensland, Australia which was written up with Graham Maxwell, a senior manager working in the locality. This chapter draws heavily on examples from the OECD study including those case studies in Canada, Denmark, New Zealand and in particular, Queensland. There was no significant differences between these countries and the others not mentioned – it is simply that these case studies provided illustrations of some emerging themes. It is important to acknowledge that the eight countries were from Europe, North America and Australasia and did not include a country that by any definition could be described as 'developing'. Furthermore, the chapter draws only on illustrative examples of policy and practice and the analysis cannot therefore be claimed to provide a comprehensive or definitive picture of the countries involved.

The OECD study provides a basis for identifying some common themes in assessment for learning policy and practice that can be compared across countries. These involve, at the most basic level, what is included in assessment for learning ('formative assessment' as it is called in the study), the nature and role of feedback, self and peer-assessment, the relationship between student grouping strategies and assessment for learning and teacher development. In addition to these classroom level issues, there are contextual factors in schools and beyond which enhance or inhibit the implementation of assessment for learning strategies. These factors, such as the role of leadership, developing schools as learning organizations and students as agents of change, are not specific to developing assessment for learning and might more appropriately be viewed as strategies for school improvement. They do, however, vary within and across different countries thus influencing the capacity for assessment for learning strategies to be effective. The links between assessment for learning at the classroom level, teacher development and school improvement are further explored in Chapter 2.

Before considering these themes, four underlying tensions are acknowledged which need to be taken into account when drawing interpretations and inferences from comparisons of assessment for learning across countries. These are: focusing on difference at the expense of similarities; the influence of cultural contexts; problems of transferability of strategies across countries; and the methodological limitations of research involving short visits to a small sector of provision in other countries. These issues have been more extensively debated in the literature on comparative education (for example Vulliamy et al., 1990), but need to be mentioned here to urge caution in drawing generalized inferences from the examples presented.

Focusing on difference at the expense of similarities

In undertaking any comparative analysis, there is a danger of focusing exclusively on differences and ignoring or under-acknowledging similarities. Throughout this chapter, an attempt is made to draw parallels between the experiences of assessment for learning across different countries and to seek multiple interpretations of both the similarities and differences observed. It is important to attempt to distinguish between differences in terminology, definitions and meaning and real differences in policy and practice. International comparisons are frequently hampered by a lack of agreed consistent terminology, which acts as a barrier to communication, development of understanding and the drawing of conclusions. For example, much greater emphasis was put in some countries on the use of test data to inform teaching as a component of formative assessment, whereas others saw this as distinctively separate from formative assessment as such.

The influence of cultural contexts

A second underlying tension concerns the need to acknowledge the cultural contexts within which assessment for learning strategies are being implemented. Attempting to understand the cultural differences between countries and indeed, between different areas within countries, is a considerable challenge extensively debated in comparative education (for example Vulliamy et al., 1990). Broadfoot et al. (1993), provided strong evidence of the influence of culture on the educational organization and processes in different countries. The interaction between national cultures and educational policies and structures adds further complexity to this. For example, national policies prescribing curricula, assessment and accountability systems provide structural contexts which may reflect, or indeed create, particular cultural contexts. Vulliamy (2004) argues that the increasing knowledge and information associated with globalization are in danger of strengthening those positivist approaches that threaten the centrality of culture in comparative education.

Problems of transferability

Thirdly, and partly related to issues of cultural context, the transferability of strategies and innovations from one country to another is a further underlying tension. The assumption that educational innovations that have an effect in one context will have the same or any effect in another has been challenged by many writers (for example Crossley, 1984). The Black and Wiliam research review (1998a), which indicated the substantial impact of assessment for learning strategies on students' learning and generated extensive international interest, drew on a large number of studies from different countries but was ultimately limited to those written in English. The OECD study included appendices of reviews of the literature in English, French and German. However, more often the findings of a single study undertaken in one country are taken as evidence for the efficacy of that strategy in another country. Furthermore, as Fielding et al. (2005) have demonstrated, the concept of 'best practice' is contested and its transfer from one individual, institution or group to another is much more complicated than national policies tend to acknowledge.

Methodological limitations of research based on short 'expert' visits

A final underlying tension is the methodological limitations of what Vulliamy et al. (1990) referred to as 'jetting in' experts or researchers to other countries for short periods. The OECD study involved 'experts' from one country visiting another country for a short time (1–2 weeks), and in partnership with 'experts' from the host country visiting schools, analysing documentation and interviewing those individuals and groups involved as consumers or providers of assessment for learning. While many comparative studies are probably similarly limited, the methodological weaknesses in research design, data collection, analysis and interpretation and of trying to identify appropriate research questions, construct a research design and implement it in a short period with limited understanding of the context, raise serious questions. Drawing inferences from a necessarily partial picture in contexts where others have determined what documents are accessed, who is interviewed and observed and perhaps the views that are conveyed, is problematic. For example, it is clear that observations undertaken in two schools in Queensland cannot be assumed to be representative of that state, let alone typical of Australia as a whole. Generalizations should therefore be minimized and interpretations treated as illustrative rather than indicative. Vulliamy et al. argue that in-depth qualitative research undertaken prior to the full study can inform the subsequent study questions and design, thereby increasing relevance, validity (for example in interpreting terminology) and understanding. They also discuss ways in which research capacity can be developed with local populations.

Despite these limitations, the OECD study provided rich descriptions of a variety of forms of practice in assessment for learning, in a range of different contexts, which offered interesting insights and suggested that some classroom practices and challenges may share more similarities than differences.

What is included in assessment for learning/formative assessment?

In the OECD study 'formative assessment' is defined as:

> ... frequent, interactive assessments of student progress and understanding to identify learning needs and adjust teaching appropriately. (2005: 21)

This definition differs significantly from that which is provided in the Introduction (ARG, 2002a) and which has been adopted in the national primary and secondary strategies in the UK. The Assessment Reform Group definition puts considerably greater emphasis on the use to be made by learners of the assessment information. The OECD definition instead stresses the adjusting of teaching in light of the assessment.

Similarities in the strategies encompassed in formative assessment across the eight countries included; establishing learning goals and tracking of individual students' progress towards these goals; ensuring student understanding (rather than just skills or knowledge) is adequately assessed; providing feedback that influences subsequent teaching; the active involvement of students in the learning process. But the emphasis given to each of these and the additional strategies which were included under the formative assessment umbrella varied considerably. For example, in the Danish case study schools there was greater emphasis on developing self-confidence and verbal competence. In New Zealand, formative assessment was linked to the Maori Mainstream Programme within which the importance of culture is emphasized through group work, co-construction of knowledge and peer solidarity (Bishop and Glynn, 1999). Several of the case studies included use of summative assessment data as part of their formative strategies, even where the use has been for whole school improvement rather than individual learning, which arguably falls outside the ARG definition given in the Introduction.

The nature and role of feedback

At one of the two schools in Queensland (Sebba and Maxwell, 2005) students were working on their individual assignments in the library using books, articles and the internet to research globalization in the context of a company they had chosen, for example Nike or McDonald's. The teacher individually saw about half of the 25 students in the group to review their progress. She asked challenging open questions to encourage them to extend and deepen their investigations and gave specific feedback on what they needed to target for improvement.

In each of the two schools, I analysed more than 20 students' files from across year groups and ability ranges (as identified by the teachers) in order to check if and how grades were used. I collected examples of comment marking and looked for evidence that students had acted upon the comments. One of the schools used no grades at all and the comment marking was characterized as very specific and almost always included targets for improvement. What distinguished it in particular from the comment marking I have experienced in England was that even positive comments were elaborated to ensure that students were left in no doubt about why a piece of work was so good. For example:

> *You girls have done a fantastic job!! Not only is your information accurate and well-researched, but you have also successfully completed the extension tasks! Try and keep an eye on the difference between 'endangered' and 'extinct' and watch your spelling. But please keep up this brilliant effort! You have all gone above and beyond in this activity!! Well done!!*

The comments, in particular for less high achieving students, were additionally often characterized by empathy and humour:

> *L, an excellent effort, I would like to join you in your mission to Mars.*

At this school, 11-year-old students said that grades or marks were never given. They felt that this helped them work to their own standard and not worry about comparing themselves to other people. They all claimed to read and act upon the comments and suggested that the teacher was always willing to discuss them. In both schools, students claimed to read and act upon comments written on work and there was some evidence of this, though there were no specific consistent strategies as observed in a few schools elsewhere, such as keeping a list of comments in the front of a book and expecting students to indicate when and where (indicated by a page reference) these have been acted upon. However, teachers and students identified lessons in which time was allocated to making revisions in response to comments given.

In Denmark (Townshend et al., 2005), one case study school put great emphasis on verbal competencies. Goal-setting and oral feedback were strong features of the formative assessment work. Oral assessment was preferred because it was quick and flexible and allowed an immediate response from the student enabling misunderstandings to be clarified rapidly. Individual student interviews took place several times a year in order to assess progress and set new goals focusing on subject outcomes, work attitudes and social skills. As in the Queensland schools, the lessons often incorporated periods of reflective feedback from students to teachers which resulted in adjustments to teaching.

Students used logbooks to record their reflections and these were used for teacher and student to enter into a dialogue. Forster and Masters (1996–2001) provide further examples of this in their materials developed in Australia on developmental assessment.

Effective feedback seems to be characterized by specific comments that focus on students' understanding rather than on quality of presentation or behaviour. Oral feedback may allow for greater exploration of understanding and be more immediate but written comments allow teachers greater flexibility to reflect on students' work and allocate more time to this process, though the dialogue may be delayed and stilted. In contexts with a strong oral tradition such as the Danish case study school, the balance was more in favour of oral than written feedback. Effective oral questioning and feedback seem to require the teacher to be confident and competent in that subject area and to have the flexibility to 'try another way' in their questioning and feedback strategies in order to ensure that the message has been understood. A much fuller account of this issue can be found in Black et al. (2003).

Self- and peer assessment

In the PROTIC programme in Quebec (Sliwka et al., 2005) teaching is organized around interdisciplinary projects with a strong emphasis on collaborative group exploration. All projects in the programme make extensive use of ICT for research, reporting and assessing. At the start of each project students identify their individual learning targets and at regular intervals they are given time for writing reflections on their own learning, their team learning and the achievement of their targets. These written reports are the basis for future target setting and choices. Peer assessment is used to give feedback on each others' regular presentations of work and on teamwork skills. Students reported needing to adjust to the level of autonomy expected compared to their previous schools: 'You understand that you are responsible, you are in charge' (Sliwka et al., 2005: 102).

In Saskatchewan (Sliwka et al., 2005), one school uses electronic learning portfolios with younger children to record their own learning. They keep exemplary pieces of work, scan in art work and are taught how to assess their own work. The same researchers noted that in a school in western Newfoundland portfolios are similarly used by students to record their best work alongside reflective journals. In pairs, they use criteria provided by the teacher to give each other feedback on ways of improving their quality of writing in English. These practices are used formatively to support continuous learning but may also contribute to summative purposes of assessment.

Teachers and students in Queensland have had to adapt to the development of an outcomes-based assessment system in which there is no testing. Teachers are trying to ensure that the students are aware of and understand the outcome-based statements and can assess themselves against the standards. When interviewed, the students described reflection time as a feature of most lessons. This involved the use of their learning journals in which questions to be addressed included 'what do you understand about … ?' They gave examples of marking each others' work and giving each other feedback on written work. Self and peer-assessment was a strong feature of the lessons observed in Queensland. Every week there was an allocated time for Year 8 and some Year 9 students to reflect on their learning, working with others and their experiences, and to write comments about it in their learning journals. Teachers were allowed to read these but not allowed to write in them.

In another lesson at this school, at the end of each activity, the students were invited to assess it on difficulty; student feedback determined whether the teacher moved on to the next activity or gave a further explanation of the previous one. Students and other staff interviewed confirmed that reflections of this type were regularly built into lessons.

In Queensland, peer assessment was less well developed than self-assessment in the lessons observed. This may reflect the additional demands on teachers and students of peer assessment and the skills that we have noted elsewhere needing to be taught (for details of the skills, see Chapters 1 and 5; also Kutnick et al., 2005). Feedback between students tended to be at the level of whether an outcome was correct or not, rather than indicating how to improve it. Students were encouraged to reflect on how effectively they had worked as a group, as well as how well they had completed the task. One student had entered the following comment into her journal:

> Yesterday my group and I made different shapes of a certain size out of newspaper. I got frustrated when nobody would listen to me. But we finished a square and two rectangles. Listen. None of our group members listened to each other. We all had ideas but wouldn't explain them. Then it would all end up in a mess.

In both schools in Queensland there was a strong ethos of developing lifelong learners rather than only getting students through school together with the Senior Certificate they received on leaving. This was reflected in a strong focus on learning to learn and on students taking responsibility for their own actions. Self- and peer assessment were seen by students and teachers to be contributing to this but it was acknowledged that they required skills that had to be taught.

The relationship between student grouping strategies and assessment for learning

Assessment for learning encourages students to develop greater responsibility for their own learning but also to regard their peers as a potential resource for learning and thus to become less dependent on the teacher. Assessment for learning requires effective group work, in particular in the area of peer assessment. Well developed peer assessment is very demanding on students' social and communication skills, in particular listening, turn-taking, clear and concise verbal and written expression, empathy and sensitivity. There is substantial evidence that group work skills need to be taught (for example, see Kutnick et al., 2005 for a review) and that highly effective group work takes a long time to develop. Teaching students to self-reflect was observed as follows in a school in Queensland:

> *Sixteen Year 9 pupils in a PSHE [personal and social health education] lesson worked in self-selected groups of four. The school had a 'buddying' system for incoming Year 7 pupils whereby they had an identified 'buddy' from Year 10 help settle them into school. Most pupils in this Year 9 class had applied to be 'buddies' and were to be interviewed to see if they are suitable for this role. The teacher asked the groups to identify what characteristics 'buddies' need. She gave them ten minutes to discuss this and draw up a list. She invited the groups to feedback. She then invited them to spend 10 minutes working out what questions the interviewers would ask them to draw out, whether they had these skills and how they would answer these questions. At the end of the third activity and feedback she asked them to assess how they worked in their groups and invited feedback.*

Despite the challenges of group work, students and teachers alike in the two Queensland schools reported beneficial outcomes of using these strategies. In interviews in one school, the students claimed that they worked in groups for about half the lessons and that this helped them to develop their understanding through testing out their ideas, examples and explanations on others. They suggested that the disadvantages of working in groups included having '… to work with people you don't like, who hold you back or mess about'. Overall, they felt that the advantages outweighed the disadvantages and favoured the mixed-ability groups that they usually experienced:

> *I reckon it's important to have people working together at different levels, then the people at higher levels can teach the people at lower levels in their own way. In the real world you work with different people, you don't always choose who you work with and working with other people you don't know helps you. (Sebba and Maxwell, 2005: 202–3)*

In a school in Denmark (Townshend et al., 2005), 'core groups' provided opportunities for reflection on goals, effort and outcomes. The students gave each other oral feedback, recorded their views in their logbooks and evaluated one another's academic achievements and presentational skills. This was done for each project that they undertook. School leaders reported that students were more competent at reflecting on their own learning, identifying their targets and engaging in social interaction.

Teacher development

The definition of formative assessment in the OECD study refers to adjusting teaching in response to feedback about learning and in this sense, formative assessment and teacher development are inextricably linked as emphasized in Chapter 2. Many of the case studies refer to evaluation of teaching. For example, in one school in Denmark Townshend et al. (2005) noted that teachers evaluated subject courses in teams as part of their departmental meetings. This enabled them to compare the same student's progress in different subjects. The focus of these evaluations was decided by prior agreement between teacher and student. In this way, teaching as well as students' progress were assessed.

In Quebec, the university teacher educators acknowledged that in the PROTIC programme (Sliwka et al., 2005) teachers have to adapt to a shift in control and responsibility for learning from teacher to student, as noted in earlier chapters. They are also required to recognize that they are not the only source of knowledge in the classroom. There is evidence that the PROTIC approach has had an impact on the teaching approaches used by other teachers, such as those in Saskatchewan who reported that whereas previously they had worked in complete isolation, they are now much more interested in working together and sharing resources and have developed a clear focus on how students learn since introducing formative assessment. This professional development issue is developed further in Chapter 2.

Teachers at one school in Queensland (Sebba and Maxwell, 2005) shared pieces of work and discussed comments they had made on them as well as the work itself. They reported that this challenged their thinking and developed their practice. Heads of department saw this as professional behaviour for moderation purposes rather than monitoring of marking for accountability purposes. It was seen as relatively easy to do in a small school in which departments are not isolated.

In the case study school in Denmark (Townshend et al., 2005) teacher development is supported through a centre for teaching innovation based in Copenhagen, established specifically to develop innovatory practices and share these with schools across Denmark. They plan and provide in-service courses for teachers, support school improvement in other schools and publish materials in accessible professional journals. Teachers are challenged by self-evaluation in that they are concerned they may be insufficiently 'objective' but there is evidence of a continuing drive for more secure and effective teaching approaches. School leaders in the case study schools acknowledged the cultural change required to implement formative assessment strategies effectively.

School improvement contextual factors

The role of leadership

It was a feature of a number of the schools in the OECD studies that the head teacher or principal had recently changed, and that the school had been restructured and significant new whole-school initiatives introduced. New managers often provided the impetus for change or were appointed to provide this, but frequent changes to senior management teams can be a threat to longer-term sustainability of new initiatives and assessment for learning strategies is not exempt from this. There was evidence in one of the schools in Queensland that the changes brought about through assessment for learning including student self-reflection, group work and comment marking had become embedded in the infrastructure of the school and could thereby 'survive' some degree of senior management change.

Developing schools as learning organizations

The schools where significant progress had been made were characterized by an ongoing commitment to further development. They did not express views suggesting they thought they had reached their targets and could reduce their energies. Consistent with research on developing schools as learning communities (for example, McMahon et al., 2004), these schools recognized the importance of engaging with the wider community beyond teachers with many, for example, having well-developed mechanisms for ongoing dialogue with parents about formative assessment. The emphasis on teachers working in teams and helping to develop one another seems to have been another feature of these schools, which is an issue considered in Chapter 2.

Students as agents of change

There was some evidence of students' awareness that their school was different to others and of linking this to aspects of formative assessment. For example, in one school in Queensland students reported that teaching strategies compared very favourably to those used in other schools attended by their friends, suggesting that other schools relied more heavily on worksheets and students received less full explanations from teachers. Students in one of the Denmark schools noted that they enjoyed better relationships with teachers and that instead of just 'getting grades', they were engaged in a process with their teachers which enabled them to get to know them better and to discuss expectations.

There was, however, little evidence from the OECD case studies of well-developed examples of students acting as change agents in their schools in the realm of formative assessment. Fielding (2001) has proposed levels of engagement for students in schools that enable them to become 'true' contributors to or even leaders of change. For example, students might be expected to challenge the school on why peer assessment opportunities provided in one subject were not created in other subjects. This would seem to be a potential next development for the schools studied.

The impact and relevance of policy

Australia has a national curriculum framework based on agreed national goals stated as providing young Australians with the knowledge, skills, attitudes and values relevant to social, cultural and economic needs in local, national and international settings. This includes a commitment to an outcomes based approach across eight key learning areas and an emphasis on developing lifelong learners. The Queensland Studies Authority published principles (QSA, 2005) that emphasize that assessing students is an integral part of the teaching and learning process and that opportunities should be provided for students to take responsibility for their own learning and self-monitoring. The syllabus documents recommend that assessment be continuous and on-going and be integrated into the learning cycle – that is, provide the basis for planning, monitoring student progress, providing feedback on teaching and setting new learning targets. One of the principles developed by the Assessment Reform Group (ARG, 2002a), and presented in the Introduction, relates to the need for assessment for learning to be part of effective planning for teaching and learning.

There is no whole-cohort external testing or examining in secondary schools in Queensland. Reporting in years 1–10 is currently a school responsibility and is unmoderated. School-based assessments for the Senior Certificate (Year 12) are currently moderated by subject-based panels of expert teachers, providing advice to schools on the quality of their assessment and judgments based on sample portfolios.

There are important contextual policy factors that seem likely to support the practices observed in the two Queensland schools. Perhaps the national curriculum framework, less prescriptive than that in England, is a useful contextual factor enabling a strong focus on formative assessment by reducing the necessity for teachers to determine what to teach. The lack of external tests and examinations passed without comment in the teacher interviews in the Queensland schools, yet as a systematic review of research on this has shown (Harlen and Deakin Crick, 2003), high-stakes testing and publication of results are associated with teachers adopting a teaching style that favours transmission of knowledge. This not only reduces the use of teaching approaches consistent with assessment for learning but is likely to consume energy that Queensland teachers could instead direct into assessment for learning. Finally, the status ascribed to teacher summative assessment in the Queensland system suggests that formative assessment is better recognized than in some other systems, for both its contribution to learning and to summative assessment. Its role as a key professional skill for teachers, as advocated in the principles in the Introduction, is recognized in this system.

In Denmark, the 2003 Education Act introduced an outcomes-based curriculum defining competencies for all students. Schools are required to publish annually the results of average grades on their websites, though these seemed not to take account of prior attainment and were therefore regarded by those interviewed as reflecting intake and not effectiveness. There was no evidence that this accountability framework was inhibiting the developments in formative assessment in the schools. At the time the case studies were conducted (2002–3) the Ministry of Education had just changed the definition of the role of headteachers, so in one of the case study schools the head had used formative assessment as part of the change strategy adopted.

Educational policy in Canada is set at province/territory level. At federal level, monitoring across the provinces takes place but curricular guidelines are produced in the provinces and territories and these often emphasize learning to learn skills. In western Newfoundland, the mandate from the Department of

Education and school district that required test (attainment) data to be the basis for school improvement has influenced the developing focus on analysing progress and addressing the needs of 'weaker' students, partly through formative assessment. Initial resistance was followed by a gradual change in culture and analysing data is now a key focus of staff development activities, closely linked to evaluation by teachers with individual students. This reflects the Assessment Reform Group principle (ARG, 2002a) of promoting a commitment to a shared understanding of the criteria by which students are assessed. The tension for teachers remains how to reconcile the demands of summative testing with formative assessment, though this does not seem to be severely limiting developments in assessment for learning.

Conclusion

Despite considerable differences in cultural contexts across the OECD case study schools, what teachers do at the classroom level may be surprisingly similar. For example, the feedback provided to students on their work, the development of self and peer-assessment and the implications of formative assessment for group work have overlapping practices across countries. Perceptions of these, however, by students, teachers, senior school managers and teacher educators may differ as a result of the considerable differences in national policy contexts. The national assessment and curriculum framework, accountability mechanisms and underlying values reflected in these about the purposes of education, lifelong learning skills and skills for employability, will enhance or inhibit to different degrees the teachers' capacity to adopt, implement and sustain formative assessment practices. Furthermore, as has been the experience of school improvement in general schools that are effective at implementing a specific strategy, in this case formative assessment, are often those which can redirect the requirements and additional resources made available through national policies to support their established plans.

Note

[1] I would like to acknowledge the extensive writing and editing that Janet Looney of OECD contributed to the report.

Assessment for Learning: A Compelling Conceptualization

John Gardner

At a seminar in 1998, hosted by the Nuffield Foundation at their London head-quarters, the Assessment Reform Group launched the Black and Wiliam review pamphlet *Inside the Black Box*. The review itself, and the pamphlet, immediately attracted critical acclaim and have continued to enjoy significant impact on assessment thinking throughout the UK and further afield to the present day. However, one moment in the event sticks out clearly in my memory. After the main presentation, a senior educational policy maker stood up and declared that he had heard it all before; we had nothing new to offer. Indicating, with a glance at his watch, that he had commitments elsewhere he promptly left the seminar before the discussion proper got underway. My immediate urge was to rush after him and say 'Yes, you are absolutely right! But it seems to us that, powerful as it might be, formative assessment is actually off the schools' and policy-makers' radar! Surely we need to do something quite urgently if we are to reap the benefits we know are there?' I resisted the urge and instead a year later, at the same venue and with the same sponsors, we injected the urgency we all felt was needed. We launched the pamphlet *Assessment for Learning: Beyond the Black Box*. This pamphlet deliberately and directly challenged official complacency and inertia.

Six years on, the Assessment Reform Group can now record an impressive list of dissemination successes and official endorsements of assessment for learning from, for example, the Scottish and Welsh governments, the curriculum and assessment agencies of England, Scotland, Wales and Northern Ireland, and from overseas jurisdictions as diverse as Hong Kong and the Canadian province of Alberta. However, in contrast to the situation in Scotland, Wales and Northern Ireland the policy agenda in England remains somewhat hamstrung, with an accountability focus driving assessment policy and specifically with schools being evaluated on the basis of the performance of their students on external assessments. The ensuing and controversial 'league tables', which purport to indicate the relative quality of education in the schools concerned, arguably increase the emphasis on 'teaching to the test' as schools focus on raising their students' performance in external tests and assessments. There is evidence that the richness of the delivered curriculum suffers and that the pedagogic techniques associated with assessment for learning are neglected.

Paradoxically, assessment for learning's central message, prompted by the research review of Black and Wiliam (1998a) and disseminated vigorously by the Assessment Reform Group, is that overall standards and individual performance may be improved by actually emphasizing formative assessment techniques such as student self-assessment, negotiation of learning goals and feedback to identify next steps. This message is now squarely on the 'radar' of English schools as it continues to generate interest at the grassroots level, attracting official endorsement in major areas such as the Key Stage 3 national curriculum and in the professional development publications of the Qualifications and Curriculum Authority (QCA, 2004).

Much progress is therefore being made, but let me return for a moment to the observations made by our disappointed seminar guest above. I readily concede that the principles and processes of assessment for learning are not novel in any real sense; indeed they have a fairly lengthy pedigree in curriculum and assessment developments in the UK. I could reflect on Harry Black's work with teachers in the early 1980s (Black, 1986) or I could cite the work by Harlen that led to the publication of professional development materials under the title *Match and Mismatch* (Harlen et al., 1977), to illustrate the point. Such sources would be in keeping with the book's primary focus on schools but I will illustrate the breadth of recognition of the principles we espouse with an example from post-compulsory (vocational) education. The quotation that follows could conceivably have appeared at any time in the last seven years since the publication of *Inside the Black Box* (Black and Wiliam, 1998b) and the subsequent Assessment Reform Group outputs: *Assessment for Learning: Beyond the Black Box* (ARG, 1999); *Assessment for Learning: 10 Principles* (ARG, 2002a) and *Testing, Motivation and Learning* (ARG, 2002b).

However, the quotation I reproduce below was actually written in 1986 by Pring as part of an analysis of developments in vocational curricula, initially sponsored by the 1979 publication of the Department of Education and Science's Further Education Unit's *A Basis for Choice*. He argued that a number of implications for assessment had begun to emerge in the wake of the various initiatives in post-compulsory qualifications and summarized them as follows:

First, what had to be assessed was different. A curriculum that stresses personal development, social awareness, cooperative learning, problem solving, is seeking to assess different qualities from those assessed in traditional forms of examination. Secondly, the purpose of assessment was different ... the main purpose of assessment was the diagnosis of learning needs with a view to promoting the process of learning. It is difficult to provide well-informed guidance, and consequent negotiation of further learning experiences, without some assessment of what the students know or can do. Therefore, it was recommended that the assessment should be part of a continuous, formative profile of the experiences and achievements of the student. Furthermore, it was envisaged that this profile would be the basis of regular teacher/student discussion and guidance of educational progress. ... The radical difference lies not only in the content of what is taught but also in the processes of learning and thus the demands upon assessment. In its

Resources Sheet ... the Joint Board [City and Guilds of London Institute and the Business and Technician Education Council] says:

'If the individual student is to be enabled to make the most of his/her programme, the quality of the assessment system and its link with supportive guidance will be critical. Most of the assessing will be formative; that is, a regular feedback on performance to the students from all *those involved ... '*

Assessment is thus tied to guidance, negotiation, and the assumption of responsibility for one's own learning. (Pring, 1986: 13–14, emphases in original)

There are many such examples, over time, of the acceptance that the classroom assessment techniques comprising assessment for learning are broadly 'good things' to do. However, the specific intention of this book has been to ground this 'goodness' in a credible argument that draws its authority and explanatory power from sound empirical and theoretical contexts. The central arguments have emerged in various ways throughout the chapters, using research evidence and theory to explain and support the points made. We have attempted to address the specific education-related aspects of assessment for learning but clearly there are many more contextual issues that have a bearing on practice, policy and indeed perception. These include the dominance in some quarters of summative assessment and the use of data from student assessments for accountability purposes. The various educational and contextual key issues may be categorized as follows:

- Classroom pedagogy;
- The essence of assessment for learning;
- Motivation of learners;
- A theory of assessment for learning;
- Assessment myths, misunderstandings and tensions;
- The complexity of influencing policy and policy makers.

Classroom pedagogy

In Chapters 1 and 2, Black and Wiliam, and James and Pedder, respectively relate insights gained from major research projects into the practice of assessment for learning techniques in the classroom. Chapter 1 offered examples of techniques for feedback, for self-assessment and classroom questioning which were developed by the teachers, but it particularly struck a chord in illustrating how '... applying research in practice is much more than a simple process of translating the findings into the classroom'. In true developmental fashion the application in practice led directly to more research insights, especially in the context of teachers' professional development. In Chapter 2, James and Pedder took up the professional development baton by conceptualizing it in terms of the ten principles for assessment for learning, with a specific focus on the principle that it should be regarded as a key professional skill for teachers.

However, they issue stern warnings that radical changes are needed in teaching and learning roles, that teachers need to learn new practices and that the various changes need to be encouraged by a supportive culture of continuous professional development. Their warnings continue: teachers' learning is not straightforward and there are serious dangers of much of the assessment for learning gains translating to superficial practice if teachers do not engage actively with the ideas and practices, and if the environments in which they work do not actively encourage inquiry-based modes of professional development in the classroom. To paraphrase one of their messages, a true assessment for learning context for teachers is one in which they take responsibility for all aspects of their professional development, giving new meaning to the old expression 'self-taught'.

The essence of assessment for learning

Almost every chapter in this book addresses at least some of the core issues of assessment for learning, including practice and theory and what some might term its antithesis – assessment of learning or summative assessment. However, it is the policy chapter by Sebba (Chapter 11) that particularly focuses on the commonality of practice in formative assessment across several national and cultural boundaries. Key ingredients of assessment for learning including peer and self-assessment, feedback to support learning and effective questioning are all in evidence, but here too Sebba issues several warnings.

These include an echo of Black and Wiliam's and James and Pedder's identification of the crucial need to ensure appropriate teachers' professional development. In terms of the students themselves, she also identifies the need to teach peer (specifically group) assessment skills in areas such as verbal expression, sensitivity, turn-taking and listening. Sebba's chapter demonstrates a welcome harmony in aspirations and understanding relating to formative assessment across a variety of cultures and organizational contexts.

Motivation of learners

A theme that plays out through every successful instance of assessment for learning is the motivation to learn that it generates among students. It is arguably uncontentious that students are motivated to learn if they participate in developing their learning activities, if they know how their work will be assessed and if they are involved in assessing it with their peers. Perhaps it is also unnecessary to point out that students' motivation is enhanced by the ability to engage readily with their teacher, to receive feedback that supports the next steps in their learning or by being involved in drawing up the criteria against which they will be assessed.

Why then are these classroom processes not more commonplace? Harlen's Chapter 4 does not seek to answer this question but she focuses research evidence on the types of circumstances in which assessment has deleterious effects on students' motivation and provides the Assessment Reform Group's conclusions on how the worst effects can be avoided and the motivation of learners enhanced.

A theory of assessment for learning

A central aim of the book has been to explore a theoretical understanding of assessment for learning and James's Chapter 3 provides an accessible foray into the main learning theories from which a putative theory of formative assessment might spring. This daunting task is then taken up by Black and Wiliam in Chapter 5. Grounding their tentative theory on the basis of the experiences of the KMOFAP project, and supported by Engeström's Activity System theory, they make no bones about the complexity of the task. That said, the four component model they expound in this chapter offers an approach to theorizing assessment for learning. Black and Wiliam are, however, the first to concede that much more needs to be done in terms of understanding practice before a more comprehensive theory can be achieved.

Assessment myths, misunderstandings and tensions

I see the offerings in this category as addressing the contextual factors that impinge on assessment for learning and its practices. First there is the relationship between assessment for learning and assessment of learning, or put another way, between formative and summative assessment. Harlen's Chapter 6 is about purposes and the manner in which the purpose ordained for any specific assessment activity will ultimately distinguish it as serving learning (assessment for learning) or as providing a measure of learning (summative assessment). This leads to a variety of tensions, not least about whether one assessment can provide evidence for both of these purposes. The optimistic view, that perhaps they can be, is unpicked in some detail by Harlen who concludes that there is an asymmetrical relationship between evidence gathered for summative and formative purposes, and that this curtails the opportunity for dual usage.

Purposes are also key determinants in the arguments for reliability and validity and this link leads to these underpinning concepts being examined in Chapters 7 (Black and Wiliam) and 8 (Stobart) respectively. Black and Wiliam's chapter provides a grounding in reliability theory, illustrated by examples, which debunk the myth that external summative testing is de facto reliable. If there exists criticism that assessment for learning is inherently unreliable because it involves teachers with their subjective biases, for example, the antithesis that summative assessment is reliable because it is more 'objective', for example, is seriously undermined. Stobart's message is equally unequivocal. He draws out the purpose of the assessment as the main driver in determining its validity. Formative assessment is by definition designed to support learning. To be considered valid, then, it must lead to further learning. It is as simple as that. Or is it?

Stobart's chapter is liberally sprinkled with caveats and cautions. The 'upstream' factors of national culture and social context can create circumstances in which some of the key assessment for learning features might actually threaten the learning support they are otherwise designed to deliver. For example, in cultures where it is the norm, individual feedback may enhance learning, while in others where task-related feedback is expected it may impact negatively on the learners. Peer assessment may simply be unacceptable in some cultures. Where high-stakes transitions exist (for example, entry to university) comment-only feedback may be seriously contentious and may struggle to achieve its aim of supporting anxious students (or their parents!) to next steps in their learning. Nevertheless, as a first approximation, the basic tenet of successfully supporting learning remains the main validity check for assessment for learning.

The complexity of influencing policy and policy makers

Herein lies the rub. It often matters little if academic researchers 'know what's right' since the resources and other support, which they or practitioners might need, may not be forthcoming if the prevailing policy is blind to the issues, or worse, understands them and deliberately ignores them. Even if the research is irrefutable, Rist warns that:

> We are well past the time when it is possible to argue that good research will, because it is good, influence the policy process. That kind of linear relationship of research to action is not a viable way to think about how knowledge can inform decision making. The relation is both more subtle and more tenuous. (2000: 1002)

It certainly helps if the professionals find ways of doing what they think is 'right' anyway and in the UK a variety of bottom-up pressures from grassroots practitioners, not least through the activities of the Assessment Reform Group and our many collaborators, has brought considerable success in influencing policy development. But the process is exceedingly complex.

Daugherty and Ecclestone's Chapter 9 spells out the complexity underlying the successes of assessment for learning to date, with theory-based explanation where appropriate and with factual detail in terms of the four countries of the UK. In essence they argue that the process of change is slow but once it grips, governments can enact quite radical policies. Wiliam's Chapter 10 paints an entirely different picture of the assessment agenda in the USA. Here change is more or less limited to refinements of long-established variations of summative assessment, much of it geared to high-stakes selection. Assessment for learning is barely on the horizon, queued behind other learning oriented activities such as portfolio assessment. Where formative assessment does appear, it is more or less a collation of frequent or continuous assessments (for example, in a portfolio) that constitute a form of summative assessment, albeit perhaps in a more valid manner than an end-of-year test.

Assessment for learning: the concept

Any book covering the practice, theory and policy relating to a given educational concept might conceivably claim to provide a comprehensive analysis of that concept. We do not make such a claim for this book on assessment for learning because the extent of existing knowledge and understanding of such a complex process and set of techniques is still in its early stages. We might claim, however, to have assembled an authoritative account of what is known today, however inadequate the extent of this knowledge and understanding might be. Drawing as it does on the work of many researchers and practitioners, as well as our own, this is not an unreasonable claim. We will leave this for others to judge. What we can say categorically about assessment for learning, however, is that it is more often than not a fundamental element of any successful learning context.

A deep appreciation of this fact was brought home to me very clearly in a recent presentation I attended on assessment for learning. The presenters were two teachers, Margo Aksalnik and Bev Hill, from a Rankin Inlet school in the Nunuvut Territory, a new province established in northern Canada in 1999. The main illustration in the talk was of the national symbol of the Inuit people, the Inukshuk. An Inukshuk is a person-like construction of medium-sized rocks, which has been used by the Inuit people for millennia as a means of guiding wayfarers in the treeless and landmark-less expanses of northern Canada. Their various uses include giving directions to good fishing waters or simply reassuring the wayfarer that others have passed the same way, and that they are on the right path. A reproduction of the illustrative model used by the two teachers is presented in Figure 12.1.

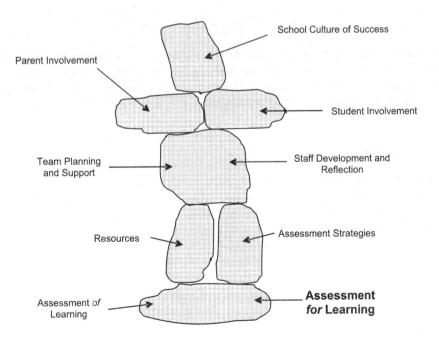

Figure 12.1: *An Inukshuk Guide to Successful Education (after Aksalnik and Hill, 2004)*

As can be seen, they placed assessment for learning squarely in the set of main ingredients designed to create a school with a culture of success. The other elements included teachers, their planning of the learning activities, their teaching and assessment strategies, their capacity to reflect about their own and their students' learning, and the resources they bring to the learning environment. Outside of the classroom, additional elements include professional development and team support for the teachers while outside of the school, the positive involvement of parents adds to the recipe for success.

It is arguable that other aspects of a successful school could be found to populate the Inukshuk's frame; successful sporting programmes or a students' council for example. No doubt they and other features of successful schools are also somewhere within the model, but the community-based context in which the two teachers introduced assessment for learning to their school dispelled any notion that its inclusion in the Inukshuk was either whimsical or contrived for the event (a seminar on assessment for learning on Vancouver Island). They recounted that:

> The Elders met to consider these new approaches and had the concept of assessment for learning explained to them. They then came up with a word to identify the dynamic – the resonance – between teaching, learning and assessment. (Aksalnik and Hill, 2004)

This new word, in the Inuktitut language of the Inuits, is

$$\Delta \subset C \triangleright \sigma d \subset \cap \sigma^{\varsigma b}$$

and is written in Roman form as Illitaunikuliriniq (or in sound form: ee-lee-tau-nee-qu-lee-ree-nee-kay). Most non-Inuit educationalists will have difficulty articulating this word but they will not fail to empathize with the assessment for learning aspirations of this small community in Canada's frozen north.

Conclusion

Throughout all of the text in this book, the aim has been to argue the case for the importance of assessment as a means of enhancing learning. The argument has been backed up by reasoned explanation, empirical evidence and theoretical analysis. Borrowing Fullan et al's phrase, we offer what we hope is a 'compelling conceptualization' (2004: 43) of a type of assessment that is specifically designed to serve learning – and which impacts positively on three key areas of education: classroom pedagogy, the quality of students' learning experiences and the insights that underpin assessment policy formation.

References

AAIA (2005a) *A Critique of the Assessment for Learning Materials in 'Excellence and Enjoyment: Learning and Teaching in the Primary Years'*. Birmingham: Association for Achievement and Improvement through Assessment.

AAIA (2005b) *Managing Assessment for Learning*. Birmingham: Association for Achievement and Improvement through Assessment.

ACCAC (2004) *Review of the School Curriculum and Assessment Arrangements 5–16: A report to the Welsh assembly government*. Cardiff: Qualifications, Curriculum and Assessment Authority for Wales.

ACT (2004) available at http://www.act.org/news/data/04/data.html

AERA/APA/NCME (1985) *Standards for Educational and Psychological Tests.* American Educational Research Association/American Psychological Association/National Council on Measurement in Education, Washington DC: American Psychological Association.

Aksalnik, M. and Hill, B. (2004) Oral presentation to 'Making Connections', Assessment for Learning Symposium, Vancouver Island: Classroom Connections, Courtenay, July.

Alexander, R. (2000) *Culture and Pedagogy: International comparisons in primary education.* Oxford: Blackwell.

Alexander, R. (2004) *Towards Dialogic Teaching: Rethinking classroom talk.* 2nd edn. Cambridge: Dialogos.

Ames, C. (1984) 'Achievement attributions and self-instructions under competitive and individualistic goal structures'. *Journal of Educational Psychology*, 76: 478–87.

Ames, C. (1992) 'Classrooms: goals, structures and student motivation'. *Journal of Educational Psychology*, 84 (3): 261–71.

Ames, C. and Archer, J. (1988) 'Achievement goals in the classroom: students' learning strategies and motivation processes'. *Journal of Educational Psychology*, 80: 260–67.

Anderson, L. W. and Bourke, S.F. (2001) *Assessing Affective Characteristics in Schools.* 2nd edn. Mahwah, NJ: Erlbaum.

Angoff, W. H. (ed.) (1971) *The College Board Admissions Testing Program: A technical report on research and development activities relating to the scholastic aptitude test and achievement tests.* 2nd edn. New York: College Entrance Examination Board.

ARG (1999) *Assessment for Learning: Beyond the black box.* University of Cambridge: Assessment Reform Group.

ARG (2002a) *Assessment for Learning: 10 principles.* University of Cambridge: Assessment Reform Group.

ARG (2002b) *Testing, Motivation and Learning.* University of Cambridge: Assessment Reform Group.

ASF (2004) *Working Paper 2, Draft 3 Summative Assessment by Teachers: Evidence from research and its implications for policy and practice.* Assessment Systems for the Future Project (see ARG website: http://www.assessment-reform-group.org).

Askew, M., Brown, M. L., Rhodes, V., Johnson, D. C. and Wiliam, D. (1997) *Effective Teachers of Numeracy: Final report.* London: King's College, School of Education.

Askew, S. and Lodge, C. (2000) 'Gifts, ping-pong and loops – linking feedback and learning', in S. Askew (ed.), *Feedback for Learning.* London: RoutledgeFalmer.

Atkinson, R. C. (2001) *The 2001 Robert H. Atwell Distinguished Lecture.* Paper presented at 83rd Annual Meeting of the American Council on Education, Washington, DC. Oakland, CA: University of California.

ATL, NUT and PAT (2004) *Reclaiming Assessment for Teaching and Learning. The future of national curriculum assessment: A way forward.* London: Association of Teachers and Lecturers/National Union of Teachers/ Professional Association of Teachers.

Ayres, E. P. (1918) 'History and present status of educational measurements', in S. A. Courtis (ed.). *The Measurement of Educational Products. The seventeenth yearbook of the National Society for the Study of Education.* Bloomington, IL: Public School Publishing Company. pp. 9–15.

Baird, J.R. and Northfield, J.R. (1992) *Learning from the PEEL Experience.* Melbourne: Monash University.

Baker, K. (1993) *The Turbulent Years: My life in politics.* London: Faber and Faber.

Ball, D. L. and Bass, H. (2000) 'Interweaving content and pedagogy in teaching and learning to teach: knowing and using mathematics', in J. Boaler (ed.), *Multiple Perspectives on Mathematics Teaching and Learning.* Westport, CT: Ablex. pp. 83–104.

Ball, S. (1990) *Politics and Policy-Making in Education: Explorations in policy sociology.* London: Routledge.

Ball, S. (1994) *Education Reform: A critical and post-structural approach.* Buckingham: Open University Press.

Ball, S. (2000) 'Performance and fabrications in the education economy: towards the performative society'. *Australian Education Researcher,* 27 (2): 1–24.

Bates, R. and Moller Boller, J. (2000) *Feedback to a Year 7 Pupil.* Unpublished research, Stockport Local Education Authority.

Benmansour, N. (1999) 'Motivational orientations, self-efficacy, anxiety and strategy use in learning high school mathematics in Morocco'. *Mediterranean Journal of Educational Studies,* 4: 1–15.

Bennis, W.G., Benne, K.D. and Chin, R. (1961) *The Planning of Change.* London: Holt, Rinehart and Winston.

Berlak, H., Newmann, F. M., Adams, E., Archbald, D. A., Burgess, T., Raven, J. and Romberg, T. A. (1992) *Towards a New Science of Educational Testing and Assessment.* Albany, NY: State University of New York Press.

Bevan, R. (2004) 'From black boxes to glass boxes: the application of computerised concept-mapping in schools'. Paper presented at the Teaching and Learning Research Project Annual Conference, Cardiff, November.

Biggs, J. (1996) 'Enhancing teaching through constructive alignment'. *Higher Education,* 32: 347–64.

Biggs, J. (1999) 'What the student does: teaching for enhanced learning'. *Higher Education Research and Development,* 18 (1): 57–75.

Biggs, J. and Tang, C. (1997) 'Assessment by portfolio: constructing learning and designing teaching'. Paper presented at the annual conference of the Higher Education Research and Development Society of Australasia, Adelaide, July.

Binet, A. and Simon, T. (1911) 'La mesure du développement de l'intelligence chez les enfants'. *Bulletin de la Société libre pour l'étude psychologique de l'enfant*, 70–1.

Bishop, R. and Glynn, T. (1999) *Culture Counts: Changing power relations in Education.* New Zealand: Dunmore Press.

Black, H. (1986) 'Assessment for learning', in D. J. Nuttall (ed.), *Assessing Educational Achievement.* London: Falmer. pp. 7–18.

Black, P. (1963) Bulletin of the Institute of Physics and the Physical Society, 202–3.

Black, P. (1990) 'APU Science – the past and the future'. *School Science Review,* 72 (258): 13–28.

Black, P. (1993) 'Formative and summative assessment by teachers'. *Studies in Science Education*, 21: 49–97.

Black, P. (1995) 'Ideology, evidence and the raising of standards'. Annual Education Lecture, London, King's College.

Black, P. (1997) 'Whatever Happened to TGAT?', in C. Cullingford (ed.), *Assessment vs. Evaluation.* London: Cassell. pp. 24–50.

Black, P. and Wiliam, D. (1998a), 'Assessment and classroom learning'. *Assessment in Education*, 5: 7–71.

Black, P. and Wiliam, D. (1998b) *Inside the Black Box: Raising standards through classroom assessment.* London: King's College (see also Phi Delta Kappan, 80: 139–48).

Black, P. and Wiliam, D. (2002) *Standards in Public Examinations.* London: King's College, School of Education.

Black, P. and Wiliam, D. (2003) 'In praise of educational research: formative assessment'. *British Educational Research Journal*, 29 (5): 623–37.

Black, P. and Wiliam, D. (2005) 'Changing teaching through formative assessment: research and practice: The King's-Medway-Oxfordshire Formative Assessment Project', in OECD: *Formative Assessment: Improving learning in secondary classrooms.* Paris: OECD.

Black, P., Harrison, C., Lee, C., Marshall, B. and Wiliam, D. (2002) *Working Inside the Black Box: Assessment for learning in the classroom.* London: NFER Nelson.

Black, P., Harrison, C., Lee, C., Marshall, B. and Wiliam, D. (2003) *Assessment for Learning: Putting it into practice.* Buckingham: Open University Press.

Black, P., Harrison, C., Osborne, J. and Duschl, R. (2004) *Assessment of Science Learning 14–19.* London: Royal Society (www.royalsoc.ac.uk/education).

Bolon, C. (2000) 'School-based standard testing'. *Education Policy Analysis Archives,* 8 (23) at http://epaa.asu.edu/epaa/v8n23/

Bowe, R., Ball, S. with Gold, A. (1992) *Reforming Education and Changing Schools: Case studies in policy sociology.* London: Routledge.

Bransford, J. D., Brown, A. L. and Cocking, R. R. (2000) *How People Learn: Brain, mind, experience and school.* Washington, DC: National Academies Press.

Bredo, E. (1994) 'Reconstructing educational psychology'. *Educational Psychologist,* 29 (1): 23–45.

Bredo, E. (1997) 'The social construction of learning', in G. D. Phye (ed.), *Handbook of Academic Learning: Construction of knowledge.* San Diego, CA: Academic Press.

Brigham, C. C. (ed.) (1926) *Scholastic Aptitude Tests: A manual for the use of schools.* New York, NY: College Entrance Examination Board.

Broadfoot, P. (1986) *Profiles and Records of Achievement: A review of issues and practice.* London: Reinehart and Wilson.

Broadfoot, P. (1996) *Education, Assessment and Society.* Buckingham: Open University Press.

Broadfoot, P. (2000) 'Empowerment or perfomativity? Assessment policy in the late twentieth century', in R. Phillips and J. Furlong (eds), *Education, Reform and the State:*

Twenty-five years of politics, policy and practice. London: RoutledgeFalmer. pp. 136–55.

Broadfoot, P., Osborn, M., Gilly, M. and Bucher, A. (1993) *Perceptions of Teaching: Primary school teachers in England and France.* London: Cassell.

Brookhart, S. and DeVoge, J. (1999) 'Testing a theory about the role of classroom assessment in student motivation and achievement'. *Applied Measurement in Education,* 12: 409–25.

Broome, E. C. (1903) *An Historical and Critical Discussion of College Admission Requirements.* New York, NY: Macmillan.

Brousseau, G. (1984) 'The crucial role of the didactical contract in the analysis and construction of situations in teaching and learning mathematics', in H. G. Steiner (ed.), *Theory of Mathematics Education: ICME 5 topic area and miniconference.* Germany: Bielefeld. Institut für Didaktik der Mathematik der Universität Bielefeld. pp. 110–19.

Bruner, J. (1996) *The Culture of Education.* Cambridge, MA: Harvard University Press.

Bryce, T. (1999) 'Could do better? Assessment in Scottish schools', in T. Bryce and W. Humes (eds), *Scottish Education.* Edinburgh: Edinburgh University. pp. 709–20.

Bryce, T. and Humes, W. (1999) *Scottish Education.* Edinburgh: Edinburgh University Press.

Butler, D. L. and Winne, P. H. (1995) 'Feedback and self-regulated learning: a theoretical synthesis'. *Review of Educational Research,* 65 (3): 245–81.

Butler, R. (1988) 'Enhancing and undermining intrinsic motivation: the effects of task-involving and ego-involving evaluation on interest and performance'. *British Journal of Educational Psychology,* 58: 1–14.

Butler, R. (1992) 'What young people want to know when: effects of mastery and ability goals on interests in different kinds of social comparison'. *Journal of Personality and Social Psychology,* 62: 934–43.

Butler, R. and Neuman, O. (1995) 'Effects of task and ego-achievement goals on help-seeking behaviours and attitudes'. *Journal of Educational Psychology,* 87 (2): 261–71.

Callaghan, D. (1995) 'The believers: politics, personalities in the making of the 1988 Education Act'. *History of Education,* 24 (4): 369–85.

Cameron, J. and Pierce, D. P. (1994) 'Reinforcement, reward, and intrinsic motivation: a meta-analysis'. *Review of Educational Research,* 64 (3): 363–423.

Carless, D. (2005) 'Prospects for the implementation of assessment for learning'. *Assessment in Education,* 12 (1): 39–54.

Carter, C. R. (1997) 'Assessment: shifting the responsibility'. *The Journal of Secondary Gifted Education,* 9 (2): 68–75.

Cattell, J. M. (1890) 'Mental tests and measurement'. *Mind,* 15: 373–81.

Cattell, J. M. and Farrand, L. (1896) 'Physical and mental measurements of the students at Columbia University'. *Psychological Review,* 3: 618–48.

CCEA (2003) *Pathways – Proposals for Curriculum and Assessment at Key Stage 3.* Belfast: Council for the Curriculum, Examinations and Assessment.

CCEA (2004) *The Revised Northern Ireland Primary Curriculum: Key Stages 1 and 2.* Belfast: Council for Curriculum, Examinations and Assessment.

Chadwick, E. (1864) 'Statistics of educational results'. *The Museum,* 3: 479–84.

Chaiklin, S. (2005) 'The zone of proximal development in Vygotsky's analysis of learning and instruction', http://www.education.miami.edu/blantonw/mainsite/componentsfromclmer/Component5/ChaiklinTheZoneOfProximalDevelopmentInVygotsky.html.

Chickering, A. W. (1983) 'Grades: one more tilt at the windmill'. *American Association for Higher Education Bulletin,* 35 (8): 10–13.

Choppin, B. and Orr, L. (1976) *Aptitude Testing at 18+.* Windsor: NFER Publishing.

Clarke, S. (1998) *Targeting Assessment in the Primary School.* London: Hodder and

Stoughton.

Clarke, S. (2001) *Unlocking Formative Assessment*. London: Hodder and Stoughton.

Clarke, S. (2005) *Formative Assessment in the Secondary Classroom*. London: Hodder Murray.

College Board (2004). *College-bound Seniors: A profile of SAT program test-takers*. New York, NY: College Entrance Examinations Board.

Conant, J. B. (1940) 'Education for a classless society: the Jeffersonian tradition'. *The Atlantic*, 165 (5): 593–602.

Conner, C. and James, M. (1996) 'The meddling role of LEAs in the interpretation of government assessment policy at school level in England'. *Curriculum Journal*, 7 (2): 153–66.

Corbett, H. D. and Wilson, B. L. (1991) *Testing, Reform and Rebellion*. Hillsdale, NY: Ablex.

Cowie, B. (2004) *Student commentary on formative assessment*. Paper presented at the annual conference of the National Association for Research in Science Teaching, Vancouver, March.

Cowie, B. and Bell, B. (1999) 'A model of formative assessment in science education'. *Assessment in Education*, 6 (1): 101–16.

Crooks, T. J. (1988) 'The impact of classroom evaluation practices on students'. *Review of Educational Research*, 58: 438–81.

Crooks, T. J. (2001) 'The validity of formative assessments'. Paper presented at the Annual Conference of the British Educational Research Association, Leeds.

Crooks, T. J., Kane M.T. and Cohen, A. S. (1996) 'Threats to the valid use of assessments'. *Assessment in Education*, 3 (3): 265–85.

Crossley, M. (1984) 'Strategies for curriculum change and the question of international transfer'. *Journal of Curriculum Studies*, 16: 75–88.

Cumming, J. and Maxwell, G. S. (2004) 'Assessment in Australian schools: current practice and trends'. *Assessment in Education*, 11 (1): 89–108.

Dale, R. (1994) 'Applied education politics or political sociology of education: contrasting approaches to the study of recent education reform in England and Wales', in D. Halpin and B. Troyna (eds), *Researching Education Policy: Ethical and methodological issues*. London: Falmer.

Daugherty, R. (1995) *National Curriculum Assessment: A review of policy 1987–1994*. London: Falmer.

Daugherty, R. (2000) 'National Curriculum assessment policies in Wales: administrative devolution or indigenous policy development?'. *The Welsh Journal of Education*, 9 (2): 4–17.

Daugherty, R. (2004) *Learning Pathways through Statutory Assessment: Final report of the Daugherty Assessment Review Group*. Cardiff: Welsh Assembly Government.

Daugherty, R. and Elfed-Owens, P. (2003) 'A national curriculum for Wales: a case study of policy-making in the era of administrative devolution'. *British Journal of Educational Studies*, 51 (3): 233–53.

Davidson, J. (2004) *Statement to plenary session of the National Assembly for Wales*, July. Cardiff: Welsh Assembly Government.

Davies, J. and Brember, I. (1998) 'National curriculum testing and self-esteem in Year 2. The first five years: a cross-sectional study'. *Educational Psychology*, 18: 365–75.

Davies, J. and Brember, I. (1999) 'Reading and mathematics attainments and self-esteem in Years 2 and 6: an eight year cross-sectional study'. *Educational Studies*, 25: 145–57.

Deakin Crick, R., Broadfoot, P. and Claxton, G. (2002) *Developing ELLI: the Effective Lifelong Learning Inventory in Practice*. Bristol: University of Bristol Graduate School of Education.

Deci, E. L. and Ryan, R. M. (1994) 'Promoting self-determined education', *Scandinavian Journal of Educational Research*, 38 (1): 3–14.

Deci, E. L., Koestner, R. and Ryan R. M. (1999) 'A meta-analysis review of experiments examining the effects of extrinsic rewards on intrinsic motivation'. *Psychological Bulletin*, 125: 627–88.

DES/WO (1988a) *Task Group on Assessment and Testing: A report*. London: Department of Education and Science and the Welsh Office.

DES/WO (1988b) *Task Group on Assessment and Testing: Three supplementary reports*. London: Department of Education and Science and the Welsh Office.

DfEE (1997) *Education for Excellence*. London: Department for Education and Employment.

Dorans, N. J. (1999) *Correspondence Between ACT and SAT I Scores*. Princeton, NJ: Educational Testing Service.

Dorans, N. J., Lyu, C. F., Pommerich, F. and Houston, W. M. (1997) 'Concordance between ACT Assessment and re-centered SAT I sum scores'. *College and University*, 73 (2): 24–34.

Dorr-Bremme, D. W. and Herman, J. L. (1986) *Assessing Student Achievement: A profile of classroom practices*. Los Angeles, CA: University of California, Center for the Study of Evaluation.

Dorr-Bremme, D. W., Herman, J. L. and Doherty, V. W. (1983) *Achievement Testing in American Public Schools: A national perspective*. Los Angeles, CA: University of California, Center for the Study of Evaluation.

Duckworth, K., Fielding, G. and Shaughnessy, J. (1986) *The Relationship of High School Teachers' Class Testing Practices to Students' Feelings of Efficacy and Efforts to Study*. Eugene, OR: University of Oregon.

Dudley, P. (2004) 'Lessons for learning: research lesson study, innovation, transfer and metapedagogy: a design experiment?' Paper presented at the ESRC TLRP Annual Conference, Cardiff, November. Available at http://www.tlrp.org/dspace/retrieve/289/Dudley+full+paper+Nov04+for+conferencev5271004.doc.

Dweck, C.S. (1986) 'Motivational processes affecting learning', *American Psychologist*, 41: 1040–48.

Dweck, C. S. (1992) 'The study of goals in psychology'. *Psychological Science*, 3: 165–7.

Dweck, C. S. (1999) *Self-Theories: Their role in motivation, personality and development*. Philadelphia: Psychology Press.

Dweck, C. S and Leggett, E. L. (1988) 'A socio-cognitive approach to motivation and personality'. *Psychological Review*, 95: 256–73.

Earl, L., Fullan, M., Leithwood, K. and Watson, N. (2000) *Watching and Learning: Evaluation of the implementation national literacy and numeracy strategies: First annual report*. London: Department for Education and Employment.

Ecclestone, K. (2002) *Learning Autonomy in Post-16 Education*. London: RoutledgeFalmer.

Ecclestone, K., Swann, J., Greenwood, M., Vobar, J. and Eldred, J. (2004) *Improving Formative Assessment in Vocational Education and Basic Skills*. Research project in progress – see www.exeter.ac.uk.

Edwards, A. (2005) 'Let's get beyond community and practice: the many meanings of learning by participating'. *The Curriculum Journal*, 16 (1): 49–65.

Elliott, E. S. and Dweck, C. S. (1988) 'Goals: an approach to motivation and achievement'. *Journal of Personality and Social Psychology*, 54: 5–12.

Engeström, Y. (1987) *Learning by Expanding: An activity-theoretical approach to developmental research*. Helsinki, Finland: Orienta-Konsultit Oy.

Engeström, Y. (1993) 'Developmental studies of work as a testbench of activity theory:

the case of primary care in medical education', in S. Chaiklin and J. Lave (eds), *Understanding Practice: Perspectives on activity and context.* Cambridge, UK: Cambridge University Press. pp. 64–103.

Engeström, Y. (1999) 'Activity theory and individual and social transformation', in Y. Engeström, R. Miettinen and R-L. Punamäki (eds), *Perspectives on Activity Theory.* Cambridge: Cambridge University Press.

Entwistle, N. (2005) 'Learning outcomes and ways of thinking across contrasting disciplines and settings in higher education'. *The Curriculum Journal,* 16 (1): 67–82.

Evans, E. and Engelberg, R. (1988) 'Students' perceptions of school grading'. *Journal of Research and Development in Education,* 21: 44–54.

Fernandez, C. (2002) 'Learning from Japanese approaches to professional development: the case of lesson study'. *Journal of Teacher Education,* 53 (5): 393–405.

Fielding, M. (2001) 'Students as radical agents of change'. *Journal of Educational Change,* 2: 123–41.

Fielding, M., Bragg, S., Craig, J., Cunningham, I., Eraut, M., Gillinson, S., Horne, M., Robinson, C. and Thorp, J. (2005) *Factors Influencing the Transfer of Good Practice.* London: DfES.

Filer, A. and Pollard, A. (2000) *The Social World of Pupil Assessment: Processes and contexts of primary schooling.* London: Continuum.

Finlay, I. (2004) 'Evolution or devolution? Distinctive education policies in Scotland'. Paper presented at the Annual Conference of the British Educational Research Association, Manchester.

Flyvbjerg, B. (2001) *Making Social Science Matter: Why social inquiry fails and how it can succeed again.* Cambridge: Cambridge University Press.

Foos, P. W., Mora, J. J. and Tkacz, S. (1994) 'Student study techniques and the generation effect'. *Journal of Educational Psychology,* 86: 567–76.

Forster, M. and Masters, G. (1996–2001) *Assessment Resource Kit* (complete set). Camberwell: Australian Council for Educational Research.

Fredericksen, J. R. and Collins, A. (1989) 'A systems approach to educational testing'. *Educational Researcher,* 18 (9): 27–32.

Frederiksen, J. R. and White, B. Y. (2004) 'Designing assessment for instruction and accountability: an application of validity theory to assessing scientific inquiry', in M. Wilson (ed.), *Towards Coherence between Classroom Assessment and Accountability: 103rd Yearbook of the National Society for the Study of Education Part II.* Chicago: National Society for the Study of Education. pp. 74–104.

Fullan, M., Bertani, A. and Quinn, J. (2004) 'New lessons for districtwide reform'. *Educational Leadership,* April: 42–6.

Galton, F. (1869) *Hereditary Genius: An inquiry into its laws and consequences.* London, UK: Macmillan.

Gardner, H. (1989) 'Zero-based arts education: an introduction to Arts PROPEL'. *Studies in Art Education: A Journal of Issues and Research,* 30 (2): 71–83.

Gardner, H. (1992) 'Assessment in context: the alternative to standardised testing', in B. R. Gifford and M. C. O'Connor (eds), *Changing Assessments: Alternative views of aptitude, achievement and instruction.* Boston, MA: Kluwer Academic Publishers. pp. 77–117.

Gardner, J. and Cowan, P. (2000) *Testing the Test: A study of the reliability and validity of the Northern Ireland transfer procedure test in enabling the selection of pupils for grammar school places.* Belfast: Queen's University of Belfast. (See also *Assessment in Education,* 14 (2): 145–65)

Gauld, C. F. (1980) 'Subject oriented test construction'. *Research in Science Education,* 10:

77–82.

Gibson, J. J. (1979) *The Ecological Approach to Visual Perception*. London, UK: Houghton Mifflin.

Gipps, C. (1994) *Beyond Testing: Towards a theory of educational assessment*. London: Falmer.

Gipps, C. and Murphy, P. (1994) *A Fair Test? Assessment, achievement and equity*. Buckingham: Open University Press.

Gipps, C., McCallum, B. and Hargreaves, E. (2001) *What Makes a Good Primary School Teacher? Expert classroom strategies*. London: Falmer.

Glassman, M. (2001) 'Dewey and Vygotsky: society, experience and inquiry in educational practice'. *Educational Researcher*, 30 (4): 3–14.

Glover, P. and Thomas, R. (1999) 'Coming to grips with continuous assessment'. *Assessment in Education*, 4 (3): 365–80.

Goddard, H. H. (1916) *Publication of the Vineland Training School* (no. 11). Vineland, NJ: Vineland Training School.

Goldstein, H. (1996) 'Group differences and bias in assessment', in H. Goldstein and T. Lewis (eds), *Assessment: Problems, developments and statistical issues*. Chichester: John Wiley. pp. 85–93.

Gordon, S. and Reese, M. (1997) 'High stakes testing: worth the price?'. *Journal of School Leadership*, 7: 345–68.

Graduate Record Examinations Board (2004) *Guide to the Use of Scores 2004–2005*. Princeton, NJ: Educational Testing Service.

Greeno, J. G. and The Middle-School Mathematics Through Applications Project Group (1998) 'The situativity of knowing, learning and research'. *American Psychologist*, 53 (1): 5–26.

Greeno, J. G., Pearson, P. D. and Schoenfeld, A. H. (1996) *Implications for NAEP of Research on Learning and Cognition: Report of a study commissioned by the National Academy of Education*. Panel on the NAEP Trial State Assessment, conducted by the Institute for Research on Learning. Stanford, CA: National Academy of Education.

Grossman, P. L. and Stodolsky, S. S. (1994) 'Considerations of content and the circumstances of secondary school teaching'. *Review of Research in Education*, 4: 179–221.

GTC(E) (2004) *Internal and External Assessment: What is the right balance for the future? Advice to the Secretary of State for Education and others*. London: General Teaching Council for England.

Hacker, D. J. Dunlosky, J. and Graesser, A. C. (1998) *Metacognition in Educational Theory and Practice*. Mahwah, NJ: Lawrence Erlbaum Associates.

Hall, C. and Harding, A. (2002) 'Level descriptions and teacher assessment in England: towards a community of assessment practice'. *Educational Research*, 44: 1–15.

Hall, K., Collins, J., Benjamin, S., Nind, M. and Sheehy, K. (2004) 'SATurated models of pupildom: assessment and inclusion/exclusion'. *British Educational Research Journal*, 30 (6): 801–18.

Hallam, S., Kirton, A., Peffers, J., Robertson, P. and Stobart, G. (2004) *Evaluation of Project 1 of the Assessment is for Learning Development Programme: Support for professional practice in formative assessment*. Edinburgh, UK: Scottish Executive.

Hargreaves, A. (1995) *Curriculum and Assessment Reform*. Buckingham: Open University Press.

Hargreaves, D. (1999) 'The knowledge creating school'. *British Journal of Educational Studies*, 47: 122–44.

Hargreaves, D. (2005) *About Learning: Report of the Learning working group*. London: Demos.

Harlen, W. (1998) 'Classroom assessment: a dimension of purposes and procedures'.

Paper presented at the annual conference of the New Zealand Association for Research in Education, Dunedin, December.

Harlen, W. (2000) *Teaching, Learning and Assessing Science 5–12*. 3rd edn. London: Paul Chapman Publishing.

Harlen, W. (2004) 'A systematic review of the reliability and validity of assessment by teachers used for summative purposes', in *Research Evidence in Education Library* Issue 1. London: EPPI-Centre, Social Sciences Research Unit, Institute of Education.

Harlen, W. (2005) 'Teachers' summative practices and assessment for learning: tensions and synergies'. *Curriculum Journal*, 16 (2): 207–23.

Harlen, W. and Deakin Crick, R. (2002) 'A systematic review of the impact of summative assessment and tests on students' motivation for learning (EPPI-Centre Review)'. In *Research Evidence in Education Library Issue 1*. London: EPPI-Centre, Social Science Research Unit, Institute of Education. Available on the website at: http://eppi.ioe. ac.uk/EPPIWeb/home.aspx?page=/reel/review_groups/assessment/review_one.htm.

Harlen, W. and Deakin Crick, R. (2003) 'Testing and motivation for learning'. *Assessment in Education*, 10 (2): 169–208.

Harlen, W. and James, M. (1997) 'Assessment and learning: differences and relationships between formative and summative assessment'. *Assessment in Education*, 4 (3): 365–80.

Harlen, W., Darwin, A. and Murphy, M. (1977) *Leader's Guide: Match and Mismatch Raising Questions and Match and Mismatch Finding Answers*. Edinburgh: Oliver and Boyd.

Harlen, W. et al. (1992) 'Assessment and the improvement of education'. *The Curriculum Journal*, 3 (3): 215–30.

Harris, S., Wallace, G. and Rudduck, J. (1995) 'It's not that I haven't learnt much. It's just that I don't really understand what I'm doing': metacognition and secondary school students'. *Research Papers in Education*, 10 (2): 253–71.

Hayward, L., Priestley, M. and Young, M. (2004) 'Ruffling the calm of the ocean floor: merging practice, policy and research in assessment in Scotland'. *Oxford Review of Education*, 30 (3): 397–415.

Henderson, V.L. and Dweck, C. S. (1990) 'Motivation and achievement', in S. S Feldman and G. R. Elliott (eds), *At the Threshold: The developing adolescent*. Cambridge, MA: Harvard University Press. pp. 308–29.

Herman, J. L. and Dorr-Bremme, D. W. (1983) 'Uses of testing in the schools: a national profile'. *New Directions for Testing and Measurement*, 19: 7–17.

Hidi, S. (2000) 'An interest researcher's perspective: the effects of extrinsic and intrinsic factors on motivation', in C. Sansone and J. M. Harackiewicz (eds), *Intrinsic and Extrinsic Motivation: The search for optimal motivation and performance*. New York: Academic Press.

Hidi, S. and Harackiewicz, J. M. (2000) 'Motivating the academically unmotivated: a critical issue for the 21st century'. *Review of Educational Research*, 70 (2): 151–79.

HMI (1999) *HM Inspectors of Schools Review of Assessment in Pre-School and 5–14*. Available online at: http://www.scotland.gov.uk/3–14assessment/rapm-00.htm.

Hodgen, J. and Marshall, B. (2005) 'Assessment for learning in mathematics and English: a comparison'. *The Curriculum Journal*, 16 (2): 153–76.

Holland, D., Lachicotte Jr, W., Skinner, D. and Cain, C. (1998) *Identity and Agency in Cultural Worlds*. Cambridge, MA: Harvard University Press.

Hubin, D. R. (1988) *The Scholastic Aptitude Test: Its development and introduction, 1900–1948*. Unpublished University of Oregon PhD thesis. Retrieved from http://darkwing.uoregon.edu/~hubin on 13.11.04.

Hufton, N. and Elliott, J. (2001) 'Achievement motivation: cross-cultural puzzles and paradoxes'. Paper presented at the British Educational Research Association Conference, Leeds.

Humes, W. (1997) 'Analysing the policy process'. *Scottish Educational Review,* 29 (1): 20–9.

Humes, W. (1999) 'Policy-making in Scottish education', in T. Bryce and W. Humes (eds), *Scottish Education.* Edinburgh: Edinburgh University Press. pp. 74–85.

Hutchinson, C. and Hayward, L. (2005) 'The journey so far: assessment for learning in Scotland'. *The Curriculum Journal,* (forthcoming).

Intercultural Development Research Association (1999) *Longitudinal Attrition Rates in Texas Public High Schools 1985–1986 to 1998–1999.* San Antonio, TX: Intercultural Development Research Association.

Isaac, J., Sansone, C. and Smith, J. L (1999) 'Other people as a sources of interest in an activity'. *Journal of Experimental Social Psychology,* 35: 239–65.

James, M. (2004) 'Assessment of learning, assessment for learning and personalised learning: synergies and tensions'. Paper presented at Goldman Sachs US/UK Conference on Urban Education, London, December.

James, M. and Brown, S. (2005) 'Grasping the TLRP nettle: preliminary analysis and some enduring issues surrounding the improvement of learning outcomes'. *The Curriculum Journal,* 16 (1): 7–30.

James, M., Pedder, D. and Swaffield, S. with Conner, C., Frost, D. and MacBeath, J. (2003) 'A servant of two masters: designing research to advance knowledge and practice'. Paper presented at the annual meeting of the American Educational Research Association, Chicago, in the symposium, *'Talking, working and learning with teachers and school leaders: the Cambridge Symposium'.* http://www.learntolearn.ac.uk/home/009_public_papers/conf_papers/003/l2l-aera-master2003.doc).

James, M., Pollard, A., Rees, G. and Taylor, C. (2005) 'Researching learning outcomes: building confidence in our conclusions'. *The Curriculum Journal,* 16 (1): 109–22.

Jessup, G. (1991) *Outcomes: NVQs and the emerging model of education.* London: Falmer.

Johnston, C. (1996) *Unlocking the Will to Learn.* Thousand Oaks, CA: Corwin Press.

Johnston, J. and McClune, W. (2000) *Selection Project Sel 5.1: Pupil motivation and attitudes – self-esteem, locus of control, learning disposition and the impact of selection on teaching and learning.* Belfast: Department of Education for Northern Ireland.

Jones, L. V. and Olkin, I. (2004) *The Nation's Report Card: Evolution and perspectives.* Bloomington, IL: Phi Delta Kappan Educational Foundation.

Kane, M. T., Crooks, T. and Cohen, A. (1999) 'Validating measures of performance'. *Educational Measurement: Issues and Practice,* 18 (2): 5–17.

Katzell, R. A. and Thompson, D. E (1990) 'Work motivation: theory and practice'. *American Psychologist,* 45: 144–53.

Kellaghan, T., Madaus, G. and Raczek, A. (1996) *The Use of External Examinations to Improve Student Motivation.* Washington, DC: AERA.

King, A. (1992) 'Facilitating elaborative learning through guided student-generated questioning'. *Educational Psychologist,* 27: 111–26.

Kluger, A. N. and DeNisi, A. (1996) 'The effects of feedback interventions on performance: a historical review, a meta-analysis, and a preliminary feedback intervention theory'. *Psychological Bulletin,* 119: 252–84.

Kohn, A. (1993) *Punished by Rewards: The trouble with gold stars, incentive plans, A's, praise, and other bribes.* Boston: Houghton Mifflin.

Koretz, D. M. (1998) 'Large-scale portfolio assessments in the US: evidence pertaining to the quality of measurement'. *Assessment in Education: Principles, Policy and Practice,* 5 (3): 309–34.

Koretz, D. M., Stecher, B. M., Klein, S. P., McCaffrey, D. and Deibert, E. (1994) *Can Port-*

folios Assess Student Performance and Influence Instruction? The 1991–92 Vermont experience. Santa Monica, CA: RAND Corporation.

Kreisberg, S. (1992) *Transforming Power: Domination, Empowerment and Education*. New York :State University of New York Press.

Krug, E. A. (1969) *The Shaping of the American High School: 1880–1920*. Madison, WI: University of Wisconsin Press.

Kutnick, P., Sebba, J., Blatchford, P. and Galton, M. (2005) *The Effects of Pupil Grouping: An extended literature review for DfES* (submitted).

Lave, J. and Wenger, E. (1991) *Situated Learning: Legitimate peripheral participation*. Cambridge: Cambridge University Press.

Lawlor, S. (ed.) (1993) *The Dearing Debate: Assessment and the national curriculum*. London: Centre for Policy Studies.

Leadbetter, C. (2004) *Personalised Learning*. London: DfES/DEMOS.

Lee, C. (2000) 'Studying changes in the practice of two teachers'. Paper presented at symposium entitled 'Getting Inside the Black Box : Formative Assessment in Practice', the British Educational Research Association 26th Annual Conference, Cardiff University. London: King's College School of Education.

Lemann, N. (1999) *The Big Test: The secret history of the American meritocracy*. New York, NY: Farrar, Straus and Giroux.

Leonard, M. and Davey, C. (2001) *Thoughts on the 11 Plus*. Belfast: Save the Children Fund.

Levine, D. O. (1986) *The American College and the Culture of Aspiration 1915–1940*. Ithaca, NY: Cornell University Press.

Lindquist, E. F. (ed.) (1951) *Educational Measurement*. 1st edn. Washington, DC: American Council on Education.

Linn, R. L. (1989) 'Current perspectives and future directions', in R. L. Linn (ed.), *Educational Measurement*. 3rd edn. London: Collier Macmillan. pp. 1–10.

Linn, R. L. (2000) 'Assessment and accountability'. *Educational Researcher*, 29 (2): 4–16.

MacBeath, J. and Mortimore, P. (eds) (2001) *Improving School Effectiveness*. Buckingham: Open University Press.

Madaus, G. F. and Kellaghan, T. (1992) 'Curriculum evaluation and assessment', in P. W. Jackson (ed.), *Handbook of Research on Curriculum*. New York, NY: Macmillan. pp. 119–54.

Marshall, B. and Hodgen, J. (2005) Formative Assessment in English. Private communication – in preparation for publication.

Marsland, D. and Seaton, N. (1993) *Empire Strikes Back: Creative subversion of the National Curriculum*. York: Campaign for Real Education.

Masters, G. and Forster, M. (1996) *Progress Maps*. Victoria, Australia: Australian Council for Educational Research.

Mathews, J. (2004) *Portfolio Assessment*. Retrieved on 30.3.05 from http://www.educationnext.org/20043/72.html.

Maxwell, G. S. (2004) 'Progressive assessment for learning and certification: some lessons from school-based assessment in Queensland'. Paper presented at the third Conference of the Association of Commonwealth Examination and Assessment Boards, March, Nadi, Fiji.

McDonald, A. S., Newton, P. E., Whetton, C. and Benefield, P. (2001) *Aptitude Testing for University Entrance: A literature review*. Slough: National Foundation for Educational Research in England and Wales.

McInerney, D. M., Roche, L. A., McInerney, V. and Marsh, H. (1997) 'Cultural perspectives on school motivation: the relevance and application of goal theory'. *American*

Educational Research Journal, 34: 207–36.

McKeown, P. (2004) 'Exploring education policy in Northern Ireland'. Paper presented at the annual conference of the British Educational Research Association, Manchester UK , September.

McMahon, A., Thomas, S., Greenwood, A., Stoll, L., Bolam, R., Hawkey, K., Wallace, M. and Ingram, M. (2004) 'Effective professional learning communities'. Paper presented at the ICSEI conference, Rotterdam.

Meier, C. (2000) 'The influence of educational opportunities on assessment results in a multicultural South Africa'. Paper presented at 26th IAEA conference, Jerusalem.

Mercer, N. (2000) *Words and Minds*. London: Routledge.

Mercer, N., Dawes, L., Wegerif, R. and Sams, C. (2004) 'Reasoning as a scientist: ways of helping children to use language to learn science'. *British Educational Research Journal*, 30 (3): 359–77.

Messick, S. (1980) 'Test validity and the ethics of assessment'. *American Psychologist*, 35 (11): 1012–27.

Messick, S. (1989) 'Validity', in R. L. Linn (ed.), *Educational Measurement*. 3rd edn. New York, NY: American Council on Education and Macmillan. pp. 13–103.

Miliband, D. (2004) Speech to the North of England Education Conference, Belfast, January available at http://www.dfes.gov.uk/speeches.

Montgomery, M. (2004) 'Key features of assessment in Northern Ireland'. Paper presented at a seminar of the Assessment Systems for the Future project, Cambridge UK, March.

National Committee on Science Education Standards and Assessment (1995) *National Science Education Standards*. Washington, DC: National Academies Press.

Natriello, G. (1987) 'The impact of evaluation processes on students'. *Educational Psychologist*, 22: 155–75.

NCTM (1989) *Curriculum and Evaluation Standards for School Mathematics*. Reston, VA: National Council of Teachers of Mathematics.

NCTM (1991) *Professional Standards for Teaching Mathematics*. Reston, VA: National Council of Teachers of Mathematics.

NUT (2004) *The NUT Approach to Assessment for England: Foundation stage and primary*. London: National Union of Teachers.

OECD (2005) *Formative Assessment: Improving learning in secondary classrooms*. Paris: OECD.

OFSTED (2005) *The Annual Report of Her Majesty's Chief Inspector of Schools for 2003/04*. Office for Standards in Education, at http://www.ofsted.gov.uk/publications/annual-report0304/annual_report.htm.

Osborn, M., McNess, E., Broadfoot, P., Pollard, A. and Triggs, P. (2000) *What Teachers Do: Changing policy and practice in primary education*. London: Continuum.

Palincsar, A.S. and Brown A.L. (1984) *Reciprocal Teaching of Comprehension Fostering and Monitoring Activities: Cognition and instruction*. Hillsdale, NJ: Erlbaum.

Paris, S., Lawton, T., Turner, J. and Roth, J. (1991) 'A developmental perspective on standardised achievement testing'. *Educational Researcher*, 20: 12–20.

Paterson, L. (2003) *Scottish Education in the Twentieth Century*. Edinburgh: Edinburgh University Press.

Pedder, D., James, M. and MacBeath, J. (2005) 'How teachers value and practise professional learning'. *Research Papers in Education*, 20 (3): (forthcoming).

Pellegrino, J. W., Baxter, G. P. and Glaser, R. (1999) 'Addressing the 'Two Disciplines' problem: linking theories of cognition with assessment and instructional practice'. *Review of Research in Education*, 24: 307–53.

Pellegrino, P., Chudowsky, N. and Glaser, R. (2001) *Knowing What Students Know: The science and design of educational assessment*. Washington, DC: National Academies Press.

Perrenoud, P. (1991) 'Towards a pragmatic approach to formative evaluation', in P. Weston (ed.), *Assessment of Pupils Achievement: Motivation and school success*. Amsterdam: Swets and Zeitlinger. pp. 79–101.

Perrenoud, P. (1998) 'From formative evaluation to a controlled regulation of learning processes. Towards a wider conceptual field'. *Assessment in Education*, 5 (1): 85–102.

Perry, N. (1998) 'Young children's self-regulated learning and contexts that support it'. *Journal of Educational Psychology*, 90: 715–29.

Phillips, M. (1996) *All Must have Prizes*. London: Little, Brown and Company.

Pollard, A. and James, M. (eds) (2005) *Personalised Learning: A commentary by the Teaching and Learning Research Programme*. Swindon: Economic and Social Research Council.

Pollard, A., Triggs, P., Broadfoot, P., McNess, E. and Osborn, M. (2000) *What Pupils Say: Changing policy and practice in primary education*. London: Continuum.

Popham, W. J. (1997) 'Consequential validity: right concern – wrong concept'. *Educational Measurement: Issues and Practice*, 16 (2): 9–13.

Pring, R. (1986) 'The developing 14–18 curriculum and changes in assessment', in T. Staden and P. Preece (eds), *Issues in Assessment, Perpectives 23*. Exeter: University of Exeter. pp. 12–21.

Project Zero (2005) *History of Project Zero*. Retrieved on 30.03.05 from http://www.pz.harvard.edu/History/History.htm.

QCA (2004) *Assessment for Learning: Research into practice*. London: Qualifications and Curriculum Authority (CD-ROM package).

QCA (2005) www.nc.uk.net (accessed 22.02.05).

QSA (2005) Queensland Studies Authority, at http://www.qsa.qld.edu.au.

Ramaprasad, A. (1983) 'On the definition of feedback'. *Behavioral Science*, 28: 4–13.

Raveaud, M. (2004) 'Assessment in French and English infant schools: assessing the work, the child or the culture?'. *Assessment in Education*, 11 (2): 193–211.

Reay, D. and Wiliam, D. (1999) 'I'll be a nothing: structure, agency and the construction of identity through assessment'. *British Educational Research Journal*, 25: 343–54.

Rees, G. (2005) 'Democratic devolution and education policy in Wales: the emergence of a national system?'. *Contemporary Wales*, 17: 28–43.

Reeves, J., McCall, J. and MacGilchrist, B. (2001) 'Change leadership: planning, conceptualization and perception', in J. MacBeath and P. Mortimore (eds), *Improving School Effectiveness*. Buckingham: Open University Press. pp. 122–37.

Reynolds, D. (2002) 'Developing differently: educational policy in England, Wales, Scotland and Northern Ireland', in J. Adams and P. Robinson (eds), *Devolution in Practice: Public policy differences within the UK*. London: Institute of Public Policy Research. pp. 93–103.

Rist, R. C. (2000) 'Influencing the policy process with qualitative research', in N. K. Denzin and Y. S. Lincoln (eds), *Handbook of Qualitative Research*. Thousand Oaks, CA: Sage. pp. 1001–77.

Robson, B. (2004) 'Built to fail: every child left behind. Minneapolis/St Paul'. *City Pages*, 25 (1214). Retrieved from http://citypages.com/databank/25/1214/article11955.asp on 31.03.05.

Roderick, M. and Engel, M. (2001) 'The grasshopper and the ant: motivational responses of low achieving pupils to high stakes testing'. *Educational Evaluation and Policy Analysis*, 23: 197–228.

Rogoff, B. (1990) *Apprenticeship in Thinking: Cognitive development in social context*. Oxford:

Oxford University Press.

Rogosa, D. (1999) *How Accurate Are the STAR National Percentile Rank Scores for Individual Students? An interpretive guide*. CSE Technical Report 509a. Los Angeles, CA: CRESST. Published on web-site : http://www.cse.ucla.edu/products/reports_set.htm.

Rousseau, J-J. ([1762] 1961) *Emile*. London: Dent.

Rowe, M. B. (1974) 'Wait time and rewards as instructional variables, their influence on language, logic and fate control'. *Journal of Research in Science Teaching*, 11: 81–94.

Sacks, P. (1999) *Standardized Minds: The high price of America's testing culture and what we can do to change it*. Cambridge, MA: Perseus Books.

Sadler, D. R. (1987) 'Specifying and promulgating achievement standards'. *Oxford Review of Education*, 13: 191–209.

Sadler, D. R. (1989) 'Formative assessment and the design of instructional systems'. *Instructional Science*, 18: 119–44.

Sadler, D. R. (1998) 'Formative assessment: revisiting the territory'. *Assessment in Education*, 5: 77–84.

Salomon, G. (ed.) (1993) *Distributed Cognitions: Psychological and educational considerations*. Cambridge: Cambridge University Press.

Schön, D. (1983) *The Reflective Practitioner*. New York: Basic Books.

Schunk, D. H. (1996) 'Goal and self-evaluative influences during children's cognitive skill learning'. *American Educational Research Journal*, 33 (2): 359–438.

Scriven, M. (1967) 'The methodology of evaluation' in R. W. Tyler (ed.), *Perspectives of Curriculum Evaluation*. Chicago: Rand McNally. pp. 39–83.

Sebba, J. and Maxwell, G. (2005) 'Queensland, Australia: an outcomes-based curriculum', in *Formative Assessment: Improving learning in secondary classrooms*. Paris: OECD.

SEED (2004a) *Assessment, Testing and Reporting 3–14: Our response*. Edinburgh: Scottish Executive.

SEED (2004b) *A Curriculum for Excellence: Ministerial response*. Edinburgh: Scottish Executive.

Serafini, F. (2000) 'Three paradigms of assessment: measurement, procedure, and inquiry'. *The Reading Teacher*, 54 (4): 384–93.

Sfard, A. (1998) 'On two metaphors for learning and the dangers of choosing just one'. *Educational Researcher*, 27 (2): 4–13.

SHA (2002) *Examinations and Assessment*. Leicester: Secondary Heads' Association.

Shayer, M. (1999) 'Cognitive acceleration through science education II: its effects and scope'. *International Journal of Science Education*, 21 (8): 883–902.

Shayer, M. and Adey, P. (1993) 'Accelerating the development of formal thinking in middle and high-school students 4. 3 years after a 2-year intervention'. *Journal of Research in Science Teaching*, 30: 351–66.

Shepard, L. A. (1997) 'The centrality of test use and consequences for test validity'. *Educational Measurement: Issues and Practice*, 16 (2): 5–8, 13.

Shulman, L. (1986) 'Those who understand: knowledge growth in teaching'. *Educational Researcher*, 15 (1): 4–14.

Shulman, L. (1987) 'Knowledge and teaching: foundations of the new reform'. *Harvard Educational Review*, 57 (1): 1–22.

Sliwka, A., Fushell, M., Gauthier, M. and Johnson, R. (2005) 'Canada: encouraging the use of summative data for formative purposes', in *Formative Assessment: Improving learning in secondary classrooms*. Paris: OECD.

Smith, E. and Gorard, S. (2005) 'They gives us our marks: the role of formative feedback in student progress'. *Assessment in Education*, 12 (1): 21–38.

SOED (1991) *Curriculum and Assessment in Scotland: Assessment 5–14*. Edinburgh: HMSO.

Starch, D. and Elliott, E. C. (1912) 'Reliability of grading high school work in English'. *School Review*, 20: 442–57.

Starch, D. and Elliott, E. C. (1913) 'Reliability of grading high school work in mathematics'. *School Review*, 21: 254–9.

Standards for Success (2003) *Mixed messages: What state high school tests communicate about student readiness for college.* Eugene, OR: Association of American Universities.

Stenhouse, L. (1975) *An Introduction to Curriculum Research and Development.* London: Heinemann Educational Books.

Stiggins, R. J. (2001) *Student-Involved Classroom Assessment.* 3rd edn. Upper Saddle River, NJ: Merrill Prentice Hall.

Stiggins, R. J. and Bridgeford, N. J. (1985) 'The ecology of classroom assessment'. *Journal of Educational Measurement*, 22 (4): 271–86.

Stiggins, R. J., Conklin, N. F. and Bridgeford, N. J. (1986) 'Classroom assessment: a key to effective education'. *Educational Measurement: Issues and Practice*, 5 (2): 5–17.

Stiggins, R. J., Frisbie, D. A. and Griswold, P. A. (1989) 'Inside high-school grading practices: building a research agenda'. *Educational Measurement: Issues and Practice*, 8 (2): 5–14.

Stigler, J. and Hiebert, J. (1999) *The Teaching Gap: The best ideas from the world's teachers for improving education in the classroom.* New York, NY: Free Press.

Stobart, G. and Gipps, C. (1990) *Assessment: A teacher's guide to the issues.* 1st edn. London: Hodder and Stoughton.

Stoll, L., Stobart, G., Martin, S., Freeman, S., Freedman, E., Sammons, P. and Smees, R. (2003) *Preparing for Change: Evaluation of the implementation of the Key Stage 3 strategy pilot.* London: DfES.

Sutton, R. (1995) *Assessment for Learning.* Manchester: Ruth Sutton Publications.

Swaffield, S. and Dudley, P. (2002) *Assessment Literacy for Wise Decisions.* London: Association of Teachers and Lecturers.

Swann, J. and Brown, S. (1997) 'The implementation of a National Curriculum and teachers' classroom thinking'. *Research Papers in Education*, 12: 91–114.

Tamir, P. (1990) 'Justifying the selection of answers in multiple choice items'. *International Journal of Science Education*, 12 (5): 563–73.

Taylor, T. (1995) 'Movers and shakers: high politics and the origins of the National Curriculum'. *The Curriculum Journal*, 6 (2): 160–84.

Terman, L. M. (1916) *The Measurement of Intelligence.* Boston, MA: Houghton-Mifflin.

Terman, L. M. (1921) 'Intelligence tests in colleges and universities'. *School and Society*, (April 28): 482.

Thatcher, M. (1993) *The Downing Street Years.* London: HarperCollins.

Thomas, G. and Egan, D. (2000) 'Policies on schools inspection in Wales and England', in R. Daugherty R. Phillips and G. Rees (eds), *Education Policy-making in Wales.* Cardiff: University of Wales Press. pp. 149–70.

Thorndike, E. L. (1913) *Educational Psychology. Volume 1: The original nature of man.* New York: Columbia University Teachers College.

Torrance, H. (1993) 'Formative assessment – some theoretical problems and empirical questions'. *Cambridge Journal of Education*, 23 (3): 333–43.

Torrance, H. and Pryor, J. (1998) *Investigating Formative Assessment: Teaching, learning and assessment in the classroom.* Buckingham: Open University Press.

Toulmin, S. (2001) *Return to Reason.* Cambridge, MA: Harvard University Press.

Towns, M. H. and Robinson, W. R. (1993) 'Student use of test-wiseness strategies in solving multiple-choice chemistry examinations'. *Journal of Research in Science Teaching*, 30 (7): 709–22.

Townshend, J., Moos, L. and Skov, P. (2005) 'Denmark: building on a tradition of democracy and dialogue in schools'. In *Formative Assessment: Improving learning in secondary classrooms*. Paris: OECD.

Travers, R. M. W. (1983) *How Research has Changed American Schools: A history from 1840 to the present*. Kalamazoo, MI: Mythos Press.

Tunstall, P. and Gipps, C. (1996) 'Teacher feedback to young children in formative assessment: a typology'. *British Educational Research Journal*, 22: 389–404.

Tymms, P. (2004) 'Are standards rising in English primary schools?'. *British Educational Research Journal*, 30 (4): 477–94.

Varon, E. J. (1936) 'Alfred Binet's concept of intelligence'. *Psychological Review*, 43: 32–49.

Vispoel, W. P. and Austin, J. R. (1995) 'Success and failure in junior high school: a critical incident approach to understanding students' attributional beliefs'. *American Educational Research Journal*, 32 (2): 377–412.

Vulliamy, G. (2004) 'The impact of globalisation on qualitative research in comparative and international education'. *Compare*, 34: 261–84.

Vulliamy, G., Lewin, K. and Stephens, D. (1990) *Doing Educational Research in Developing Countries: Qualitative strategies*. London: Falmer.

Vygotsky, L. S. (1978) *Mind in Society: The Development of Higher Psychological Process*. Cambridge, MA: Harvard University Press.

Vygotsky, L. S. (1986) *Thought and Language*. Cambridge, MA: Harvard University Press.

Vygotsky, L. S. (1998 [1933/4]) 'The problem of age', in R. W. Rieber (ed.), *The Collected Works of L. S. Vygotsky: Vol. 5. Child Psychology* (trans. by M. Hall). New York: Plenum Press. pp. 187–205.

Watkins, C., Carnell, E., Lodge, C., Wagner, P. and Whalley, C. (2000) *Learning about Learning*. London: Routledge.

Watkins, C., Carnell, E., Lodge, C., Wagner, P. and Whalley, C. (2001) *NSIN Research Matters No.13: Learning about learning enhances performance*. London: Institute of Education.

Watkins, D. (2000) 'Learning and teaching: a cross-cultural perspective'. *School Leadership and Management*, 20 (2): 161–73.

Webb, N. L. (1999) *Alignment of Science and Mathematics Standards and Assessments in Four States*. Washington, DC: Council of Chief State School Officers.

Weeden, P., Winter, J. and Broadfoot, P. (2002) *Assessment: What's in it for schools?* London: RoutledgeFalmer.

Weiner, B. (1979) 'A theory of motivation for some classroom experiences'. *Journal of Educational Psychology*, 71: 3–25.

Wenger, E. (1998) *Communities of Practice: Learning, meaning and identity*. Cambridge: Cambridge University Press.

White, B. Y. and Frederiksen, J. R. (1998) 'Inquiry, modeling and metacognition: making science accesible to all students'. *Cognition and Instruction*, 16 (1): 3–118.

White, E. E. (1888) 'Examinations and promotions'. *Education*, 8: 519–22.

White, J. (2004) Unpublished report on the CCEA 'Pathways' proposals. London: University Institute of Education.

Whitty, G. (2002) *Making Sense of Education Policy*. London: Paul Chapman Publications.

Wiliam, D. (1992) 'Some technical issues in assessment: a user's guide'. *British Journal for Curriculum and Assessment*, 2 (3): 11–20.

Wiliam, D. (2000) 'Recent developments in educational assessment in England: the integration of formative and summative functions of assessment'. Paper presented at SweMaS, Umea, Sweden, May.

Wiliam, D. (2001) 'Reliability, validity and all that jazz'. *Education 3–13*, 29 (3): 17–21.

Wiliam, D. (2003) 'The impact of educational research on mathematics education' in A. Bishop, M. A. Clements, C. Keitel, J. Kilpatrick and F. K. S. Leung (eds), *Second International Handbook of Mathematics Education*. Dordrecht, Netherlands: Kluwer Academic Publishers. pp. 469–88.

Wiliam, D. and Black, P. (1996) 'Meanings and consequences: a basis for distinguishing formative and summative functions of assessment?'. *British Educational Research Journal*, 23 (5): 537–48.

Wiliam, D., Lee, C., Harrison, C. and Black, P. (2004) 'Teachers developing assessment for learning: impact on student achievement'. *Assessment in Education*, 11: 49–65.

Wilson, M. (1990) 'Measurement of developmental levels', in T. Husen and T. N. Postlethwaite (eds), *International Encyclopedia of Education: Research and studies (Supplementary volume)*. Oxford: Pergamon Press.

Wilson, M. and Sloane, K. (2000) 'From principles to practice: an embedded assessment system'. *Applied Measurement in Education* (forthcoming).

Wilson, M., Kennedy, C. and Draney, K (2004) *GradeMap* (Version 4.0) [computer program]. Berkeley, CA: University of California, BEAR Center.

Wilson, S. M. and Berne, J. (1999) 'Teacher learning and the acquisition of professional knowledge: an examination of research on contemporary professional development', in A. Iran-Nejad and P. D. Pearson (eds), *Review of Research in Education*. Washington, DC: American Educational Research Association. pp. 173–209.

Wood, D. (1998) *How Children Think and Learn: The social contexts of cognitive development*. 2nd edn. Oxford: Blackwell.

Wood, D., Bruner, J. S., and Ross, G. (1976) 'The role of tutoring in problem solving'. *Journal of Child Psychology and Psychiatry and Allied Disciplines*, 17: 89–100.

Yarroch, W. L. (1991) 'The implications of content versus item validity on science tests'. *Journal of Research in Science Teaching*, 28 (7): 619–29.

Zenderland, L. (2000) *Measuring Minds: Henry Herbert Goddard and the origins of American intelligence testing*. Cambridge: Cambridge University Press.

Zimmerman, B. J. and Schunk, D. H. (eds) (1989) *Self-Regulated Learning and Academic Achievement: Theory, research, and practice*. New York: Springer.

Author index

Subject index

Added to the page reference 'f' denotes a figure.

activity systems, subject classrooms as 83–4, 94–7
activity theory 56–8, 59
American College Testing (ACT) 176
ARG (Assessment Reform Group) 1, 5, 10, 157, 197
'Assessment is for Learning' (AifL) programme 160–2
assessment for learning 2–3, 197–204
 'compelling conceptualization' 204
 concept 202–4
 as a cycle of events 104–5
 definition 2
 distinctions between summative assessment and 4, 103–6
 educational and contextual issues 199–202
 and inquiry-based learning by teachers 40–2
 OECD study see OECD study
 principles 3, 28, 29, 108
 and professional learning see professional development/learning
 and student grouping strategies 191–2
 UK policy see UK policy
 US policy see US policy
 see also formative assessment
assessment for learning in the classroom 9–25
 future issues 23–5
 KMOFAP see KMOFAP (King's-Medway-Oxfordshire Formative Assessment Project)
 research review 9–12
assessment of learning
 distinctions between assessment for learning and 103–6
 see also summative assessment
Assessment Reform Group (ARG) 1, 5, 10, 157, 197
attribution theory 12
 and locus of control 66

Australia
 impact and relevance of policy 194–5
 see also Queensland

BEAR (Berkeley Evaluation and Assessment Research) project 110
 contrast with KMOFAP (King's-Medway-Oxfordshire Formative Assessment Project) 97–8
 patterns of influence 95
behaviourist theories 54–5, 59, 67

Canada
 impact and relevance of policy 195–6
 professional development/learning 193
 self- and peer assessment 190
classical test theory 48
classroom dialogue 14
 framing and guiding 89
 studies 98–9
classroom discourse 11
classroom practice 2–3, 11, 199–200
 application of research 18–21, 199
 links with professional development 24
 examples 50–2
 and KMOFAP (King's-Medway-Oxfordshire Formative Assessment Project) 84–94
classroom roles
 changes 17–18
 implications of assessment for learning 27–30
 see also student's role; teacher's role
classrooms
 assessment for learning in see assessment for learning in the classroom
 as communities of practice 82–3
 as figured worlds 82–3
 see also subject classrooms
cognitive acceleration initiative 98
cognitivist theories 55–6, 59, 85
 see also constructivist theories
comment marking 15, 142–3
 in Queensland 189

225